The Essential Sociology Reader

Robert Thompson
Editor
Minot State University

Allyn and Bacon
Boston • London • Toronto • Sydney • Tokyo • Singapore

Editor in Chief, Social Sciences: Karen Hanson
Executive Marketing Manager: Suzy Spivey
Editorial Production Service: Chestnut Hill Enterprises, Inc.
Manufacturing Buyer: Megan Cochran
Cover Administrator: Jennifer Hart

Copyright © 1998 by Allyn & Bacon
A Viacom Company
160 Gould Street
Needham Heights, Massachusetts 02194

Internet: www.abacon.com
America Online: Keyword: College Online

Library of Congress Cataloging-in-Publication Data

The essential sociology reader / edited by Robert Thompson.
     p.   cm.
   Includes bibliographical references (p.).
   ISBN 0–205–28309–8
   1. Sociology.   2. Social Problems.   3. United States–Social
conditions—1980–   I. Thompson, Robert.
HM51.E89   1997
301—dc21   97–40010
                                                        CIP

Printed in the United States of America

10   9   8   7   6   5   RRD-VA   02   01   99

Contents

Chapter 1

The Sociological Perspective

Perhaps the most enjoyable aspect of sociology is the hands-on experience of doing research, and it is the real "stuff" of the discipline. While your textbook describes six distinct methods of research, actual research designs are often mixtures of methods. In this selection, Shively uses both a modified experiment and written questionnaires to explore a fascinating phenomenon—the fact that both whites and Native Americans enjoy Western movies, even when the film clearly portrays white heroes triumphing over evil Indians. As you read the article, notice how the author controls the influence of variables other than those she wishes to explore. Note the choice of the movie she used, as well as the makeup of the two groups of subjects.

Shively's findings are also quite interesting, since common sense would predict just the opposite, which left the author with the task of discovering why this was true. Since the explanations provided by earlier researchers in this area could not account for these findings, Shively's analysis of the data had to draw out an alternative, and also surprising, conclusion.

Cowboys and Indians
Perceptions of Western Films among American Indians and Anglos*

JOELLEN SHIVELY
University of Michigan

The dominant approach to understanding cultural products typically selects a particular popular genre for analysis in the hope of generating conclusions about the societal values expressed in the cultural product (some exceptions are Radway 1984; Griswold 1987; and Liebes and Katz 1990).[1] For example, Cawelti (1970,1976), on the basis of his reading of Western novels, concluded that these novels are a vehicle for exploring value conflicts, such as communal ideas versus individualistic impulses, and traditional ways of life versus progress. Cawelti argued that Westerns are formulaic works that provide readers with a vehicle for escape and moral fantasy.

In the major sociological study of Western films, Wright (1977) used his own viewing of most popular Western movies from 1931 to 1972 to argue that Westerns resemble primitive myths. Drawing on Levi-Strauss, Wright developed a cognitive theory of mythic structures in which "the receivers of the Western myth learn how to act by recognizing their own situation in it" (p. 186). Wright's main thesis is that the narrative themes of the Western resolve crucial contradictions in modern capitalism and provide viewers with strategies to deal with their economic worlds. The popularity of Westerns, Wright argued, lies in the genre's reflection of the changing economic system, which allows the viewers to use the Western as a guide for living.

These explanations of the Western's popularity attend to cultural texts but ignore the viewers, whose motives and experiences are crucial. The lack of solid data about audience

Shively, JoEllen. Cowboys and Indians: Perceptions of Western Films among American Indians and Anglos. *American Sociological Review, 57,* 6, 1992, 725–734. By permission of The American Sociological Association.

[1]Much work has involved literary and film studies. However, literary theories such as reader-response theory (Iser 1974; Fish 1980), pertain mostly to an "implied reader" within the text, and psychoanalyze what ethnicity, gender, religion, etc., in films mean (Friedman 1991). This work is interesting, but irrelevant for a study of how real audiences actually respond.

interpretations of various formulas renders existing models of the cultural significance of Westerns and other genres speculative.

While growing up on an Indian reservation in the Midwestern United States, I observed that fellow Indians loved Western movies and paperbacks. Subsequently, I observed this phenomenon on Indian reservations in Oregon and North Dakota, as well as among Indians who lived off the reservations. As scholars have noted (McNickle 1973; Cornell 1987; Snipp 1991), American Indians have always lived in a culturally, economically, and politically marginal subculture and are ambivalent about American values of achievement and acquisition of material wealth. Thus, it seemed unlikely that Indians who like Westerns would need them as conceptual guides for economic action as Wright alleged. The popularity of Westerns among Indians must be explained in other ways.

In an argument similar to Wright's, Swidler (1986) suggested that cultural works are tools used by people to contend with immediate problems. Swidler discussed "culture" in a broad sense as comprising "symbolic vehicles of meaning including beliefs, ritual practices, art forms, ceremonies as well as language, gossip, stories and rituals of daily life" (p. 272). Swidler was concerned with how culture shapes action and with how people "use" culture. Assuming that Western movies are a story or an art form, how do American Indians use this cultural product?

I address several issues that previous studies have made assumptions about, but have not addressed clearly. One issue is the general question of how different groups appropriate and find meaning in cultural products. In particular, does Wright's theory about the cultural use of Westerns hold true for American Indians watching a "cowboys vs. Indians" film? Is the mythic structure of a drama—the "good guy/bad guy" opposition in the Western—more salient than the ethnic aspect of the cultural product, or do Indians in the audience identify with Indians on the screen, regardless of who the good guys and bad guys are? Do Indians prefer Westerns that portray sympathetic and positive images of Indians, e.g., *Broken Arrow* and other movies described by Aleiss (1987) and Parish and Pitts (1976)? Do Indians like only Westerns that show a tribal group other than their own as the villains? Fundamentally, how do Indians link their own ethnic identity to the Western, or limit this identity so they can enter the narrative frame of the Western?

Research Design

Matched samples of 20 Indian males and 20 Anglo[2] males living in a town on an Indian reservation on the Western Plains of the United States watched a Western film, *The Searchers*. Ethnically pure groups were assembled by one Anglo informant and one Indian informant who invited five ethnically similar friends to their homes to watch the film. Written questionnaires were administered immediately after the film, followed by focus-group interviews. An Anglo female conducted the focus-group interviews with Anglos; I conducted the focus-group interviews with Indians. (I am Chippewa.) (Transcripts of the focus interviews are available from the author on request.)

---

[2]"Anglo" refers to non-Indian white Americans and does not include those of Spanish or Mexican descent.

Respondents were asked why they liked or did not like *The Searchers* in particular and Western movies in general. Basic demographic questions included racial identification, including "blood quantum" for Indians.

The research site is the second largest town on the reservation and has a population of about 1,200. Equal numbers of Indians and Anglos live in the town.[3] According to the Tribal Headquarters Enrollment Officer (Bighorn, 12 May 1988), of the 600 Indians, approximately 40 percent are Sioux, 10 percent are Assiniboine, 10 percent are Indians of mixed Indian origins, and approximately 40 percent of the self-identified Indians are "mixed-blood," i.e., Indian and white ancestry. Because I wanted to avoid the possible ambiguity of asking how mixed-bloods understand Westerns, all Indians in my sample claim to be "full-blood" Sioux, and all Anglos claim to be white.[4] Because the Western genre is primarily about males, only males were included in the sample.[5]

The respondents did not constitute a representative sample, but were assembled in an effort to create roughly matched groups. I attempted to match Indians and Anglos on age, income, years of education, occupation, and employment status, but succeeded in matching mainly on age, education, and occupation, and was less successful on income and employment status.[6] In the analysis, neither employment status nor income appear to affect the dependent variables. Matching Indians and Anglos on education required me to exclude college-educated respondents.[7] (All subjects were between the ages of 36 and 64—the average age of Indian respondents was 51, and the average age of Anglo respondents was 52. Most of the respondents were married.[8]

---

[3]Of the approximately 50,000 residents living on the 7 federally recognized reservations in this state in 1980, 48.5 percent are Indian and 51.5 percent are Anglo (Confederation of American Indians 1986, pp. 125–34). Under the 1887 General Allotment Act, more than 100 Indian Reservations on the Plains, along the Pacific Coast, and in the Great Lakes states, were divided up and allotted to individual Indians. The remaining land was declared "surplus" and opened up to white homesteaders. Under the terms of this Act, Indians were eventually dispossessed of almost 90 million acres (Talbot 1981, pp. 111–12). Today, whites continue to own land and live on these reservations where their land is "checker-boarded" between Indian-owned land. On some of these reservations, non-Indians own as much or more land than the tribe or Indians do, and the proportion white is equal to or higher than the proportion Indian. The research site is on one of these reservations.

[4]I have observed that "mixed-blood" Indians acknowledge and respect both their Indian and white ancestries. To avoid speculation about whether the findings might be associated with the self-identified Indians' "Indianness" or "whiteness," I included only full-bloods.

[5]My data show that the Western genre is popular among women, but because the major focus of this study is on racial differences and because I had a limited budget, I controlled for gender by looking at males only.

[6]The median annual household income for the Indians was $9,000; the median annual household income for the Anglos was $13,000. Seven of the 20 Indian men were unemployed at the time of the research compared to 3 of the Anglo men. Of currently employed Indians, four were working part-time; three of currently employed Anglos were working part-time. There are no significant differences between the Indians in my study and the 1980 Census data on income and unemployment (U.S. Bureau of the Census 1986, Tables 9, 10, 25; U.S. Bureau of the Census 1988, Table 234). Occupations of the Indians included bartender, farm worker, mechanic, factory worker, carpenter, and food-service worker. Occupations of the Anglos included janitor, school bus driver, bartender, store clerk, factory worker, carpenter, mechanic, foreman, and postal worker.

[7]Indians and Anglos differed in the proportion who completed high school, but this difference had no effect on the analysis. Among Indian respondents, 25 percent had completed high school and 60 percent had some high school. For Anglo respondents, 80 percent had completed high school and 20 percent had some high school.

[8]To obtain matched 20-person samples, 11 groups comprising 30 Indians and 25 Anglos watched the film. Of these, 2 Indians and 3 Anglos had "some college education" and 8 Indians and 2 Anglos were mixed-blood. These respondents' questionnaires were not used and the respondents were not involved in the focus interviews.

I chose *The Searchers* (1956) as the Western film to show because its major conflict is between cowboys and Indians. According to Wright (1977), *The Searchers* was one of the period's top-grossing films, a sign of mythical resonance. The film stars John Wayne—a critical advantage for a Western according to Indian and Anglo informants. Briefly, *The Searchers* is about Indian-hating Ethan Edwards's (John Wayne) and Martin Polly's (Jeff Hunter) five-year search to find Debbie Edwards, Ethan's niece (Natalie Wood), who has been kidnapped by Comanche Chief Scar (Henry Brandon). In the end, Scar is killed, and Debbie, who was married to Scar, is taken back to the white civilized world.

Findings

I began my research with the assumption that people understand movies based on their own cultural backgrounds. Therefore, the experience of watching Western movies should be different for Indians and Anglos, especially when watching scenes in which Indians are portrayed in distorted, negative ways. My most striking finding, however, is an overall similarity in the ways Indians and Anglos experienced *The Searchers*.

All respondents—Indians and Anglos—indicated that they liked Western movies in general. Furthermore, in the focus interviews, they said they wished more Westerns were being produced in Hollywood. I asked the respondents to rank the three types of films they most liked to watch from a list of 10 (musical, gangster, horror, and so on). All 40 subjects—both Anglo and Indian—ranked Westerns first or second; the Western was far and away the most popular genre. Seventy-five percent ranked Westerns first. Combat movies were a distant second, and science fiction movies were third.

On both the written questionnaires and in the focus interviews, all respondents indicated that they liked *The Searchers* and considered it a typical Western. One Indian and two Anglos reported that they had seen the film before.

In response to the question, "With whom did you identify most in the film?," 60 percent of the Indians and 50 percent of the Anglos identified with John Wayne, while 40 percent of the Indians and 45 percent of the Anglos identified with Jeff Hunter.[9] None of the Indians (or Anglos) identified with the Indian chief, Scar. Indians did not link their own ethnic identity to Scar and his band of Indians, but instead distanced themselves from the Indians in the film. The Indians, like the Anglos, identified with the characters that the narrative structure tells them to identify with—the good guys. In the focus-group interviews, both Indians and Anglos reiterated their fondness for John Wayne. For both audiences, the Indians in the film were either neutral or negative. What stood out was not that there were Indians on the screen, but that the Indians were the "bad guys." For example, in the focus groups respondents were asked. "Do you ever root for the Indians?" Both Indians and Anglos consistently responded, "Sometimes, when they're the good guys." Their responses suggest that there is no strong ethnic bias governing whom the respondents root for and identify with. Instead, antagonism is directed against the bad guys. The structure of oppositions that defines the heroes in a film seems to guide viewers' identification with the characters in the film and overrides any ethnic empathy.

---

[9]One Anglo identified with Laurie, Jeff Hunter's girlfriend. It was difficult to tell why.

The Indians' identification with the good guys in the film is similar to Jahoda's (1961, p. 104) observations of African audiences reacting to films set in Africa that portray Africans as "rude, barbaric savages." Jahoda found that the majority of Africans did not identify with the Africans on the screen—only a minority of highly-educated Africans identified with the Africans.

Although Indians and Anglos relied on cues in *The Searchers* about whom to identify with, in other ways the fictional frame of the film did not completely capture these viewers. When discussing *The Searchers,* Indians and Anglos rarely used the main characters' story names. Instead they used the actors' names—John Wayne and Jeff Hunter—which suggests a strong "star effect." Although John Wayne plays different characters in different films, these audiences associated his "cowboy" personality with the off-screen John Wayne, not with specific movie characters. On one level, they saw the actor as embodying all his movie roles. For example, when asked, "Why do you think Ethan Edwards hated the Indians in this movie?" the Indians and Anglos responded in similar ways:

Indians:

Well, John Wayne might have hated Indians in this movie, but in other movies he doesn't hate them. (Mechanic, age 51)

Well, they've killed his brother and his brother's wife. He doesn't hate Indians in all his movies. (Cook, age 56)

Anglos

John Wayne doesn't like the Indians here because they've killed his brother's family. But in other movies, he's on their side. He sticks up for them. (Foreman, age 56)

Sometimes he fights for the Indians like in Fort Apache. (Bartender, age 48)

Both Indians and Anglos reported that they liked all of John Wayne's movies, whether he played a boxing champion, a pilot, or a cowboy. In all of his films, they see the strong personality characteristics of "the Duke," or "Dude," as some of the respondents referred to him. For both Indians and Anglos on this reservation, being called "cowboy" or one of John Wayne's nicknames, often "Dude" or "Duke," is a token of respect. Indians often see themselves as "cowboys," greeting each other with, "How ya doing, cowboy?," or "Long time no see, cowboy," and refer to their girlfriends or wives as "cowgirls." Fixico (1986) described a similar emulation of the cowboy among reservation Indians in Arizona and South Dakota.

The respondents talked about John Wayne as if he were one of them and they knew him personally—like a good friend. Believing in John Wayne the man is part of the charisma attached to the cowboy role. It is a self-reinforcing cycle: Because John Wayne always plays good guys characters with whom viewers empathize—it is easy to identify with John Wayne and all he represents. Levy (1990) noted that, "because acting involves actual role playing and because of the 'realistic' nature of motion pictures, audiences sometimes fail to separate between players' roles onscreen and their real lives offscreen. The difference between life on and offscreen seems to blur" (p. 281). For respondents, John Wayne *is* the Cowboy, both in his movies and in real life. This focus on "John Wayne in real life" is similar to Liebes and Katz's (1990) finding that when retelling episodes of the TV series "Dallas," Americans and Kibbutzniks talk about the "real life" (behind-the-scene) personalities of the actors.

The Real and the Fictional: Patterns of Differences

Although Anglos and Indians responded in similar ways to the structure of oppositions in the narrative, the two groups interpreted and valued characteristics of the cultural product differently once they "entered" the narrative. The narrative was (re)interpreted to fit their own interests. Although both Indians and Anglos saw some aspects of *The Searchers* as real and others as fictional, the two groups differed on what they saw as authentic and what they saw as fictional.

Table 1.1 hows how the two groups responded when asked to rank their three most important reasons for liking the film. The Kendall rank-order correlation coefficient of $\tau = .29$ indicates that Indians' and Anglos' reasons often differed. The two groups agreed on the importance of "action and fights," "it had cowboys and Indians," and "the scenery and landscape" as reasons for liking the film. They also agreed that "romance" was not an important reason for liking the film. But the differences between Indians and Anglos in Table 1.1 are striking: None of the Indians ranked "authentic portrayal of the Old West" as an important reason for liking the movie, while 50 percent of the Anglos ranked it as the most important reason.

The results in Table 1.1 suggest that the distinctive appeal of the Western for Indians has two elements: (1) the cowboy's way of life—the idealized Western lifestyle seems to make this cultural product resonate for Indians; and (2) the setting of the film, the beauty

TABLE 1.1 Ranks of Reasons for Liking *The Searchers*, by Ethnicity

Reason	American Indians				Anglos			
	Ranked 1st	Ranked 2nd	Ranked 3rd	Weighted Sum of Ranks*	Ranked 1st	Ranked 2nd	Ranked 3rd	Weighted Sum of Ranks*
Action/fights	2	4	5	19	2	6	4	22
John Wayne	5	3	2	23	2	3	0	12
It had cowboys and Indians	6	5	3	31	3	2	5	18
Scenery/landscape	6	3	2	26	3	5	6	25
Humor	1	5	6	19	0	1	1	3
Romance	0	0	1	1	0	0	1	1
Authentic portrayal of Old West	0	0	0	0	10	3	3	39
Other	0	0	1	1	0	0	0	0

*Ranks are weighted: 1st × 3; 2nd × 2; 3rd × 1.

of the landscape (Monument Valley) moves Indian viewers. When asked in the focus groups, "Why did you like this film, and what makes Westerns better (or worse) than other kinds of movies?" Indians reported: "Westerns relate to the way I wish I could live"; "The cowboy is free"; "He's not tied down to an eight-to-five job, day after day"; "He's his own man"; and "He has friends who are like him." What makes Westerns meaningful to Indians is the fantasy of being free and independent like the cowboy and the familiarity of the landscape or setting.

The setting also resonated for Anglos, but Anglos perceived these films as authentic portrayals of their past. In the focus groups, Anglos, but not Indians, talked about Westerns as accurate chronicles of their history. When asked, "Why did you like this film, and what makes Westerns better (or worse) than other kinds of movies?" Anglos said, "My grandparents were immigrants and Westerns show us the hard life they had"; "Westerns are about my heritage and how we settled the frontier and is about all the problems they had"; "Westerns give us an idea about how things were in the old days"; and "Westerns are true to life." What is meaningful to Anglos is not the fantasy of an idealized lifestyle, but that Western films link Anglos to their own history. For them, Western films are like primitive myths: They affirm and justify that their ancestors' actions when "settling this country" were right and good and necessary.[10]

Indians seemed ambivalent about how the Old West was portrayed in *The Searchers*. In the focus groups, I asked Indians if the film was an authentic portrayal of the Old West and they responded:

> *As far as the cowboy's life goes, it's real, but you don't get to know the Indians, so it's hard to say it's totally authentic. (Bartender, age 42)*

> *I think it's real in some ways, like when you see the cowboy and how he was. (Mechanic, age 51)*

> *The cowboys are real to me. That's the way they were. But I don't know about the Indians 'cause you never see much of them. (Farm worker, age 50)*

> *Yeah, the movie is more about the good guys than the bad guys. I mean, the bad guys are there, but you don't get to know them very well. Mostly the movie is about the cowboys, the good guys, anyway. (Carpenter, age 48)*

For Indians, the film was more about cowboys than about Indians. This does not hinder their enjoyment of the film or make it less meaningful, because they did not view the Indians on the screen as real Indians.

Both Indians and Anglos were asked, "Are Indians and cowboys in this film like Indians and cowboys in the past?" and, "Are they like Indians and cowboys today?" Anglos replied:

---

[10]Describing the role of the myth among Trobriand Islanders, Malinowski (1948) wrote: "The *myth* comes into play when rite, ceremony, or a social or moral rule demands justification, warrant of antiquity, reality, and sanctity" (pp. 84–85).

I think the cowboys and the settlers are pretty much like those in the old days. It's hard to say if the Indians are like Indians in the past. (Mechanic, age 39)

They're not like Indians today. (Foreman, age 56)

Indians don't go around kidnapping white women and children these days. (Bartender, age 48)

Probably they're similar to how some of the Indians were in the past, I mean Indians really did scalp white men. (Postal worker, age 49)

Yeah, and they kidnapped white children and white women. My grandparents used to tell stories about how their parents told them to be careful when they played outside. They had to stay close to their homes, 'cause the Indians used to kidnap children. (Bus driver, age 49)

Anglos thought the cowboys in the Western were similar to cowboys of the past, and they suggested that Indians in the film were similar to Indians in the past. However, they did not think Indians today are like Indians in the film.

When asked the same questions about whether Indians and cowboys in the film are like Indians and cowboys today and in the past, Indians replied somewhat differently:

The cowboys are like cowboys in the past. Maybe some Indians in the past were like the Indians in the films. (Bartender, age 58)

They're not like Indians today. I mean, the only time Indians dress up is for pow-wows. (Cook, age 60)

In this movie and other movies with Indians, you don't get to know them. I mean, they're not really people, like the cowboys are. It's hard to say they're like Indians in the past. For sure they're not like Indians today. (Bartender, age 42)

The Indians aren't at all like any of the Indians I know. (Unemployed factory worker, age 44)

Indians today are the cowboys. (Bartender, age 42)

The phrase "Indians today are the cowboys," means that contemporary Indians are more like cowboys than Anglos are, in the sense that it is Indians who preserve some commitment to an autonomous way of life that is not fully tied to modern industrial society. Indians want to be, and value being, independent and free—separate from society—more than Anglos do.

Because *The Searchers* portrays Indians not as human beings, but as "wild, blood-thirsty animals," Indians might be expected to report that the Indians on the screen are not like Indians they know today or like Indians in the past. How could they identify with the Indians on the screen when Indians are portrayed in such a caricatured fashion? The only connections that Indians made between the Indians on the screen and Indians of the past and present were with the costumes worn by the Indians on the screen.

On some deeper level, however, Indian respondents may have identified with the Indians on the screen. For example, when asked in the focus groups, "What's a bad Western like?" Indians reported that they like all Westerns except for films like *Soldier Blue.* All of the Indian respondents were familiar with this film. *Soldier Blue* is a 1970 film based on the Sand Creek massacre of 1864, when Colonel Chivington of the U.S. Cavalry ambushed and slaughtered a village of peaceful Arapaho and Cheyenne children, women, and men in Colorado. In all of die Indian focus groups, this title was mentioned as one Western they did not like. This suggests that when films are too realistic and evoke unpleasant emotions, they are no longer enjoyable. This finding resembles Radway's (1984, p. 184) findings about "failed" romance novels. A "failed" romance is one that evokes overly intense feelings of anger, fear, and violence. Such novels are discarded by readers because they are not enjoyable. *Soldier Blue,* however, is sympathetic to the Indians, and the narrative leads the viewer to empathize with the Indians. Unlike the Indians, Anglos reported that they like all Westerns and could not think of an example of a bad Western.

Another striking difference revealed in Table 1.1 is that Indians cited "humor" as an important reason for liking the film, while Anglos did not. In the focus groups, Indians talked about several comic scenes in the film. When asked if humor was important in Western films, they all said. "Yeah." They reported that they liked humor and wit in Western movies and valued this trait in their friends. Humor is a source of joy for them—a gift.

Anglos, in contrast, never mentioned John Wayne's humor. Why did Indians and not Anglos respond to the humor? If Anglos perceived the film as an authentic story of their past, they may have concentrated on the serious problems in the film, i.e., getting the white girl back. Perhaps Anglos were so preoccupied with the film as an affirmation of their past that they were unable to focus on the intended humor, or at least other characteristics of the film were more important. On the other hand, Indians, who did not see the film as an authentic story of their own past, may have focused more on the intended humor in the film.

Ideal Heroes

Indians and Anglos also valued individual traits of the cowboy differently. Table 1.2 shows how the two groups responded when asked to rank the three most important qualities that make a good hero in a good Western. A Kendall rank-order correlation coefficient of $\tau = .167$ shows little agreement between Indian and Anglo rankings. Indians ranked "toughness" and "bravery" as the two most important qualities of a good hero in a good Western, whereas Anglos ranked "integrity/honesty" and "intelligence" as most important. Perhaps audiences look for exceptional characteristics in a good hero—qualities they would like to see in themselves. To live free and close to the land like Indians wish to live, exceptional bravery and toughness are necessary. Because Anglos do not want to live like cowboys, bravery and toughness are not as important. Responses of Indians in Table 1.2 are similar to responses in Table 1.1 and to the oral responses. For example, when the Indians described John Wayne as a reason why they liked *The Searchers,* they concentrated on John Wayne's toughness.

While the two groups differed on the qualities that make a good hero, Indians and Anglos tended to agree on the characteristics of a good Western. When asked what characteristics they liked in a good Western, a Kendall's rank-order correlation coefficient

TABLE 1.2   Ranks of Qualities That Make a Good Hero in a Good Western, by Ethnicity

Quality	American Indians				Anglos			
	Ranked 1st	Ranked 2nd	Ranked 3rd	Weighted Sum of Ranks*	Ranked 1st	Ranked 2nd	Ranked 3rd	Weighted Sum of Ranks*
Bravery	8	6	4	40	3	4	1	18
Integrity/honesty	2	2	0	10	8	9	5	47
Independence	0	0	2	2	0	0	1	1
Toughness	8	8	4	44	0	0	0	0
Sense of humor	0	2	8	12	0	1	1	3
Strength	2	0	0	6	0	0	0	0
Loyalty	0	0	0	0	1	0	7	10
Intelligence	0	2	2	6	8	6	5	41
Other	0	0	0	0	0	0	0	0

*Ranks are weighted: 1st × 3; 2nd × 2; 3rd × 1.

between Indian and Anglo responses was high, $\tau = .78$, i.e., there were no pronounced differences between Indians and Anglos. For both groups, the three most important characteristics of a good Western were: "a happy ending"; "action/fights"; and "authentic portrayal of Old West." Like the ranking of "a happy ending" as the most important ingredient in a good romance novel (Radway 1984, p. 59), Indian and Anglo viewers ranked "a happy ending" as the most desirable characteristic of a good Western. The essential happy ending for my respondents may be related to Cawelti's (1976, p. 193) "epic moment" when the villain is conquered, the wilderness is subdued, and civilization is established. The importance of the "happy ending" may also support Wright's (1977) contention that the outcome of the Western narrative is important.

For Indians, the importance of a "happy ending" in a good Western film also reflects on their evaluation of *Soldier Blue* as a bad Western—*Soldier Blue* does not fulfill the "happy ending" criterion of a good Western. Although Indians like action or fights, they are discerning about what kinds of action or fights they enjoy.

For both Anglos and Indians, the three least liked characteristics of a good Western were: "hero rides off into the sunset alone"; "Indians as bad guys"; and "romance between hero and woman." Both groups preferred that "the hero settles down." In some ways, the characteristics the respondents like to see in a good Western support Cawelti's assumptions about the cultural significance of the Western.[11]

[11]I collected some data in the field on female reservation Indians and female Anglos. These data reveal gender differences as well as differences, by ethnicity. For example, women identified with the women in the film, while the men did not. Women ranked "romance" as one of the most important reasons for liking the film, whereas the men ranked it as the least important reason. Women ranked "action/fights" as one of the least important reasons for liking the film, while the men ranked it as one of the most important reasons. Like Anglo men, Anglo women saw the film as an authentic portrayal of the past, while the Indian women, like the Indian men, did not. Indian women, like Indian men, also distanced themselves from the Indians on the screen.

The Politics of Perception

Some Indians *do* identify with the Indians in the Western and are not affected by the film's signals about whom to identify with. Before taking my research procedures into the field, I pretested them with 15 American Indian college students at a West Coast university (10 males, 5 females). Because Indians in the reservation sample differed in important characteristics from the Indians in the pretests (9 of the Indian students were "mixed-bloods"), systematic comparisons were not possible.

However, Indian students responded differently from Indians in the reservation sample. Ethnicity was a salient issue for the majority of the students. The narrative of *The Searchers* did not "work" for the students and they were unable to fully enter the drama. For example, unlike the reservation Indians, a majority of the Indian students identified with and rooted for Scar and his Indians or Debbie, the kidnapped girl. They thought Debbie should have been allowed to stay with Scar and that the search should not have taken place at all.

Like the reservation Indians, the college-educated Indians did not view *The Searchers* as an authentic portrayal of the "Old West" and were quick to point out stereotypical portrayals of Indians in the film. They reacted against the negative message in the film that "the only good Indian is a dead one." They also pointed out many inaccuracies in the film, such as the use of Navajos and the Navajo language for Comanche, "Comanche" Indians wearing Sioux war bonnets, and Indians sometimes wearing war bonnets while fishing. Neither the Indians nor the Anglos in the reservation sample mentioned any of these inaccuracies.

All students but one reported that they liked Westerns in general, but preferred Westerns whose plots are about "cowboys vs. cowboys" or "Indians vs. Indians," or a "cowboys vs. Indians" plot in which the Indian point of view is shown. Several male students indicated that they and their friends often rent Western videos and named the video stores nearest the university that had the best selection of Westerns.

None of the students particularly liked John Wayne. Like the reservation sample, the students talked about John Wayne in "real life" and referred to what they considered racist statements he made off-screen in various interviews.

I asked each student, "Do Indians back home on the reservation like Westerns?" and "Do they root for the cowboys?" All of them said, "Oh yeah, sure." One Sioux student said his father had most of John Wayne's films on video, and a Chippewa said that his uncle was named after John Wayne. One Navajo said of his reservation town, "Ever since they closed down the movie theater several years ago, every Friday night they show a movie in the cafeteria room at the high school, and most of the time it's a Western. Everybody goes."

The heightened ethnic awareness of the college students interferes with, or overrides, their responses to the Western so that they do not get caught up in the structure of oppositions in the narrative. Because they identify with their ethnic group, they see *The Searchers* through a different lens. Education increases their awareness of anti-Indian bias in the film, producing a "revised eye" that frames these films in ethnic terms. In this context, ethnicity is a construct of a particular culture or subculture.

Conclusion

Although it would seem problematic for Indians to know which characters to identify with in *The Searchers,* it was not a problem for them at all—they identified with the cowboy and his lifestyle. Indians did not focus on the Indians, who are often portrayed on-screen as a faceless, screaming horde. Instead, they saw the cowboys as they want to see themselves—as the good guys.

What appears to make Westerns meaningful to Indians is the fantasy of being free and independent like the cowboy. In addition, the familiarity of the setting is important. Anglos, on the other hand, respond to the Western as a story about their past and their ancestors. The Western narrative becomes an affirmation of their own social experience— the way they are and what their ancestors strove for and imposed on the West are "good." Thus, for Anglos, the Western resembles a primitive myth. But it is not a myth in this sense for Indians—Indians do not view the Western as authentic.

Both Indians and Anglos find a fantasy in the cowboy story in which the important parts of their ways of life triumph and are morally good, validating their own cultural group in the context of a dramatically satisfying story. Perhaps this motive for ethnic group validation is more general and not peculiar to cowboy movies.

Oppositions in the Western narrative are important to viewers. Indians and Anglos both root for and identify with the good guys. The strength of the narrative lies in its Levi-Straussian oppositions, and Wright (1977) correctly focused on them. However, Wright's thesis, that viewers see their own economic situation in Westerns and use its messages to deal with their economic world, is not supported here. Both Indians and Anglos respond to "their own situation," but not in Wright's sense. Wright's sociological explanation of the cultural significance of Westerns does not entirely contradict Cawelti (1976). Although Cawelti's discussion is too nonspecific, and therefore more difficult to refute, my evidence is more compatible with Cawelti's argument that viewers use Westerns as a fantasy for exploring value conflicts (e.g., traditional ways of life versus progress) and to affirm the value of their ideals and way of life. Cawelti's nonspecificity and Wright's incorrect explanation may have resulted from their failure to ask viewers or readers *why* they like Westerns.

The Indian college students, who by attending college have opted for some of the values of white society, find other meanings in *The Searchers.* Because they are immersed in the intellectual world of the university, the symbolic importance of the film for them lies in its false representation of their ancestry and history.

References

Aleiss, Angela. 1987. "Hollywood Addresses Post-war Assimilation: Indian/White Attitudes in *Broken Arrow.*" *American Indian Culture and Research Journal* 11:67–79.

Bighorn, Spike N. 1988. Personal communication with author. 12 May.

Cawelti, John. 1970. *The Six-Gun Mystique.* Bowling Green, OH: Bowling Green State University Popular Press.

———. 1976. *Adventure, Mystery and Romance.* Chicago: University of Chicago Press.

Confederation of American Indians. 1986. *Indian Reservations: A State and Federal Handbook.* Jefferson, NC: McFarland.

Cornell, Stephen. 1987. "American Indians, American Dreams, and the Meaning of Success." *American Indian Culture and Research Journal* 11:59–70.

Fish, Stanley. 1980. *Is There a Text in This Class?* Cambridge, MA: Harvard University Press.

Fixico, Donald L. 1986. "From Indians to Cowboys: The Country Western Trend." Pp. 8–14 in *American Indian Identity: Today's Changing Perspectives,* edited by C. E. Trafzer. Sacramento, CA: Sierra Oaks Publishing Company.

Friedman, Lester D., ed. 1991. *Unspeakable Images: Ethnicity and the American Cinema.* Chicago: University of Illinois Press.

Griswold, Wendy. 1987. "The Fabrication of Meaning: Literary Interpretation in the United States, Great Britain, and the West Indies." *American Journal of Sociology* 92:1077–117.

Iser, Wolfgang. 1974. *The Implied Reader: Patterns of Communication in Prose Fiction from Bisnyan to Beckett.* Baltimore, MD: Johns Hopkins University Press.

Jahoda, Gustav. 1961. *White Man: A Study of the Attitudes of Africans to Europeans in Ghana before Independence.* London: Oxford University Press.

Levy, Emanuel. 1990. *And the Winner Is . . . : The History and Politics of the Oscar Awards.* New York: Continuum.

Liebes, Tamar and Elihu Katz. 1990. *The Export of Meaning: Cross Cultural Readings of DALLAS.* New York: Oxford University Press.

McNickle, D'Arcy, 1973. *Native American Tribalism: Indian Survivals and Renewals.* New York: Oxford University Press.

Malinowski, Bronislaw. 1948. *Magic, Science, and Religion and Other Essays.* Glencoe, IL: The Free Press.

Parish, James R. and Michael R. Pitts. 1976. *The Great Western Pictures.* Metuchen, NJ: The Scarecrow Press, Inc.

Radway, Janice A. 1984. *Reading the Romance: Women, Patriarchy, and Popular Literature.* Chapel Hill, NC: University of North Carolina Press.

Snipp, C. Matthew. 1991. *American Indians: The First of This Land.* New York: Russell Sage Foundation.

Swidler, Ann 1986. "Culture in Action: Symbols and Strategies." *American Sociological Review* 51:273–86.

Talbot, Steve. 198 1. *Roots Of Oppression: The American Indian Question.* New York: International Publishers.

U.S. Bureau of the Census. 1986. *1980 Census of Population. American Indians, Eskimos, and Aleuts On Identified Reservations and in The Historical Areas of Oklahoma.* Vols. 1–2, Subject Report prepared by the U.S. Department of Commerce. Washington, DC: U.S. Government Printing Office.

———. 1988. *1980 County and City Data Book.* Prepared by the U.S. Department of Commerce. Washington, DC: U.S. Government Printing Office.

Wright, Will. 1977. *Sixguns and Society: A Structural Analysis of the Western.* Berkeley, CA: University of California Press.

Discussion Questions

1. Which among the three theoretical perspectives discussed in this chapter best fits Shively's research? How might the research design be changed to fit each of the other two perspectives?

2. How might research similar to Shively's be designed using other methods? Could other methods be combined to study the same topic? Do you think a change in research design would yield different results? If so, why?

C h a p t e r 2

Culture

Perhaps no society with any complexity has been free of countercultures. The legend of Robin Hood and his band might be an example of a counterculture in Feudal England. In her article, Fox looks at the fascinating world of "punk." She combines participant observation and interviews to explore the makeup of people embracing the punk lifestyle to various degrees.

From a distance, the punk scene seems like an unorganized, if not disorganized, mass of young people who are held together only by their attraction to lifestyles represented by various kinds of rock bands. However, Fox found far more than that—pointing out three layers of organized adherents, in addition to those who were mere spectators. As researchers have found with other groups, the difference among that layers in based primarily on commitment to the cause.

It would be easy to focus the research merely on the differences among punks, but Fox extends her analysis by asking what functions each group performed for the counterculture as well as how they represented antiestablishment groups in general. Findings from this kind of research can do much to dispel the kind of us-against-them mentality people often assume when facing groups that are markedly different from themselves.

Subcultures and Countercultures
Real Punks and Pretenders: The Social Organization of a Counterculture

KATHRYN JOAN FOX

Modern Western Society has been characterized by a variety of antiestablishment style countercultures following in succession (i.e., the Teddy Boys of 1953–1957, the Mods and Rockers of 1964–1966, the Skinheads of 1967–1970, and the Punk Rockers of the late 1970s; Taylor, 1982). The punk culture is but the latest in this series. Since most studies of youth- and style-oriented groups are British (Frith, 1982), very little has been written from a sociological perspective about punks in the United States. This study is an attempt to fill that void.

Whether or not the punk scene in the United States could be legitimately classified as a social movement is debatable. Most writers on this contemporary phenomenon agree that American punks have a more amorphous, less articulated ideological agenda than punks elsewhere (Brake, 1985; Street, 1986). While the punk scene in England responded to youth unemployment and working-class problems, the phenomenon in the United States was more closely connected to style than to politics. Street (1986: 175) notes that even for English punks, "politics was part of the style." I would argue that this was even more the case for American punks. The consciousness of the youth in the United States did not parallel the identification with the plight of youth found in Europe. Nonetheless, the "style" code for punks in the United States contained an insistent element of conflict with the dominant value system. The consensual values among the punks, as ambiguous as they were, could best be understood by their contradictory quality with reference to mainstream society. In this respect, punk in America fit the definition of a "counterculture" offered by Yinger (1982: 22–23). According to this definition, the salient feature of a counterculture is its contrariness. Further, as opposed to individual deviant behavior, punks constituted a counterculture in that they shared a specific normative system. Certain behaviors were con-

Fox, Kathryn Joan. Real Punks and Pretenders: The Social Organization of a Counterculture. *Journal of Contemporary Ethnography, 16,*3, Oct. 1987, 344–370. By permission of Sage Publications.

16

sidered punk, while others were not. Indeed, style was the message and the means of expression. Observation of behaviors that were consistent with punk sensibilities were viewed as indicative of punk "beliefs." These behaviors, along with verbal pronouncements, verified commitment. Within the groups of punks I studied, the degree of commitment to the counterculture lifestyle was the variable that determined placement within the hierarchy of the local scene.

Previous portrayals of youthful, antiestablishment style cultures have discussed their norms and values (Berger, 1967; Davis, 1970; Hebdige, 1981; Yablonsky, 1968), their relationship to conventional society (Cohen, 1972; Douglas, 1970; Flacks, 1967), their focal concerns and ideology (Flacks, 1967; Miller, 1958), and their relationship to social class (Brake, 1980; Hall and Jefferson, 1975; Mungham and Pearson, 1976). With the exception of Davis and Munoz (1968), Kinsey (1982), and Yablonsky (1959), few of the studies of antiestablishment, countercultural groups discuss their implicit stratification. In this essay I will describe and analyze the various categories of membership in the punk scene and show how members of these strata differ with regard to their ideology, appearance, taste, lifestyle, and commitment.

I begin by discussing how I became interested in the topic and the methods I employed to gain access to the group and to gather data. I then offer a description of the setting and the people who frequented this scene. Next I offer a structural portrayal of the social organization of this punk scene, showing how,the layers of membership form. I then examine each of the three membership categories (hardcore punks, softcore punks, and preppie punks), as well as the spectator category, focusing on the differences in their attitudes, behavior, and involvement with this antiestablishment style culture. I conclude by outlining the contributions each of these types of members makes to the continuing existence of the punk movement, and, more broadly, by describing the relation between the punk counterculture and conventional society.

Methods

My interest in the punk movement dates back to 1978. At that time, I attended a local punk bar fairly regularly and wore my hair and clothing in "punk" style, albeit not the radical version. I also visited a major northeastern city at about the same time, when the punk scene was in full flower, and spent several nights visiting what are now famous punk hangouts. My early interest and involvement in this scene laid the groundwork for this study, as it permitted me to gain knowledge of the punk vernacular, styles, and motives. The research continued, with active, weekly participation, through the middle of 1986. I have continued to keep a close watch on national trends and developments in punk culture. Further, I continually frequent local punk bars in an effort to deepen my understanding and to observe the decline of this counterculture. However, I conducted the bulk of my interviews in the fall of 1983 over a period of about two months. During that time, I attended "punk night" at a local bar once a week. In addition, I was invited to other punk functions, such as parties, midnight jam sessions, and public property destruction events. I thereby observed approximately 30 members of this movement with some degree of regularity. I used mainly observational techniques, along with some participation. Although I frequented numerous punk gatherings, my participatory role was constrained by the limited time I spent there. I also had to tread a line between covert and overt roles. While some people knew I was researching this setting, I could not reveal this to others because they might have denied me further access to the group. This created a problem, much the same as that experienced by Henslin (1972) and Adler (1985), in that I had to be careful about what I said and to whom I confided my research interests. This "tightrope effect" severely limited my active participation in the scene.

Nevertheless, by following the investigative research techniques advocated by Douglas (1976), I was able to gain the trust of some key members. I tried to establish friendly relations by running errands for them, buying them drinks and food, and driving them to pick up their welfare checks and food stamps. After several weeks, when I began to be recognized, I was able to broach the topic of doing interviews with several people. I formally interviewed nine people at locations outside the bar. These tape-recorded interviews were unstructured and open-ended. Additionally, I conducted 15 informal interviews at the bar. Finally, I had countless conversations with members, nonmembers, interested bystanders, and social scientists who had an interest in the punk counterculture. In all, my somewhat punk appearance, similar age, regularity at the scene, and apparent acceptance of their lifestyle allowed me to move within the scene freely and easily.

Setting

The research took place in a small cowboy bar, "The Glass Gun," which was transformed into a punk bar one night a week. The bar was situated in a southwestern city with a population of about 500,000. The city itself is located in the "Bible Belt," characterized by conservative religious and political views. The bar was a small, dark, and dilapidated place. There was a stage area where the bands played, surrounded by a wooden rail. Wobbly tables and torn chairs formed a U-shape around the stage. There was a pool table in the corner, which the punks rarely used. Most of the patrons of the club stood at or near the bar.

For the punks in this city, the Glass Gun was the only place to congregate regularly at that time. On these designated nights, local punk bands played to an audience of about 20 people; some were punks, others were not. The typical audience ranged in age from about 16 to 30, although a few were younger or older. Basically, the punk counterculture was a youth phenomenon. It seemed to attract young, single, mobile people. Snow et at. (1980) have suggested that these characteristics make a person more, "structurally available" for movement recruitment. Within the punk scene the number of men and women was fairly equal.

The punk style codes were somewhat diverse. Different styles existed for different kinds of punk. Pfohl (1985: 381) has referred to Hebdige's description of punk style as "the outrageous disfigurement of commonsensical images of aesthetics and beauty and the abrasive, destructive codes of punk style. These are aesthetic inversions of the normal, or consensus-producing, rituals of the dominant culture's style." The basic identifiable element was a subculturally accepted punk hairstyle. These ranged from a very short, uneven haircut, sticking straight up in front, to an American Indian mohawk style, to a shaven head. Along with the haircut, a punk fashion prevailed. The two were inextricably associated. The fashion ranged from torn, faded jeans, T-shirts, and army boots to expensive leather outfits.

The punk dress code was also fairly androgynous. There was no real distinction between male and female fashions. Both men and women wore faded jeans, although leather pants and miniskirts were also quite common among the women. The middle-class punk women, who tended to be students, dressed in a more traditionally feminine manner, glorifying and exaggerating the "glamour girl" image reminiscent of the sixties. This included tight skirts, teased hair, and dark, heavy makeup. The other punk women identified with a more masculine, working-class image, deemphasizing their feminine attributes. Both sexes also wore and admired leather jackets. It was also quite common to see both men and women with multiple pierced earrings all the way around the outside of their ears. Men sometimes wore eye makeup as well. (One man wore miniskirts, makeup, and rhinestones. However, this type of behavior occurred infrequently.) Basically, punk style ran counter to what the dominant culture would deem aesthetically pleasing. One major reason punks dressed as they did was to set themselves apart and to make themselves recognizable. The image consisted of dark, drab clothing, short, spiky, "homemade" haircuts, and blank, bored, expressionless faces reminiscent of those of concentration camp prisoners.[1] The punks created a new aesthetic that revealed their lack of hope, cynicism, and rejection of societal norms.

The Social Organization of the Punk Scene

Like the youth gangs that Yablonsky (1962) studied, members of this local punk scene constituted a "near-group." The membership was impermanent and shifting, members' expectations were not always clearly defined, consensus within the group was problematic, and the leadership was vague. Yet out of this uncertainty surfaced an apparent consensus about the stratification of the local community and the roles of the three types of members and peripheral hangers-on who participated in this scene. These four typologies can be hierarchically arranged by the presence (or absence) and intensity of their commitment to the punk counterculture and their consequent display of the punk affectations and belief system. They thus formed a series of outwardly expanding concentric circles, with the most committed members occupying the core, inner roles, and the least involved participants falling around the periphery.

Starting from the center, the number of members occupying each stratum progressively increased as the commitment level of the participants diminished. The categories to which I refer come from the terms used by the participants themselves.[2] The *hardcore punks* were the most involved in the scene, and derived the greatest amount of prestige from their association with it. They set the trends and standards for the rest of the members. The *softcore punks* were less dedicated to the antiestablishment lifestyle and to a permanent

---

[1] I am indebted to David Matza and John Torpey for this analogy.

[2] With the exception of the term *softcore,* all of the distinctions between categories came directly from the participants. The members did make a distinction between hardcore and what I am calling softcore punks. However, the softcores were referred to simply as "punks" by the hardcores, in an effort to distinguish the "hardcore" quality they attributed to themselves. I chose to refrain from using the term *punk* to apply to one specific category so that I can use the term more freely and generally, and to avoid confusion.

association with the counterculture, yet their degree of involvement was still high. They were greater in number, and, while highly respected by the less committed participants, did not occupy the same social status within the group as the hardcores. Their roles were, in a sense, dictated by the hardcores, whom they admired, and who defined the acceptable norms and values. The *preppie punks* were only minimally committed, constituting the largest portion of the actual membership. They were held in low esteem by the two core groups, following their lead but lacking the inner conviction and degree of participation necessary to be considered socially desirable within the scene. Finally, the *spectators* made up the largest part of the crowd at any public setting where a punk event transpired. They were not truly members of the group, and therefore did not necessarily revere the actions and dedication of the hardcores as did the two intermediary groups. They did not attempt to follow the standards of those committed to this near-group. They were merely outsiders with an interest in the punk scene.

These four groups constituted the range of participants who attended and were involved with, to varying degrees, the punk counterculture. I will now examine in greater detail their styles, beliefs, practices, intentions, and roles in the scene.

Punks and Commitment

At the time of this study, the group of punks was small and disorganized. The number of people at any given punk event had steadily declined since my first encounters with the scene in 1978. Punk was no longer a new phenomenon, and this particularly conservative community did not provide a very conducive atmosphere for a large countercultural group to flourish. Every member of the group expressed dissatisfaction and boredom with the events (or rather, lack of events) within the scene. Even within the limits necessitated by the relatively small size of the group, there was a great deal of variation in terms of punk roles and characteristics. The qualities attributed to the different roles were based upon commitment to the scene. The punks' perceptions of levels of commitment were based principally on their evaluation of physical appearances and lifestyles. The punks categorized members of the scene on these bases and invented terms to describe them. The four types of participants, described above, varied according to their level of commitment to the scene.

Hardcore Punks

Hardcore punks made up the smallest portion of the scene's membership. In the eyes of the other punks, though, they were the essence of the local movement. The hardcores expressed the greatest loyalty to the punk scene as a whole. Although the hardcores embodied punk fashion and lifestyle codes to the highest degree, their commitment to the counterculture went much deeper than that. As one hardcore punk said:

> *There's been so much pure bullshit written about punks. Everyone is shown with a safety pin in their ear or blue hair. The public image is too locked into the fashion. That has nothin' to do with punk, really. . . .For me, it is just my way of life.*

The feature that distinguished hardcore punks from other punks was their belief in, and concern for, the punk counterculture. In this sense, the hardcore punks had gone beyond commitment; they had undergone the process of conversion (Snow et al., 1986). In other words, not only did they have membership status, but they believed in and espoused the virtues and ideology of the counterculture. Although many hardcores differed on what the counterculture's core values were, they all expressed some concern with punk ideology. These values were ambiguous at best, but included a distinctly antiestablishment, anarchistic sentiment. Street (1986: 175) has described punk as celebrating chaos and "a life lived only for the moment." The associated value system of punk was understood by the incorporation of cynicism and a distrust of authority. In keeping, with other subcultures that intentionally distinguish themselves from the dominant culture, the punk aesthetic, lifestyle, and worldview directly confronted those of the larger society and its traditions. While the other types of punks made no reference to group beliefs or values, the hardcores revered the counterculture. For them, being punk had a profound effect on all aspects of their lives. As one hardcore said:

> *There are a lot of punks around, even real punks, who don't mean it. At least, not all the way, like I do. Sometimes I feel so good about punk that I cry. And when I see people getting into some band with real punk lyrics, it's like a religious experience.*

It was precisely this belief in "punk" as an external reality, like a higher good, that set the hardcores apart. Similar to Sykes and Matza's (1958) "appeal to higher loyalties," hardcore punks based their rejection of conventional society on their commitment to their antiestablishment lifestyles and beliefs. This imbued their self-identity with a sense of seriousness and purpose. Unlike other punks, they did not view their punk identity as a temporary role or a transitory fashion, but as it permanent way of life. As one hardcore member said:

> *Punk didn't influence me to be the way I am much. I was always this way inside. When I came into punk, it was what I needed all my life. I could finally be myself.*

Without exception, the hardcores reported having always held the values or qualities associated with the punk counterculture. The local scene, in fact, was just a convenient way of expressing these ideas collectively. Perhaps the most essential value professed by the punks was a genuine disdain for the conventional system. Their use of the term *system* here referred to a general concept of the way the material world works: bureaucracies, power structures, and competition for scarce goods. This "system" further referred to the ethic of deferred gratification, conventional hard work for profit, and the concept of private property. While this bears some similarity to Flacks's (1967) discussion of the student movement and Davis's (1970) portrayal of hippies, hardcore punks generally had a disdain for these earlier youth subcultures. There was a general attitude among punks of the need to create and maintain their own distinctive style. Kinsey found this same feature in the antibourgeois "killum and eatum" subculture. According to Kinsey (1982: 316), "K and E offered an attractive setting as its ideology presented an excellent vehicle for expressing hostility toward conventional society." This contempt for authority and the conventional culture was, in fact, such an essential value for the punks that if one expressed prosystem sentiments or support for the present administration, one could not be considered a committed member, no matter how well one looked the part. Overt behavioral and physical attributes, though, were major ways hardcore punks showed disdain for the system. Particular characteristics were essential for consideration as hardcores. Most fundamentally, a verbal commitment to punk values and the punk scene, in general, was required. For example, John, the epitome of a hardcore punk, claimed to hate the system. He talked about the inequality of the system quite often. In John's words:

> *Punk set me free. It let me out of the system. I can walk the streets now and do what I want and not live by the demands of the system. When I walk the streets, I am a punk, not a bum.*

However, this verbal pronouncement had to be backed by a certain lifestyle that further indicated commitment to the group. This lifestyle consisted of escaping the system in some way. Almost all of the hardcores were unemployed and lived in old, abandoned houses or moved into the homes of friends for periods of time. Some survived from the charity of sycophantic, less committed punks. Others worked in jobs that they considered to be outside the system, such as musicians in rock bands or artists.

Another central feature of the lifestyle was the hardcores' use of dangerous drugs. Many hardcores indulged heavily in sniffing glue. Glue was inexpensive and readily available to the punks. Its use also symbolized the self-destructive, nihilistic attitude of hardcores and their desire to live outside of society's norms.

As one member said:

> *It is kind of like a competition, a show-off thing. . . . See who has the most guts by seeing who can burn his brain up first. It is like a total lack of care about anything, really.*

This closely corresponds to Davis and Munoz's (1968) description of "freaks." Both punks and freaks were "in search of drug kicks as such, especially if [their] craving carries [them] to the point of drug abuse where [their] health, sanity and relations with intimates are jeopardized" (Davis and Munoz, 1968: 306). Again, here we see a rejection of anything the larger society sees as "sensible."

However, the most salient feature of the hardcore lifestyle was the radical physical appearance. In every case, people who were labeled as hardcore had drastically altered some aspect of their bodies. For example, in addition to the hairstyles discussed earlier, they often had tattoos, such as swastikas, on their arms or faces. Brake (1985: 78) has referred to the use of the swastika as a symbol for punks that was actually devoid of any political significance. Rather, the swastika was a "symbol of contempt" employed as a means of offending the traditional culture. The hardcore punks did their best to alienate themselves from the larger society.

According to Kanter (1972), the first requisite in the principle of a gestalt sociology is that a group forms maximum commitment to this higher ideal by sharply differentiating itself from the larger society. The hardcore members did this by going through the initiation rite of passage: semipermanently altering their appearance. As one hardcore said:

Did you see Russell's mohawk? I'm so glad for him. He finally decided to go for it. Now he is a punk everywhere . . . no way he can hide it now.

This was similar to certain religious cults, such as the Hare Krishnas, where a drastic change in appearance was required for consideration as a total convert (Rochford, 1985). The punk counterculture informally imposed the same prerequisite. By doing something so out of the ordinary to their appearance, the punks voluntarily deprived themselves of some of the larger society's coveted goods. For example, many of the hardcores were desperately poor. They said that they knew all they would have to do to obtain a job would be to grow their hair into a conventional style; yet they refused. This kind of action based on commitment was what Becker (1960) has called "side bets," where committed people act in such ways that affect their other interests separate and apart from their commitment interests. By making specific choices, people who are committed sacrifice the possible benefits of their other roles. An important characteristic of Becker's notion of side bets is that people are fully aware of the potential ramifications of their actions. This point was illustrated by one punk:

Some of my friends that aren't punk say, "Why don't you get a job? All you'd have to do is grow your hair out or get a wig and you could get a job." I mean, I know I could. Don't they think I knew that when I did it? It was a big step when I finally cut my hair in a mohawk.

For the hardcore punk, being punk was worth the sacrifices; it was perceived as an inherently good quality. In this respect, the hardcores differed from other types of punks. They held the larger punk scene in esteem. As one loyal member said:

It really pisses me off when people act like ours is the only punk group in the world. They don't even care what bigger and better groups exist. If this whole thing ended tomorrow, they wouldn't care what happened to the whole punk scene.

The hardcores continually expressed their disgust with the local scene. Much like the hippies studied by Davis (1970), "the scene," in itself, was the message. While not enough people joined the group to satisfy the punks, they were, nonetheless, grateful that they had any kind of group environment to which they could attach themselves. The Glass Gun, with its regularly scheduled "punk night," nonhostile attitude toward them, and coterie of interested bystanders, at least gave them a place to express their values collectively. It was essential in maintaining the group's solidarity and social organization.

Softcore Punks

The softcore punks made up a larger portion of the local scene than the hardcores. There were around fifteen softcore punks. There was one fundamental difference between the hardcore and softcore punks. For the hardcores, it was not sufficient just to be antiestablishment or to wear one's hair in a certain way. Rather, one had to embody the punk lifestyle and ideology in all possible ways. As one hardcore punk put it:

Everybody thinks she is hardcore because she looks so hardcore. I mean, yeah, she has a mohawk, and she won't get a job and she says she's for anarchy, but she doesn't care that much about being punk. She likes all these different kinds of music and stuff. She seems sometimes like she is just in it for fun. She even says she'll be whatever's in when punk goes out!

The softcore punks lived similar lifestyles to the hardcores. However, the element of "seriousness" about the scene, so pervasive among the hardcores, was absent among the softcores. Visually, the two types were basically indistinguishable. They were different only in their level of commitment. The commitment for softcores was to the lifestyle and the image only, not to "punk" as an ideology or an intrinsically valuable good. The softcores made no pretense of concern for either the larger counterculture or the feeling of permanence about their punk roles. As one softcore, Beth, said:

Everyone thinks I am so serious about it because I have a mohawk. Some people just can't get past it. Sometimes I get tired of it. Other times, I like to play jokes on people; like another friend of mine who has a mohawk, we'll walk down the street and point at someone with regular hair and say, "Wow! Look at him, he's weird, he doesn't have a mohawk." The fact is, if everyone did have one, I'd do something different to my hair.

The softcores identified with the punk image only temporarily. This distinguished their level of commitment from the *conversion* of the hardcores. The softcores' interest in the scene had only to do with what it could offer them at the present time. While participating, they did what was considered a good job of being "punk." However, if a new cultural trend surfaced. it would be just as likely that they would use their energy effectively to create that particular image. As one softcore punk said:

I've spent time identifying myself as a hippie, then as a women's libber, then an ecologist, and now as a punk. I'm punk now, but I am in the process of changing into something else. I don't know what. I'm getting bored with this scene. But for now, if I'm gonna do it, I'll do it right.

The softcore punks were somewhat committed in that they participated in some of the more drastic elements of punk lifestyle. For example, softcores had their hair cut in severe ways, just like the hardcores. They were, at least temporarily, committed to being punk (or playing punk) in that they "cut" themselves off from some of society's goods as well. However, the softcores did not share the self-destructive bent of the hardcores. The drugs that they consumed, such as marijuana, alcohol, and amphetamines, were not so potentially dangerous. Yet, because of their apparent visual commitment, and because of the lip service they gave to punk values, softcores were viewed as members in good standing. The hardcores liked and respected the softcores; the two groups associated freely. Some hardcores considered softcores to be simply members in transition. Lofland and Stark (1965) have suggested that movements themselves play a role in promoting the ideology in the new members, rather than the members coming to the movement because its ideology coincides with their own established beliefs. This was the case for the softcore punks. They did not claim to have held punk values before becoming punk. As Anne, a softcore, recalled:

It was scary to me at first. The hype from the magazines and stuff—all this weird shit, y'know. Then I went there and just hung out. The reason it was frighten-

ing is that a lot of people had different ideas about life than me. And I had to change myself to be with them. I had to be more intense, be an outcast. It was exciting because there seemed to be an element of danger in it—like living on the edge.

A process of simply happening onto the scene was typical of softcore members. Many recounted the feelings of purposelessness that preceded the drift into the punk scene. This drift is similar to the drifts that occur in other deviant lifestyles (Matza, 1964). What Matza called the "mood of desperation" often caused people to drift into delinquency or deviant lifestyles. As Joanie said:

I was really doing nothing with my life and I just kinda accidentally came into the punk scene. I gradually got involved in it that way. The music, and the people to an extent, really raised my consciousness about the system.

Softcores' verbal recognition of punk attitudes, such as awareness of the system, helped to validate their punk performances. Hardcores felt that verbal commitment was an essential first step to further commitment. For this reason, the hardcores accepted the softcores and considered them to be genuine and authentic in their punk identity. Such identification with punk values, along with a typical punk lifestyle, made the distinction between hardcores and softcores difficult. Again, the distinction became clear only with regard to the level of commitment, or seriousness, of the two types. One softcore made this qualification more apparent:

They get mad at me and think I'm insincere or whatever 'cause I like to have fun. I take my politics serious, too, but I feel if you are here, you might as well enjoy it. They think being punk is so serious, they are depressed or stoned all the time.

This statement indicates that the hardcores defined the situation for the local scene. The hardcores decided what differentiated real punks (or committed punks) from pretenders. The hardcores considered only themselves and the softcores to be real. The "realness" of a punk was based on the level of commitment. The level was judged on the basis of willingness to sacrifice other identities for the punk identity. To prove this, a member would have to make permanent his or her punk image. What the punk identity offered was status within its own subculture for those who could not or would not achieve it in conventional society (Cohen, 1955). However, commitment to the deviant identity did not stem from a forced label. On the contrary, commitment to the punk identity was a "self-enhancing attachment" (Goffman, in Stebbins, 1971). The punks' self-esteem was enhanced by the approval they received. It would follow, then, that the more consistent one's behavior was with the superficial signs of commitment, the more prestige one would be able to obtain. Doug, a softcore, commented on this aspect of subculture prestige among the punks:

In their own way, they're elitist. It's kind of like because they're not part of the general run of things, because they've actually chosen to be rejected in a lot of cases, they've kind of set up their own little social order. It seems to me like it's based on, like a contest, who can be more cool than who. With the really hardcore punks, it's who can self-destruct first; in the name of punk, I guess.

The hardcores and the softcores used the same criteria to judge commitment. Both types agreed that the difference between them was their levels of commitment. Both types fully realized that the softcores did not share the same loyalty to, and identification with, the punk counterculture as a whole. Although both types expressed some commitment to the punk identity and lifestyle, they both realized that the hardcores viewed their own identities as permanent and the softcores' as temporary.

Preppie Punks

The preppie punks made up an even larger portion of the crowd at punk events. The preppies frequented the scene, but approached it similarly to a costume party. They were concerned with the novelty and the fashion. The preppies bore some resemblance to Yablonsky's (1968) "plastic hippies" in that they were drawn to the excitement of the scene. Whereas the core members acted nonchalant and natural about being punk, the preppies could not hide their enthusiasm about being part of the scene. This feature contributed to the core members' perceptions of preppies as "not real" punks. As one core member said:

> It really kills me when these preppie girls come up to me and say "Oh, wow, you're so punk; you're so new wave," like I'm really trying or something.

Preppie punks did not lead the lifestyle of the core members. The preppie punks tended to be from middle-class families, whereas the core punks were generally from lower- or working-class backgrounds.[3] Preppie punks often lived with their parents; they tended to be younger, and were often in school or in respectable, system-sanctioned jobs. This quasi-commitment meant that preppies had to be able to turn the punk image on and off at will. For example, a preppie punk hairstyle, although short, was styled in such a versatile way that it could be manipulated to look punk sometimes and conventional at other times. Preppie fashion was much the same way. Mary, a typical preppie punk, put her regular clothes together in a way she thought would look punk. She ripped up her sorority T-shirt. She bought outfits that were advertised as having the "punk look." Her traditional bangs transformed into "punk" bangs, standing straight up using hair spray or setting gel. The distinguishing feature of preppie punks was the manufactured quality of their punk look. This obvious ability to change roles kept the preppies from being considered real or committed. The preppies were not willing to give anything up for a punk identity. As one softcore said:

> They come in with their little punk outfits from Ms. Jordan's [an exclusive clothing store] and it's written all over 'em: money. They think they can have their nice little jobs and their semipunk hairdo and live with mom and dad and be a real punk, too. Well, they can't.

Another said of preppies:

---

[3] Very little information is provided in this text about the class, race, and ethnicity of these participants. The community from which these data come is relatively homogeneous. The few references to class are more impressionistic; that is, based upon knowledge of family occupations, school districts, and so on. However, the dearth of this kind of data stems from the fact that I was more interested in the features the members had in common than in the distinctions between them, with the exception of their differing levels of commitment and their styles.

It's a little hard to take when you have nothing and they try to have everything. Having all that goes against punk. They gotta choose to not have it. Otherwise, they're just playing a game.

The preppies liked to disavow their punk association in situations that would sanction them negatively for such association. This state of "dual commitments," in which they never had to reject the conventional world in order to be marginally a part of the group, was characteristic of preppie punks (Cohen, 1955). Kanter (1972) has described a process of conversion and commitment that is commonly found in communes. The first step in the process was the renunciation of previous identities. According to this model, the preppie punks would not be considered committed at all. Thus they could not have been categorized as punks in any meaningful sense. As one core member said, "Being 'punk' to them is like playing cowboys and Indians."

Criticizing and joking about the preppies made up a large portion of core members' conversations. Some truly disliked the preppies and others were flattered by their feeble attempts at imitation of core behavior. For example, when a preppie punk approached one core member, he rolled his eyes and said, "Here comes my fan club," with a half-embarrassed smile and a distinct look of pleasure on his face.

Also, the financial function that the preppies served to core members made them more tolerable. Preppies almost always had jobs or survived by their parents' support. Many of the core members subsisted on the continued generosity of their devout fans. The preppies were more than willing to help the other punks. Preppies sometimes offered hardcores financial help in the form of buying them groceries, driving them places, and providing them with cigarettes, alcohol, and other drugs. Because of this, many punks felt that they could not afford to reject outwardly those who were less committed. As Anne said, "One of these days, this kindness is going to dry up."

Yet the joking and poking fun at preppies was a constant activity. It served to separate, for the committed punks, "us" from "them." It reinforced their sense of being the only real punks. Again the distinction made by core members was grounded in the preppies' attempts to play numerous roles. Haircut and clothing were the decisive clues. The real punks could spot a preppie from a distance; they never had to say a word. As one core member said,

Oh look, she's punked out her hair. Yes, we're impressed. Tomorrow she'll look just like a Barbie doll again.

Perhaps the most definitive statement separating the real punks from the preppies referred to lifestyle:

All I know is that I live this seven days a week, and they just do it on weekends.

The preppies, though, while definitely removed from core members, still played an important role in the scene.

Spectators

The category of spectators referred to everyone who observed the scene fairly regularly, but were not punks themselves. This type consisted of, literally, "everyone else." They made up the largest portion of the crowd at the Glass Gun on any given night. They were different from the preppie punks in that they did not try to look punk. They made no pretense of commitment to the scene at all. They did not identify themselves as punks; they had no stake in the scene. Spectators consisted of all different types of people and varied in their occupations, clothes, and reasons for being there. The only common denominator this group shared was the desire to stand back and watch, rather than to participate actively in punk activities. One spectator said of his involvement in this scene:

> *People on the fringe are usually voyeurs of a sort. They like to be on the receiver's end of what's happening. Maybe punk is really their alter-ego. And maybe that need is satisfied just by watching and pretending. That's how it is with me, anyway.*

The spectators liked to observe the fashion, to listen to the music, and to be "in the know" about the scene. They were, in other word, punk appreciators.

For the most part, spectators on the fringe were ignored by the core members. They never received the attention that preppies did because they made no attempts to "play punk." However, if a spectator appeared on the scene looking completely antithetical to punk, core members would simply laugh or say something derogatory about them and drop the subject. For example, one time a hippie-looking character came in and one punk said, "Oh my God, I think we're in a time warp," to which another punk responded, "Maybe we should tell him that Woodstock's over and that it is 1983."

Following such statements, the punks would watch the spectator's reaction to the scene. For the most part, except as a diversion, the punks were uninterested in the spectators. They did not generally associate with them or talk about them much. Presumably this was the case because of the tremendous turnover in spectator membership.

Most spectators either slowly began to identify with the group (most core members started out as spectators) or stopped frequenting the punk events. There were, however, some loyal spectators. They would frequent the club. They knew most of the punks at least slightly. The punks generally liked this sort of spectator because they provided the punks with an audience. Every type of punk thrived on an audience. The punks needed people to shock. The spectator served that function. The attitude that the members had toward the spectators was one of tolerance and indifference. As one core member said of them:

> *They're into it for the novelty. It's like going to the circus for them, to be a part of something new and exciting. But that's okay. I like going to the circus, too; I just like being in it better.*

Thus though spectators were only peripheral to the scene they provided an alternative set of norms that functioned to delineate the social boundaries of the counterculture.

Conclusion

In this essay I have depicted a contemporary counterculture composed of identity-seeking youths. Typical of the rebelliousness displayed by individuals questioning the values of society and their parents and seeking to establish their own selves, such youths engaged in deviant behavior and lifestyles. As a result, these youths have congregated into interrelations characterized by Best and Luckenbill (1982) as "deviant peers," engaging in deviant activities together and scrutinizing each other's actions. As deviant peers, they set their own standards for evaluating each other and used these as criteria for determining their membership status (Higgins and Butler, 1982).

The typologies they have articulated were based on the individual's commitment to the ideology, lifestyle, taste, and appearance of the movement. A hierarchy existed that ranged from the most involved, central members (hardcores and soft cores) to the less involved, leisure members (preppies) to the peripheral nonmembers (spectators). Members of these different groups had different roles and served different functions for the local scene as a whole. Central members provided ideology, leadership, and entertainment for peripheral participants. They served as role models for the value system associated with the counterculture. The drama and shock value of their antiestablishment appearance and lifestyle added a further allure for peripheral members. Their function for the counterculture was most central and obvious.

The role of the peripheral members was more subtle. On the one hand, they served to *insulate* central members from society (Higgins and Butler, 1982). While central members functioned within the same society as conventional people, they lived in an isolated social world. They did not associate socially with "nonpunks." They did associate, though, with peripheral members. These people formed the audience, fan club, foil, and following for central members. The peripheral members thus served to nourish the egos of the central members and reinforce their punk image. They were the only noncentral members whom the hardcores and softcores accepted socially, albeit as followers more than as friends. On the other hand, the peripheral members also served as a conduit between central members and conventional society. They helped sustain the core members' existence financially. They provided such assitance both directly, in the form of handouts of food or cigarettes, and indirectly by patronizing their club (thus helping it continue to exist) and driving them to pick up their welfare checks. It is, I believe, characteristic of antiestablishment countercultures in general for members to subsist parasitically on the societies that they oppose. Further, the peripheral members served as a conduit to conventional society by contributing an acceptable degree of societal norms to the group. It is characteristic of countercultures to have their share of hangers-on, or unauthentic members (Yinger, 1982). However, these members serve definite functions for the maintenance of the whole. The peripheral groups thus filled ironically polarized roles: buffering the central members from contact, yet, at the same time, maintaining contact for them with the conventional society.

The punks I studied seemed to share many of the characteristics of countercultural groups in general. A counterculture's expression occurs in response to the specific conditions of modern society, or the culture in particular of which it is critical. The state of consciousness or ideology of a counterculture functions as what Brake (1985: 15) has called a "magical" solution, in that the viability of the alternative is more imaged than real. However, their rather inneffectual form of protest is functional for the larger society as well. These manifestations of discontent serve to appease the disgruntled by convincing them of the validity of their solution, while remaining fundamentally nonthreatening to the structure of the dominant culture.

Presumably it is characteristic for countercultures to have varying levels of commitment within them. The most committed segment of a counterculture is necessarily the most disengaged from the dominant society. However for a counterculture to have any significant effect on a society, there must be some degree of interplay between these polarized groups. The marginally committed stratum, which continues to operate and function within conventional society, serves as the connection between the two factions. This stratum serves as the mediator between the dominant culture and the counterculture, informing both of the other side's presence and position. Thus the marginal group plays an essential role in the efflorescence of a counterculture. Without this indirect link to the larger society, a counterculure, by virtue of its definitive elements, would exist in insignificant isolation. The intent of the counterculture is to be recognized and responded to by the society. Thus for a counterculture to be effective and useful, for both itself and the dominant culture, the different levels of commitment are necessary. The core stratum provides the "counter" ideology and the opposition to the status quo. The marginal stratum facilitates the dialogue between the counterculture and the dominant culture that it opposes.

Many other structural analyses have been conducted about youth countercultures in the past, examining the members' roles and functions for the group. Future researchers on the subject could investigate the relationship between different levels of commitment within a deviant subculture and the members' class, educational, and ethnic backgrounds as well as the process by which they become committed to the counterculture.

References

Adler, P. A. 1985. *Wheeling and Dealing.* New York: Columbia Univ. Press.

Becker, H. S. 1960. "Notes on the concept of commitment," *Amer. J. of Sociology* 66: 32–40.

Berger, B. 1967. "Hippie morality—more old than new." *Transaction* 5: 19–27.

Best, J. and D. Luckenbill. 1982. *Organizing Deviance.* Englewood Cliffs, NJ: Prentice-Hall,

Brake, M. 1980. *The Sociology of Youth Culture and Youth Subcultures.* London: Routledge.

Brake, M. 1985. *Comparative Youth Culture: The Sociology of Youth Culture and Subcultures in America, Britain, and Canada.* London: Routledge.

Cohen, A. 1955. *Delinquent Boys.* Glencoe, IL: Free Press

Cohen, S. 1972. *Folk Devils and Moral Panics.* New York: St. Martin's.

Davis, F. 1970. "Focus on the flower children: why all of us may be hippies some day," pp. 327–340 in J. Douglas (ed.) *Observations of Deviance.* New York: Random House.

Davis, F. and L. Munoz. 1968. "Heads and freaks: patterns and meanings of drug use among hippies," *J. of Health and Social Behavior* 9: 156–164.

Douglas, J. 1970. *Youth in Turmoil.* Washington, DC: National Institute of Mental Health.

Douglas, J. 1976. *Investigative Social Research.* Newbury Park, CA: Sage.

Flacks, R. 1967. "The liberated generation: an exploration of the roots of student protest." *J. of Social Issues* 23: 52–75.

Flacks, R. 1971. *Youth and Social Change.* Chicago: Markham.

Frith S. 1982. *Sound Effects.* New York: Pantheon.

Hall, S. and T. Jefferson [eds.]. 1975. *Resistance Through Rituals.* London: Hutchinson.

Hebdige, D. 1981. *Subcultures: The Meaning of Style.* New York: Methuen.

Henslin, J. 1972. "Studying deviance in four settings: research experiences with cabbies, suicides, drug users, and abortionees," pp. 35–70 in J. Douglas (ed.) *Research on Deviance.* New York: Random House.

Higgins, J. and R. Butler. 1982. *Understanding Deviance.* New York: McGraw-Hill.

Kanter, R. M. 1972. *Commitment and Community: Communes and Utopia in Sociological Perspective.* Cambfidge, MA: Harvard Univ. Press.

Kinsey, B. A. 1982. "Killum and eatum: identity consolidation in a middle class poly-drug abuse subculture." *Symbolic Interaction* 5: 311–324.

Lofland, J. and R. Stark. 1965. "Becoming a world saver: a theory of conversion to a deviant perspective." *Amer. Soc. Rev.* 30: 862–875.

Matza, D. 1964. *Delinquency and Drift.* New York: John Wiley.

Miller, W. 1958. "Lower class culture as a Generating milieu of gang delinquency." *J. of Social Issues* 14: 5–19.

Mungham, G. and G. Pearson [eds.]. 1976. *Working Class Youth Culture.* London: Routledge.

Pfohl, S. 1985. *Images of Deviance and Social Control.* New York: McGraw-Hill.

Rochford, E. B., Jr. 1985. *Hare Krishnas in America.* New Brunswick, NJ: Rutgers Univ. Press.

Snow, D. A., E. B. Rochford, Jr., S. K. Worden, and R. D. Benford. 1986. "Frame alignment and mobilization." *Amer. Soc. Rev.* 51: 464–481.

Snow, D. A., L. Zurcher, Jr., and S. Ekland-Olson. 1980. "Social networks and social movements: a micro-structural approach to differential recruitment." *Amer. Soc. Rev.* 45: 787–801.

Stebbins, R. A. 1971. *Commitment to Deviance.* Westport, CT: Greenwood. Street, J. 1986.

Street, J. 1986. Rebel Rock: *The Politics of Popular Music.* Oxford: Basil Blackwell.

Sykes, G. and D. Matza. 1957. "Techniques of neutralization." *Amer. Soc. Rev.* 22: 664–670.

Taylor, I. 1982. "Moral enterprise, moral panic, and law-and-order campaigns," pp. 123–149 in M. M. Rosenberg et al. (eds.) *A Sociology of Deviance.* New York: St. Martin's.

Yablonsky, L. 1959. "The delinquent gang as a near-group." *Social Problems* 7:108–117.

Yablonsky, L. 1962. *The Violent Gang.* New York: Macmillan.

Yablonsky, L. 1968. *The Hippie Trip.* New York: Pegasus.

Yinger, J. M. 1982. *Countercultures: The Promise and Peril of a World Turned Upside Down.* New York: Free Press.

Young, J. 1973. "The hippie solution: an essay in the politics of leisure," pp. 182–208 in I. Taylor and L. Taylor (eds.) *Politics and Deviance.* Harmondsworth, England: Penguin.

Discussion Questions

1. Can you think of any other countercultures active in the United States now? What do they have in common with the punks? How do they differ from them? Are there any countercultures that might be overlooked because they are less visible than the punks?

2. Do there tend to be more countercultures in highly industrialized societies than others? If so, what is there about this kind of society that brings this about? What might be some benefits and dangers of countercultures to society?

$Chapter$ 3

Socialization

Often when we think of socialization, we think only of childhood. But as you have discovered from your textbook, the process is lifelong. In fact, your college experience is an excellent example of adult socialization.

Another example is found in this classic article by Becker and Geer, which discusses their findings concerning socialization in medical school. Part of a much larger study, the research reported here asks a fairly simple question: What happens to the shining idealism of first-year medical students in the pursuit of their degree? That idealism dulls—some would say to cynicism—in medical and other professional socialization seems evident. Becker and Geer are able not only to substantiate this general tendency, but also to indicate why it happens. They also add the intriguing idea that the outcome is not as simple as a movement from idealism to cynicism. The resurgence of an informed idealism in the fourth year is used as evidence to suggest what really happens to the initial naive attitudes of first-year students. So take a look at this sociological detective story and find out the real fate of idealism in medical school.

The Fate of Idealism in Medical School*

HOWARD S. BECKER   BLANCHE GEER

Community Studies, Inc., Kansas City, Missouri

It makes some difference in a man's performance of his work whether he believes whole-heartedly in what he is doing or feels that in important respects it is a fraud, whether he feels convinced that it is a good thing or believes that it is not really of much use after all. The distinction we are making is the one people have in mind when they refer, for example, to their calling as a "noble profession" on the one hand or a "racket" on the other. In the one case they idealistically proclaim that their work is all that it claims on the surface to be; in the other they cynically concede that it is first and foremost a way of making a living and that its surface pretensions are just that and nothing more. Presumably, different modes of behavior are associated with these perspectives when wholeheartedly embraced. The cynic cuts comers with a feeling of inevitability while the idealist goes down fighting. *The Blackboard Jungle* and *Not as a Stranger* are only the most recent in a long tradition of fictional portrayals of the importance of this aspect of a man's adjustment to his work.

Professional schools often receive a major share of the blame for producing this kind of cynicism—and none more than the medical school. The idealistic young freshman changes into a tough, hardened, unfeeling doctor; or so the popular view has it. Teachers of medicine sometimes rephrase the distinction between the clinical and pre-clinical years into one between the "cynical" and "pre-cynical" years. Psychological research supports this view, presenting attitude surveys which show medical students year by year scoring lower on "idealism" and higher on "cynicism."[1] Typically, this cynicism is seen as developing in response to the shattering of ideals consequent on coming face-to-face with the realities of professional practice.

In this paper, we attempt to describe the kind of idealism that characterizes the medical freshmen and to trace both the development of cynicism and the vicissitudes of that ideal-

Becker, Howard S. and Blanche Geer. The Fate of idealism in Medical School. *American Sociological Review, 23,* 1, 1958, 50–56. By permission of the American Sociological Association.

[1]Leonard D. Eron, "Effect of Medical Education on Medical Students," *Journal of Medical Education,* 10 (October, 1955), pp. 559–566.

ism in the course of the four years of medical training. Our main themes are that though they develop cynical feelings in specific situations directly associated with their medical school experience, the medical students never lose their original idealism about the practice of medicine; that the growth of both cynicism and idealism are not simple developments, but are instead complex transformations; and that the very notions "idealism" and "cynicism" need further analysis, and must be seen as situational in their expressions rather than as stable traits possessed by individuals in greater or lesser degree. Finally, we see the greater portion of these feelings as being collective rather than individual phenomena.

Our discussion is based on a study we are now conducting at a state medical school,[2] in which we have carried on participant observation with students of all four years in all of the courses and clinical work to which they are exposed. We joined the students in their activities in school and after school and watched them at work in labs, on the hospital wards, and in the clinic. Often spending as much as a month with a small group of from five to fifteen students assigned to a particular activity, we came to know them well and were able to gather information in informal interviews and by overbearing the ordinary daily conversation of the group.[3] In the course of our observation and interviewing we have gathered much information on the subject of idealism. Of necessity, we shall have to present the very briefest statement of our findings with little or no supporting evidence.[4] The problem of idealism is, of course, many-faceted and complex and we have dealt with it in a simplified way, describing only some of its grosser features.[5]

The Freshman

The medical students enter school with what we may think of as the idealistic notion, implicit in lay culture, that the practice of medicine is a wonderful thing and that they are go-

---

[2]This study is sponsored by Community Studies, Inc., of Kansas City, Missouri, and is being carried on at the University of Kansas Medical School, to whose dean, staff, and students we are indebted for their wholehearted cooperation. Professor Everett C. Hughes of the University of Chicago is director of the project.

[3]The technique of participant observation has not been fully systematized, but some approaches to this have been made. See, for example, Florence R. Kluckhohn, "The Participant Observer Technique in Small Communities," *American Journal of Sociology,* 45 (November, 1940), pp. 331–343; Arthur Vidich, "Participant Observation and the Collection and Interpretation of Data," *ibid.,* 60 (January, 1955), pp. 354–360; William Foote Whyte, "Observational Field-Work Methods," in Maria Jahoda, Morton Deutsch, and Stuart W. Cook (editors), *Research Methods in the Social Sciences,* New York: Dryden Press, 1951, II, pp. 393–514; and *Street Cornor Society* (Enlarged Edition), Chicago: University of Chicago Press, 1955, pp. 279–353; Rosalie Hankey Wax, "Twelve Years Later: An Analysis of Field Experience" *American Journal of Sociology,* 63 (September, 1957), pp. 133–142; Morris S. Schwartz and Charlotte Green Schwartz, "Problems in Participant Observation," *ibid,,* 60 (January, 1955), pp. 343–353; and Howard S. Becker and Blanche Geer, "Participant Observation and Interviewing: A Comparison," *Human Organization* (forthcoming). The last item represents the first of a projected series of papers attempting to make explicit the operations involved in this method. For a short description of some techniques used in this study, see Howard S. Becker, "Interviewing Medical Students," *American Journal of Sociology,* 62 (September, 1956), pp. 199–201.

[4]A fuller analysis and presentation of evidence will be contained in a volume on this study now being prepared by the authors in collaboration with Everett C. Hughes and Anselm L. Strauss.

[5]Renee Fox has shown how complex one aspect of this whole subject is in her analysis of the way medical students at Cornell become aware of and adjust to both their own failure to master all available knowledge and the gaps in current knowledge In many fields. See her "Training for Uncertainty," in Robert K. Merton, George G. Reader, and Patricia L. Kendall, *The Student Physician: Introductory Studies in the Sociology of Medical Education,* Cambridge: Harvard University Press, 1957, pp. 207–241.

ing to devote their lives to service to mankind. They believe that medicine is made up of a great body of well-established facts that they will be taught from the first day on and that these facts will be of immediate practical use to them as physicians. They enter school expecting to work industriously and expecting that if they work hard enough they will be able to master this body of fact and thus become good doctors.

In several ways the first year of medical school does not live up to their expectations. They are disillusioned when they find they will not be near patients at all, that the first year will be just like another year of college. In fact, some feel that it is not even as good as college because their work in certain areas is not as thorough as courses in the same fields in undergraduate school. They come to think that their courses (with the exception of anatomy) are not worth much because, in the first place, the faculty (being Ph.D.'s) know nothing about the practice of medicine, and, in the second place, the subject matter itself is irrelevant, or as the students say, "ancient history."

The freshmen are further disillusioned when the faculty tells them in a variety of ways that there is more to medicine than they can possibly learn. They realize it may be impossible for them to learn all they need to know in order to practice medicine properly. Their disillusionment becomes more profound when they discover that this statement of the faculty is literally true.[6] Experience in trying to master the details of the anatomy of the extremities convinces them that they cannot do so in the time they have. Their expectation of hard work is not disappointed; they put in an eight-hour day of classes and laboratories, and study four or five hours a night and most of the weekend as well.

Some of the students, the brightest, continue to attempt to learn it all, but succeed only in getting more and more worried about their work. The majority decide that, since they can't learn it all, they must select from among all the facts presented to them those they will attempt to learn. There are two ways of making this selection. On the one hand, the student may decide on the basis of his own uninformed notions about the nature of medical practice that many facts are not important, since they relate to things which seldom come up in the actual practice of medicine; therefore, he reasons, it is useless to learn them. On the other hand, the student can decide that the important thing is to pass his examinations and, therefore, that the important facts are those which are likely to be asked on an examination; he uses this as a basis for selecting both facts to memorize and courses for intensive study. For example, the work in physiology is dismissed on both of these grounds, being considered neither relevant to the facts of medical life nor important in terms of the amount of time the faculty devotes to it and the number of examinations in the subject.

A student may use either or both of these bases of selection at the beginning of the year, before many tests have been given. But after a few tests have been taken, the student makes "what the faculty wants" the chief basis of his selection of what to learn, for he now has a better idea of what this is and also has become aware that it is possible to fail examinations and that he therefore must learn the expectations of the faculty if he wishes to stay in school. The fact that one group of students, that with the highest prestige in the class, took this view early and did well on examinations was decisive in swinging the whole class around to this position. The students were equally influenced to become "test-wise" by the fact that, although they had all been in the upper range in their colleges, the class average on the first examination was frightening low.

[6]Compare Fox' description of student reaction to this problem at Cornell (*op. cit.*, pp. 209–221).

In becoming test-wise, the students begin to develop systems for discovering the faculty wishes and learning them. These systems are both methods for studying their texts and short-cuts that can be taken in laboratory work. For instance, they begin to select facts for memorization by looking over the files of old examinations maintained in each of the medical fraternity houses. They share tip-offs from the lectures and offhand remarks of the faculty as to what will be on the examinations. In anatomy, they agree not to bother to dissect out subcutaneous nerves, reasoning that it is both difficult and time-consuming and the information can be secured from books with less effort. The interaction involved in the development of such systems and short-cuts helps to create a social group of a class which had previously been only an aggregation of smaller and less organized groups.

In this medical school, the students learn in this way to distinguish between the activities of the first year and their original view that everything that happens to them in medical school will be important. Thus they become cynical about the value of their activities in the first year. They feel that the real thing—learning which will help them to help mankind—has been postponed, perhaps until the second year, or perhaps even farther, at which time they will be able again to act on idealistic premises. They believe that what they do in their later years in school under supervision will be about the same thing they will do, as physicians, on their own; the first year had disappointed this expectation.

There is one matter, however, about which the students are not disappointed during the first year: the so-called trauma of dealing with the cadaver. But this experience, rather than producing cynicism, reinforces the student's attachment to his idealistic view of medicine by making him feel that he is experiencing at least some of the necessary unpleasantness of the doctor's. Such difficulties, however, do not loom as large for the student as those of solving the problem of just what the faculty wants.

On this and other points, a working consensus develops in the new consolidated group about the interpretation of their experience in medical school and its norms of conduct. This consensus, which we call *student culture,*[7] focuses their attention almost completely on their day-to-day activities in school and obscures or sidetracks their earlier idealistic preoccupations. Cynicism, griping, and minor cheating become endemic, but the cynicism is specific to the educational situation, to the first year, and to only parts of it. Thus the students keep their cynicism separate from their idealistic feelings and by postponement protect their belief that medicine is a wonderful thing, that their school is a fine one, and that they will become good doctors.

Later Years

The sophomore year does not differ greatly from the freshman year. Both the work load and anxiety over examinations probably increase. Though they begin some medical activities, as in their attendance at autopsies and particularly in their introductory course in physical diagnosis, most of what they do continues to repeat the pattern of the college science

---

[7]The concept of student culture is analyzed in some detail in Howard S. Becker and Blanche Geer, "Student Culture in Medical School," *Harvard Educational Review* (forthcoming).

curriculum. Their attention still centers on the problem of getting through school by doing well in examinations.

During the third and fourth, or clinical years, teaching takes a new form. In place of lectures and laboratories, the students' work now consists of the study of actual patients admitted to the hospital or seen in the clinic. Each patient who enters the hospital is assigned to a student who interviews him about his illnesses, past and present, and performs a physical examination. He writes this up for the patient's chart, and appends the diagnosis and the treatment that he would use were he allowed actually to treat the patient. During conferences with faculty physicians, often held at the patient's bedside, the student is quizzed about items of his report and called upon to defend them or to explain their significance. Most of the teaching in the clinical years is of this order.

Contact with patients brings a new set of circumstances with which the student must deal. He no longer feels the great pressure created by tests, for he is told by the faculty, and this is confirmed by his daily experience, that examinations are now less important. His problems now become those of coping with a steady stream of patients in a way that will please the staff man under whom he is working, and of handling what is sometimes a tremendous load of clinical work so as to allow himself time for studying diseases and treatments that interest him and for play and family life.

The students earlier have expected that once they reach the clinical years they will be able to realize their idealistic ambitions to help people and to learn those things immediately useful in aiding people who are ill. But they find themselves working to understand cases as medical problems rather than working to help the sick and memorizing the relevant available facts so that these can be produced immediately for a questioning staff man. When they make ward rounds with a faculty member they are likely to be quizzed about any of the seemingly countless facts possibly related to the condition of the patient for whom they are "caring."

Observers speak of the cynicism that overtakes the student and the lack of concern for his patients as human beings. This change does take place, but it is not produced solely by "the anxiety brought about by the presence of death and suffering."[8] The student becomes preoccupied with the technical aspects of the cases with which he deals because the faculty requires him to do so. He is questioned about so many technical details that he must spend most of his time learning them.

The frustrations created by his position in the teaching hospital further divert the student from idealistic concerns. He finds himself low man in a hierarchy based on clinical experience, so that he is allowed very little of the medical responsibility he would like to assume. Because of his lack of experience, he cannot write orders, and he receives permission to perform medical and surgical procedures (if at all) at a rate he considers far too slow. He usually must content himself with "mere" vicarious participation in the drama of danger, life, and death that he sees as the core of medical practice. The student culture accents these difficulties so that events (and especially those involving patients) are interpreted and reacted to as they push him toward or hold him back from further participation in this drama. He does not think in terms the layman might use.

[8]Dana L. Farnsworth, "Some Observations on The Attitudes and Motivations of the Harvard Medical Student," *Harvard Medical Alumni Bulletin,* January, 1956, p. 34.

As a result of the increasingly technical emphasis of his thinking the student appears cynical to the non-medical outsider, though from his own point of view he is simply seeing what is "really important." Instead of reacting with the layman's horror and sympathy for the patient to the sight of a cancerous organ that has been surgically removed, the student is more likely to regret that he was not allowed to close the incision at the completion of the operation, and to rue the hours that he must spend searching in the fatty flesh for the lymph nodes that will reveal how far the disease has spread. As in other lines of work, he drops lay attitudes for those more relevant to the way the event affects someone in his position.

This is not to say that the students lose their original idealism. When issues of idealism are openly raised in a situation they define as appropriate, they respond as they might have when they were freshmen. But the influence of the student culture is such that questions which might bring forth this idealism are not brought up. Students are often assigned patients for examination and follow-up whose conditions might be expected to provoke idealistic crises. Students discuss such patients, however, with reference to the problems they create for the *student*. Patients with terminal diseases who are a long time dying, and patients with chronic diseases who show little change from week to week, are more likely to be viewed as creating extra work without extra compensation in knowledge or the opportunity to practice new skills than as examples of illness which raise questions about euthanasia. Such cases require the student to spend time every day checking on progress which he feels will probably not take place and to write long "progress" notes in the patient's chart although little progress has occurred.

This apparent cynicism is a collective matter. Group activities are built around this kind of workaday perspective, constraining the students in two ways. First, they do not openly express the lay idealistic notions they may hold, for their culture does not sanction such expression; second, they are less likely to have thoughts of this deviant kind when they are engaged in group activity. The collective nature of this "cynicism" is indicated by the fact that students become more openly idealistic whenever they are removed from the influence of student culture—when they are alone with a sociologist as they near the finish of school and sense the approaching end of student life, for example, or when they are isolated from their classmates and therefore are less influenced by this culture.[9]

They still feel, as advanced students, though much less so than before, that school is irrelevant to actual medical practice. Many of their tasks, like running laboratory tests on patients newly admitted to the hospital or examining surgical specimens in the pathology laboratory, seem to them to have nothing to do with their visions of their future activity as doctors. As in their freshman year, they believe that perhaps they must obtain the knowledge they will need in spite of the school. They still conceive of medicine as a huge body of proven facts, but no longer believe that they will ever be able to master it all. They now say that they are going to try to apply the solution of the practicing M.D. to their own dilemma: learn a few things that they are interested in very well and know enough about other things to pass examinations while in school and, later on in practice, to know to which specialist to send difficult patients.

Their original medical idealism reasserts itself as the end of school approaches. Seniors show more interest than students in earlier years in serious ethical dilemmas of the

[9]See the discussion in Howard S. Becker, "Interviewing Medical Students," *op. cit.*

kind they expect to face in practice. They have become aware of ethical problems laymen often see as crucial for the physician—whether it is right to keep patients with fatal diseases alive as long as possible, or what should be done if an influential patient demands an abortion—and worry about them. As they near graduation and student culture begins to break down as the soon-to-be doctors are about to go their separate ways, these questions are more and more openly discussed.

While in school, they have added to their earlier idealism a new and peculiarly professional idealism. Even though they know that few doctors live up to the standards they have been taught, they intend always to examine their patients thoroughly and to give treatment based on firm diagnosis rather than merely to relieve symptoms. This expansion and transformation of idealism appear most explicitly in their consideration of alternative careers, concerning both specialization and the kind of arrangements to be made for setting up practice. Many of their hypothetical choices aim at making it possible for them to be the kind of doctors their original idealism pictured. Many seniors consider specialty training so that they will be able to work in a limited field in which it will be more nearly possible to know all there is to know, thus avoiding the necessity of dealing in a more ignorant way with the wider range of problems general practice would present. In the same manner, they think of schemes to establish partnerships or other arrangements making it easier to avoid a work load which would prevent them from giving each patient the thorough examination and care they now see as ideal.

In other words, as school comes to an end, the cynicism specific to the school situation also comes to an end and their original and more general idealism about medicine comes to the fore again, though within a framework of more realistic alternatives. Their idealism is now more informed although no less selfless.

Discussion

We have used the words "idealism" and "cynicism" loosely in our description of the changeable state of mind of the medical student, playing on ambiguities we can now attempt to clear up. Retaining a core of common meaning, the dictionary definition, in our reference to the person's belief in the worth of his activity and the claims made for it, we have seen that this is not a generalized trait of the students we studied but rather an attitude which varies greatly, depending on the particular activity the worth of which is questioned and the situation in which the attitude is expressed.

This variability of the idealistic attitude suggests that in using such an element of personal perspective in sociological analysis one should not treat it as homogeneous but should make a determined search for subtypes which may arise under different conditions and have differing consequences. Such subtypes presumably can be constructed along many dimensions. There might, for instance, be consistent variations in the medical students' idealism through the four years of school that are related to their social class backgrounds. We have stressed in this report the subtypes that can be constructed according to variations in the object of the idealistic attitude and variations in the audience the person has in mind when he adopts the attitude. The medical students can be viewed as both idealistic and cynical, depending on whether one has in mind their view of their school activities or the future they envision for themselves as doctors. Further, they might take one or another of these positions depending on whether their implied audience is made up of other students, their instructors, or the lay public.

A final complication arises because cynicism and idealism are not merely attributes of the actor, but are as dependent on the person doing the attributing as they are on the qualities of the individual to whom they are attributed.[10] Though the student may see his own disregard of the unique personal troubles of a particular patient as proper scientific objectivity, the layman may view this objectivity as heartless cynicism.[11]

Having made these analytic distinctions, we can now summarize the transformations of these characteristics as we have seen them occuring among medical students. Some of the students' determined idealism at the outset is reaction against the lay notion, of which they are uncomfortably aware, that doctors are money-hungry cynics; they counter this with an idealism of similar lay origin stressing the doctor's devotion to service. But this idealism soon meets a setback, as students find that it will not be relevant for awhile, since medical school has, it seems, little relation to the practice of medicine, as they see it. As it has not been refuted, but only shown to be temporarily beside the point, the students "agree" to set this idealism aside in favor of a realistic approach to the problem of getting through school. This approach, which we have labeled as the cynicism specific to the school experience, serves as protection for the earlier grandiose feelings about medicine by postponing their exposure to reality to a distant future. As that future approaches near the end of the four years and its possible mistreatment of their ideals moves closer, the students again worry about maintaining their integrity, this time in actual medical practice. They use some of the knowledge they have gained to plan careers which, it is hoped, can best bring their ideals to realization.

We can put this in propositional form by saying that when a man's ideals are challenged by outsiders and then further strained by reality, he may salvage them by postponing their application to a future time when conditions are expected to be more propitious.

Discussion Questions

1. Do you think the process of moving from idealism to cynicism and then to realism describes the experience of most undergraduate students? The authors suggest that their findings may not hold constant in the face of such variables as social class. Do you think social class makes a difference in the process among undergraduates? For example, would the process be different at an Ivy League school and a small state college? Why?

2. How might Becker's and Geer's findings be interpreted by a functional theorist? A conflict theorist? A symbolic interactionist? Which interpretation do you think provides the most useful analysis? Why?

---

[10]See Philip Selznick's related discussion of fanaticism in *TVA and the Grass Roots,* Berkeley: University of California Press, 1953, pp. 205–213.

[11]George Orwell gives the layman's side in his essay, "How the Poor Die" in *Shooting an Elephant and Other Essays,* London: Secker and Warburg, 1950, pp. 18–32.

Chapter 4

Social Structure
and Social Interaction

Sociologists often assume that technological change almost always benefits the powerful. After all, they are the ones who can afford the latest advancements and usually control the information necessary to exploit them. But as so often is true, sociological research casts new light on that general conclusion. As he raises questions about the actual use of the importance of a new technology, Fischer provides an example of research into micro-level social interaction by analyzing historical data on telephone use. While the phone was seen primarily as a business tool, it seems it did much more. In his analysis, Fischer provides evidence on how women created social networks by using the telephone, beginning as early as the turn of the century.

The article is also relevant to another question raised in Chapter 4. The broad question of what holds society together is partly answered by the "sociability" bonds made possible by the telephone. If women formed personal networks without depending on face-to-face communication, they created new links that strengthened the web of society.

Gender and the Residential Telephone, 1890–1940
Technologies of Sociability*

CLAUDE S. FISCHER
University of California, Berkeley

The telephone is one of the most prominent technologies to enter the American home in the twentieth century, an era of rapid change both in technology and in women's roles. The residential telephone has been associated, in popular stereotype and in (sometimes misogynist) humor, with women. This paper explores gender differences in telephone use during the half-century before World War II, the social meaning of those differences, and its implication for understanding the nexus of gender

Two prefatory comments are needed. One: This topic *does* have a humorous dimension. It also carries for some, as it did for leaders of the early telephone industry, an implied derogation of women: that chatting on the telephone is "one more female foolishness." Social scientists know better. Conversation, even so-called "gossip," is an important social process, serving, among other ends, to renew networks and communities (see, for example, Paine, 1967; di Leanardo, 1984:194ff; Spacks, 1986). Those who might treat the subject as trivial or focus on its apparent sexism would be echoing, ironically, the dismissive attitude of male critics who ignored the seriousness with which women themselves took conversation.

Two: As a historical study, this paper must rely on evidence that is necessarily fragmentary and often impressionistic—reports in industry archives, advertising copy, comments of journalists, testimonials, and the like. We are fortunate, however, in also having a few governmental studies and other surveys to draw upon. While we might wish for more data that meet modern standards, we must use what we can. In addition to the archives and studies, I draw upon Lana Rakow's (1987) interviews about telephone use with women in a small,

Fischer, Claude S. Gender and the Residential Telephone, 1890–1940: Technologies of Sociability. *Sociological Forum, 3,* 2, 1988, 211–233. By permission of the Plenum Publishing Corp.

midwestern town and upon a handful of oral histories conducted by John Chan in San Rafael, California.[1]

The argument, in brief, is that women "appropriated" a practical, supposedly masculine technology for distinctively feminine ends. This "gendering" of the telephone may have simultaneously reinforced gender differences and also amplified women's abilities to attain both their normatively prescribed and personally preferred ends.

The Study of Domestic Technologies

In recent years, historians of women have energized the study of technology and society. In household tools and the gender division of labor, social historians are seriously examining, both empirically and theoretically, the neglected topic of consumer technologies in everyday life (see Cowan, 1987; Fischer, 1985). Most of this scholarship has contested the notion that mechanization of housework "liberated" women—notions promulgated by advertisers, Progressive-era commentators, home economists, and many women themselves. "Verily," wrote a Women's Club leader in 1905, "the march of mechanical invention has been the emancipation of women. The freeing of their hands has led to the freeing of their minds" (quoted by Wilson, 1979:95; see also Andrews and Andrews, 1974; Marchand, 1985). Instead, argue recent scholars, "industrialization of the home," although easing the arduousness of housework, nevertheless continued and even solidified women's disproportionate responsibility for domestic labor. For example, advances in cleaning technology raised the standards for cleanliness that housewives must attain (Cowan, 1983; Strasser, 1982; Vanek, 1978; Bose, Bereano, and Malloy, 1984; Walker, 1964; Thrall, 1982; McGaw, 1982; Bereano, Bose, and Arnold, 1985).

As a debunking literature, some of this work understandably tends to be contentious. Rothschild (1983:79) asserts: "Technology has aided a capitalist-patriarchal political order to reinforce the gender division of labor and lock women more firmly into their traditional roles in the home." And she provides speculative scenarios for how that might have happened.[2] Even Ruth Cowan, who firmly rejects such functionalist explanations (1983:147–150), stresses the burdens that household mechanization placed on women in contrast to the burdens they lifted from men.

Having gained much from the openings these studies provided, we should perhaps now move on to ask more complex and probing questions: How did people actually *use* domestic technologies? For what purposes? With what results? And specifically with regard to

---

[1]Chan conducted these interviews as part of a larger project on the telephone in community history headed by the author.

[2]Rothschild (1983:85) asks, "*How has* technology continued to play a role in reinforcing the gender division of labor and the control of women's household labor?" [emphasis added] and provides many credible but unproven answers—for example, that "technology helps the corporate economy to appropriate the housewife's time. New products and processes demand that the housewife educate herself about them, shop for them and comparison shop, and experiment with them." These speculations, however, beg the prior issues of documenting the causal link. (Another logical problem in this and similar lines of arguments, is anthropomorphisizing technology—e.g., "new products . . . demand" [cf. Winner, 1977].)

gender, how did men and women differ in their reactions to and uses of new tools, with what consequences for technological change and gender roles (Cowan, 1979)?

The Telephone

The case I examine here is the *telephone* in North America, briefly glancing at two other technologies later. The concern is with the residential telephone, setting aside the role of telephone use in economic organizations. The telephone, for all its pervasiveness in the contemporary home, has been subject to virtually no serious study as a household tool; even students of the domestic sphere have made, at best, only passing remarks about it. And yet there appears to be something—as suggested by the popular stereotypes—that links the domestic telephone more to women than to men.

We focus on 1890 to 1940, when the telephone became common, outside the South in middle-class urban homes and on very many farms, as well. The percentage of all homes in the United States with telephones grew from about 2 percent in 1890 to 35 in 1920 and 41 in 1930, shrinking to 31 in 1933 and then rebounding to 37 percent in 1940 (U.S. Bureau of Census, 1975:783). Household budget studies indicate that home economists expected to find telephones in urban middle-class homes beginning about the 1910s (see Horowitz, 1985). At the same time, many farm households outside the South and especially in the Midwest and West had also obtained telephones. By 1920, farm households were *more* likely, at 39 percent, to have telephones than were urban households; in the Plains region, the farm subscription rate was about 70 percent.[3] It was not until the 1960s and 1970s that telephones became virtually universal in North America, but in the pre-war era people developed what the industry termed the "telephone habit" and gender differentiation emerged.

An "Affinity" for the Telephone

Although apparently no one has conducted a public opinion poll on the matter, North Americans seem to associate women with extensive use of the telephone. Anecdotal observations suggest so, and more systematic contemporary data do, as well.

Research, largely by American Telephone and Telegraph (AT&T), indicates that today women are more likely to have telephones at home than are men (Wolfe, 1979); that the

---

[3]These averages mask great variations by region, place, and class. In 1930, for example, estimated telephone subscription rates ranged from 12 percent in Mississippi and South Carolina to over 65 percent in Iowa, Kansas, and Nebraska (Untitled Report, Chief Statistician's Division, AT&T, 27 July, 1932, courtesy AT&T Historical Archives; on differential state diffusion, see Fischer and Carroll, 1988). Community differences were also great, varying from 22 to 65 percent subscription rates among the one hundred largest AT&T exchanges in 1927 (Wilson, 1928:7). Because they are based on specific locales, estimates by economic strata are quite diverse. In 1927, in one Michigan exchange, 24 percent of the bottom quartile (measured by rents paid) had telephones, 48 percent of those in the middle half, and 65 percent of the top quintile had telephones (Wilson, 1928:7). In a "typical" southern New England exchange in 1930, half the homes in the bottom two-thirds of the income distribution had telephones, while 93 percent of those in the top third did (Harrell, 1931). While these (and similar) estimates are necessarily rough, they suggest that most urban households in the United States above the median income and outside the South had gotten telephones by the Depression. During the Depression, many households, especially those on farms, gave up telephones (sec Fischer, 1987a, 1987b).

number of women or teenage girls in a household predict its frequency of calling (Mayer, 1977:231; Brandon, 1981:Ch. 1); and that women initiate most of households' long-distance calls (Arlen, 1980:46–47). An Ontario survey of people forty and older showed that women were two to three times more likely to telephone their friends than were men, although less than one-and-a-half times more likely than men to see their friends face-to-face (Synge, Rosenthal, and Marshall, 1982). And Lana Rakow (1987:142) found that in rural Wisconsin, "both women and men generally perceive the telephone to be part of women's domain." The comments of a younger woman with whom Rakow spoke give the flavor of the perceived gender difference:

> *I never remember my dad talking on the phone. To this day, if I call up and say, "What are you up to," he'll say, "Nothin', you wanna talk to Mom?" He's real hard to talk to on the phone . . . That was one of the things my [ex-] husband said later. . . . "One of the things I hated the most was that you were on the phone from nine until I went to bed at night: you were on the phone with your mother." I never knew it bothered him, never. I said "John, you never said anything." He said, "I hated that. It was just like you were ignoring me." I'm sure if he had said something I would have cut down at least. . . . [Question: Did he use the telephone?] Very seldom, other than to make plans, but never just to visit. I would even say, "Call your mom up." He'd say, "Well, you call her." My son is the same way. (Rakow, 1987:267–270)*

Comparable historical research is harder to come by, but a few items point to a similar affinity two or three generations ago. As part of a larger project, we used 1900 and 1910 U.S. Census manuscripts to randomly sample a few hundred households in three northern California towns: Antioch, Palo Alto, and San Rafael. We then identified those that had residential telephones. In 1900, only 12 of 351 households had phones. None of the 39 households with unmarried male heads had residential telephones; 3 percent of the 203 households with male heads with wives but no daughters eighteen or older at home did; but 9 percent of the 35 households with husbands, wives, and at least one adult daughter had telephones. In 1910, the estimates were 12 percent of the 33 households headed by single males, 28 percent of the 229 with husband and wife but no adult daughters, and 44 percent of the 27 households with husband, wife, and daughter had telephones. (Households headed by females were few and unusual. These were excluded.) In other words, the probability of a residential telephone increased noticeably with the number of adult women in the home.

Logit analysis of the 1900 data showed that the number of adult women, but not of adult men, in the household correlates with telephone subscription. Adding controls for socioeconomic variables makes the effect of women drop just below statistical significance, but the patterns are maintained. Including or excluding households headed by females makes no difference. Regression analyses of the 1910 data showed the same pattern: significant or near-significant independent effects of adult women on residential telephone subscription with nil (or even negative) independent effects of the number of adult men on probability of subscription. For 1920, 1930, and 1936, we drew samples for the towns from city directories and voter lists. Again, the presence of a spouse added to the odds of having a telephone. Unfortunately, we did not record the genders of additional adults in the household. Nevertheless, the number of adults strongly predicted telephone subscription. Given the patterns for 1900 and 1910, it is likely that women in the household contributed most to the effect.

National data collected during World War I provides different, yet confirmatory, results. In 1918 and 1919, the Bureau of labor Statistics surveyed the spending patterns of over twelve thousand families headed by wage earners and low-level salaried workers (Bureau of Labor Statistics, 1924). We randomly drew 20 percent of the cases from the original list, yielding a working sample of 2,588. We defined telephone subscription as a reported expenditure on telephones in the prior twelve months of at least five dollars. The range of household types was limited to husband-and-wife families with at least one child who were above severe poverty and not recent immigrants. Those households with at least one adult son at home were *less* likely to have a telephone than were those without an adult son (15.4 percent versus 20.4; p < .05). But households with an adult daughter were *more* likely to have a telephone than those families without such a daughter at home (26.5 percent versus 19.8; p < .05). We also performed OLS regression analyses, controlling for income, region, housing and demographic factors. In these equations, the curious result was that additional household members of *any* kind *depressed* the probability of telephone subscription—but males did so far more than females. An adult son at home depressed the probability by –.17, a daughter by a nonsignificant –.05; a male lodger changed it by –.09, a female lodger by a nonsignificant +.01. In any event, a shift in the gender *proportion* of the family toward women increased the odds of a telephone.

A massive survey conducted by the General Federation of Women's Clubs in the early 1920s revealed that more homes had telephones and automobiles than had toilets. Club president Mary Sherman attributed that to women: "Before toilets are installed or washbasins put into homes, automobiles are purchased and telephones are connected . . . because the housewife for generations has sought to escape from the monotony rather than the drudgery of her lot" (Sherman, 1925:98). And two small surveys of farm families reported that wives made the great bulk of the households' calls, even those for farm business (Borman, 1936; Robertson and Amstutz, 1949:18).

This "affinity" of women for the telephone apparently bothered the nineteenth-century men who developed the industry. Emerging from the telegraph trade, telephone companies for many years considered their major market to be businessmen—calling one another or clients, calling home from the office, or calling the office from home or a resort. Women— that is, the wives of the businessmen—were also a market, but a more limited one.

Telephone advertisements counseled women to use the instrument at home to manage the household, in particular to order supplies, call service, people, and issue and respond to invitations (see Steele, 1905). A 1904 advertisement by the Delaware and Atlantic Company depicts a homemaker in an elegant Victorian dress speaking into a wall-mounted telephone. The text reads: "The modern way is to save one's time and temper by telephoning. The telephone makes housekeeping simple and emergencies no longer terrifying."[4] Themes of emergency and crime also appeared in advertisements before World War II. Bell com-

---

[4]Copy in "Advertising and Publicity" folder, AT&T Historical Archives, New York.

panies recommended that a man order an extension telephone for his wife's bedside should she hear a prowler while he was away on business. But the dominant theme in marketing the telephone to women in the the 1920s (Fischer, 1988) was the suggestion that women, in their roles as "chief executive officers" of the household, use the instrument to order goods and services. This was consistent with the emerging image of the housewife-administrator in both advertising and home economics (Marchand, 1985; Cowan, 1983). At the same time, the industry stimulated this use of the telephone from the other end: It encouraged merchants to organize, invite, and advertise telephone ordering (see, for example, Printers' Ink, 1910; Shaw, 1934).

The stereotypical woman's telephone call of today—a *conversation* with friends or family—was a problem for the industry at the turn of the century (Fischer, 1988). And it was general source of hostile humor. For example, a contributor to *Lippincott's Monthly* wrote in 1909: "Has not the telephone become the favorite pastime of the woman with nothing to do? It has. Does it not accelerate gossip? Aid the flirt and the wayward, constantly? It does. . . . A telephone in a residence should be for the convenience of the user, for imperative needs, for exceptional social emergencies. . . . But for the exchange of twaddle between foolish women . . . it has become an unmitigated domestic curse" (Antrim, 1909:125–126; Bennett, 1912).

From the 1910s into the Depression, however, women appeared increasingly often in the advertising copy and the literature of telephone advertising. And they appeared increasingly in more roles than only that of household manager. Advertisements began showing the woman as a lonely wife called by her hardworking husband or as a grandmother at the ancestral home enjoying a call from her upwardly-mobile children in the city. In the 1920s and 1930s, advertising copy depicted her as a socially active young woman managing her farflung network or as an anxious teenager courting by wire.[5] A sales manual for Bell Canada in the late 1920s advised the following "pitch" to its canvassers: "With her name in the directory, a housewife is in ready contact with friends. They can easily reach her to invite her to teas and other social activities of her circle" (Bell Canada, 1928).

By World War II, industry men viewed women as at least coequal users of the telephone, although sales personnel still seemed to assume that men would usually decide whether the household would subscribe to the service. Today, the industry considers women to be the main users of residential telephones (as noted earlier).

What Did Women Do *with the Telephone?*

Why did women so quickly outpace men as customers for the residential telephone? To answer that, we initially asked what it was that women used the telephone for. They did use

[5]This summary is based on revive much telephone advertising of the period, found in various sources (see Fischer, 1988), including archival collections: AT&T Historical Archives, New York City (thanks to Robert Lewis and Mildred Ettlinger); archives of the Pioneer Telephone Museum, San Francisco (Don Thrall, Ken Rolin, Norm Hawker); Museum of Independent Telephony (Peggy Chronister); Bell Canada Historical, Montreal (Stephanie Sykes, Nina Bederian-Gardner). Illinois Bell Information Center (Rita Lapka and the N. W. Ayer Collection, Smithsonian, Washington—supplemented by excerpts from a few northern California newspapers gathered by John Chan, Steve Derne and Barbara Loomis.

it for the purposes that the early salesmen of the technology advertised: managing the household. But how extensive, in fact, was this use? Despite passing remarks that shopping by telephone was commonplace (Cowan, 1976; Asmann, 1980:279–280), evidence suggests that fewer than half of urban women with telephones ordered goods over the lines. In material circulated to merchants in 1933, the Bell Company claimed that over 50 percent of housewives in Washington "would rather shop by telephone than in person" (Printers' Ink, 1933). A 1930s Bell survey of 4,500 households in one city found that 40 percent of subscribers were "willing" to buy over the telephone, while in another survey, a bare majority of 800 subscribers answered yes to the question, "Do you like to shop by telephone." The same source reported that telephone orders represented just 5 percent of business in large department stores (Shaw, 1934). Discounting these claims somewhat for the obvious self-interest of the telephone company leads to the conclusion that telephone shopping was probably a minority practice, as late as the 1930s.

Few women interviewed by Rakow (1987) or Chan mentioned using the telephone for ordering, although many did mention emergencies. A contemporary—although limited—survey in London, Ontario (Canada), found that only 30 percent of the respondents liked ordering goods by telephone (Singer, 1981). Telephone shopping did not become nearly as common, at least in urban America, as the industry expected or tried to stimulate. Even today, in the era of toll-free numbers and credit cards, some researchers claim that the desire to handle the merchandise and for social activity will always circumscribe "tele-shopping" (see Salomon, 1986).

If women were developing an "affinity" for the telephone but not using it that much in their roles as homemakers, what were they using it for? Social purposes—that is, to *converse* with family and friends.

Some original data illustrating the point come from an unusual time-budget study of homemakers conducted in 1930. As part of a widespread, if unsystematic, survey of how women spent their time, federal government home economists asked "Seven Sisters" alumnae to complete time-budgets for a week.[6] I randomly sampled the forms sixty-two respondents had completed for a total of 250 days and tabulated listings of telephone calls. There were only eighty-three such entries, which, considering the probability that virtually all of these high-status housewives had telephones, implies that for most telephone use was unremarkable. (Only one woman mentioned using a neighbor's telephone.) Of all the reported outgoing calls, 30 to 50 percent apparently involved orders for goods and services, and 30 to 50 percent of the outgoing calls involved personal or social matters. Of all noted calls, in- or out-going 25 to 40 percent were commercial and 30 to 50 percent were social.

Since the women often listed telephone calls with little or no explanation of the purpose, I could only estimate ranges. The low estimates assume that calls fell into a category only if they were explicitly labeled (for example, "called friend"), while the high estimates

---

[6]The time-budget forms and related materials are in Box 653, Record Group 176, Bureau of Human Nutrition and Home Economics, "Use of Time on Farms Study, 1925–1930," Washington National Records Center, Suitland, MD. Despite the title, the raw data that have survived are *not* from farms, but largely from a select sample of urban and suburban housewives. Barbara Loomis alerted me to these records. Kneeland (1929) and U.S.D.A. (1911) summarize some of the data. This sample is obviously unrepresentative of American women generally and the data are vulnerable to numerous errors, particularly for this paper, underreporting of calls. Nevertheless, it provides a rare of the daily routines of upper middle-class women over a half-century ago, in ways more systematic and comprehensive than even the diaries relied upon by many historians.

rest on bolder assumptions (for example, an unexplained outgoing call after 6 P.M. was likely to be social rather than commercial). Almost all the plausible biases in the data would reduce reporting of social calls: the study was explicitly done to assess homemaking, to see just how "hard" women were working (Kneeland, 1929); the instructions to respondents clearly imply that the primary interest was in tabulating homemaking activities; the sample is of affluent and busy women (many had part-time paid or unpaid jobs), just the sort presumably most likely to find shopping by telephone attractive; the evident status concerns in some of the responses (one woman noted that her evening's reading was in Greek, another that it was on psychology) probably lead many to minimize what might appear frivolous, and in the period, telephone "visiting" probably still had the lingering stigma, fostered by the telephone industry, of triviality (Fischer, 1988). On the other hand, perhaps the onerousness of the time-budget task led to an overselection of women with time on their hands. (But shopping by telephone was probably *not* underreported simply because shopping was commonplace; entries describing in-person marketing are very frequent, averaging perhaps one every other day.) In sum, it is reasonable to assume that, even among these upper middle-class and presumably skilled home managers, social use of the telephone was the most common use.

The most explicit reports about women's uses of the telephone concern *farm* women. Repeatedly, observers claimed that telephoning sustained the social relations—and even the sanity—of women on dispersed homesteads.[7] Industry men who sold equipment or service to farmers also claimed this; for example, the North Electric Company, of Cleveland, in 1905: "The evil and oppression of solitude on woman is eliminated" (Telephony, 1905: 303); and an officer of an Ohio telephone company, the same year:

> *When we started . . . the farmers thought that they could get along without telephones. . . . Now you couldn't take them out. The women wouldn't let you even if the men would. Socially, they have been a godsend. The women of the county keep in touch with each other, and with their social duties, which are largely in the nature of church work (Kemp, 1905:433).*

The U.S. Census Bureau made a similar claim in 1910:

> *There is a sense of community life impossible without this ready means of communication. This is an immense boon in the life of women on the farm, who for days at a time during planting and harvesting seasons may be left alone in the house during working hours . . . The sense of loneliness and insecurity felt by farmers' wives under former conditions disappears, and an approach is made to the solidarity of a small country town (U.S. Bureau of the Census, 1910:78).*

Official investigations of rural life, especially of farm women, emphasized its isolation and boredom, and—as in the 1909 Country Life Commission (U.S. Senate, 1909:

---

[7]This has been repeated so often in the telephone literature that it has of course been exaggerated. For example, Brooks (1976:94), in his history of telephony, writes, "By the end of the 1880s, telephones were beginning to save the sanity of remote farm wives by lessening their sense of isolation." But at the end of the 1880s, very few farm homes, effectively no remote ones, *had* telephones.

45ff)—recommended or applauded improved communications, including the telephone. A 1915 inquiry, "Social and Labor Needs of Farm Women" (U.S. Department of Agriculture, 1915), highlighted the "loneliness, isolation, and lack of social and educational opportunity" described by its respondents (p. 11) and relayed requests by farm women for improved communications. Most asked for better roads, but some women also mentioned telephones, such as this one from Arkansas: "The worst trouble we have is isolation. Absence of social life. We would rather have free telephones and moving pictures than free seed" (p. 14). Five years later, Florence Ward (1920:6–7) reported on a survey of ten thousand "representative" northern and western farm families: "Marked progress has been made during the past few years. . . . The telephone [in 72 percent of the homes] and the automobile [62 percent] in large measure free the farm family from isolation."

The many claims and the related anecdotes[8] suggesting that the telephone ended farm women's isolation do not, of course, prove that this was so—only that many people believed it was so. But these accounts do strengthen the assertion that farm women were using the telephone for social purposes—despite, one should note, the usual rural problems of poor sound quality, shared party lines, and poverty. In a typical rural community, subscribers shared lines of four or more parties. This worked against social conversations, both because the lines were in demand and because of frequent eavesdropping. On the other hand, companies usually charged a flat rate for unlimited local calls; this would encourage telephone visiting. The evidence suggests that, on the whole rural callers—mostly women, we have seen—exerted themselves, financially and otherwise, to make these calls. (Rakow's [1987] oral histories provide more ambiguous evidence, as noted later.)

If farm women persevered to use the telephone socially, what about urban women? There are no comparable testimonies about nor investigations of the communications needs of urban women. Fragments of evidence suggest that the town residents also emphasized the use of telephone for sociability—although perhaps to a lesser degree. These include the advertising pitches of the later years, which featured, for example, drawings of urbane women in affluent settings and texts suggesting calls to friends. They include evidence of a popular perception that women chatted on the telephone.[9] They include the alumnae survey described earlier.

Also, well-off urban women used the telephone to pursue organizational activities. In her study of Chicago "society women," Rosher (1968) found that by 1895 one-fourth of those who were officers in reform groups had telephones, compared to less than one percent Chicagoans generally; 66 percent of women activists had telephones by 1905, versus 3 percent of Chicagoans. Rosher argues that the club women were quick to adopt the telephone and suggests that it may have been a major factor in the increasing civic activity of Chicago women (1968:110).

[8]For example, in 1917, the Whitehead Telephone Company pressed the Indiana Public Service Commission to allow an extra charge for lengthy calls so as to discourage gossip on their rural, eight-party lines. But Whitehead's customers packed the hearing and testified that they had no objection to gossip. The Commission found against the company. A similar case occurred in Oregon (MacMeal, 1934:224).

[9]For instance, a 1926 item from the London, Ontario, *Free Press:* "An anti-telephone gossip union is about to see the light of day in London whose specific purpose is to obtain legislation to charge all telephone gossips after five minutes of the wire, $1.00 a minute. . . . Roughly 10,000 members have already signed on the dotted line in the Forest City, 90 percent of whom are men." Most of the complaints targeted women (1926:11 February, from "London Community File," Bell Canada Historical).

Records of women's clubs in affluent Palo Alto, California, provide other illustrations of telephone organizing. For example, the *Bulletins* of the Palo Alto Womens' Business and Professional Club, 1929 to 1933, include entries such as: "Phone the club house for reservations not than . . ."; "If you can help Grace Martley's trip arrangements, call 21745"; "Last Saturday we had a food sale. . . . Mrs. Baldwin did the telephoning"; and "If this is your first notice that you are already named on the committee, it is because you don't answer the telephone."[10]

Courting was another social use of the telephone (see Rothman, 1984:233ff). An etiquette column in 1930 warns "Patty" that if she wants her boyfriend to "respect and admire her, she does not call him up during business or working hours . . . [and at home] she should not hold him up to the ridicule of his family by holding an absurdly long telephone conversation" (Richardson, 1930). (Catherine Bertho [1981:243] claims that in France during "la Belle Epoque," the telephone was viewed as an instrument of seduction and adultery, because it allowed the voice of an "other" man secretly to enter the home.) In Palo Alto, the telephone company found in 1934 that they had to add a switchboard to the Stanford Union, because "with eighty women residing this year in the Union, the telephone congestion has been so great during the 'dating' hours around lunch and dinner that service has been slow."[11] (Of course, in this case, half the speakers were men. But the point here is to determine what women were doing with the telephone.)

These items of evidence ranging from anecdotes to surveys of thousands of women suggest that farm and middle-class women commonly used the telephone for social, personal, civic, and recreational ends. About working-class women we know least. They were least likely to have telephones at home, even less so than comparable farm women. And they were of least interest as customers to the marketers of telephone service. Nevertheless, it seems reasonable to assume that those who had telephones in their own homes used it at least as often for social conversations as for shopping, since they would have been less able to afford the tariff for the delivery of goods. Surveys today indicate that, in the general population, telephones are used far more often for social purposes than for household management. For example, over ten thousand respondents to a survey of Pacific Telephone customers (Field Research Corporation, 1985:42) estimated that 74 percent of their calls were "personal or social," versus 12 percent for household matters such as repairs or orders and 14 percent for business.

In Singer's (1981) London, Ontario, survey, 77 percent of respondents reported that their calls of the day had been for personal or social reasons versus 20 percent for commercial or business purposes. A small study of thirty-one women in the Bronx in 1970 who were heavy users of the telephone pointed to their isolation in the home and their consequent need to call both service providers and friends and kin as the explanation for their high use (Maddox, 1976:263).

To this evidence of female sociability on the telephone, we must add John Chan's and Lana Rakow's (1987) oral histories, which include several elderly women who had been raised on farms. Most interviewees claimed that the telephone was *not* used very much then,

---

[10]"Palo Alto Womens' Business and Professional Club" folder, Palo Alto Historical Association; collected by Steve Derne.

[11]*Palo Alto Times,* 1934:15 November.

from about 1915 to 1940; that when it was used, it was largely for "serious" purposes; that people did not visit on the telephone as often or for as long as they do "nowadays"; and that party lines, poor sound, the lack of someone with a telephone to call, and simple etiquette kept subscribers from having lengthy chats. While visiting by telephone was probably *less* frequent and *briefer* the farther back in time one goes, so that the contrast with current practice is notable, the interviewees nevertheless reported that social calls *did* occur regularly, were considered important, and were *more often women's calls than men's* (see, for example, Rakow, 1987:230).[12]

The best estimate as to what women actually *did* with the telephone is that, while they used it for emergencies on rare occasions and while many used it regularly for shopping and other household management tasks, they used it most—and in a gender-specific way—as an instrument of sociability. The volume of such use was probably less before World War II than it is now, but it probably took precedence over "practical" uses then, too. Some might criticize the *quality* of telephone sociability, contending that it lacks the intimacy of face-to-face conversation (Strasser, 1982:305), but its popularity among women is undoubtable. About men's use of the telephone at home we know comparatively little. The evidence suggests that they used it less often, valued it less, and were perhaps more shy of it than women.

Women and a Technology of Sociability

In sum, North American women seemed to have a special affinity for the household telephone and that affinity seemed to involve sociability. Why?

A simple but insufficient answer is that men had equal appetites for telephone conversation but satisfied it at work. Relatively few men, however, had access to telephones at work. Farmers in the field did not, blue-collar workers rarely did, and probably only a small minority of white-collar workers could chat on the telephone while at work.[13] The great majority of men, too, would have needed the home telephone (or at least, a pay telephone) for their personal calls. Furthermore, bits of data suggest that men and women in comparable situations still differ in telephone use, for pie, farm men and women and working men and women (Rakow, 1987; Synge, Rosenthal, and Marshall, 1982).

I will suggest three mutually compatible answers for the gender differentiation of telephone use. One locates the source in women's structural positions, another in normative gender rules, and the third in personality differences.

---

[12]Chan's respondents similarly downplayed the amount of telephone use, but a common recollection—at least among the men—was the use of the telephone by mothers and sisters for social purposes. Some men reported that they had made rendezvous by telephone, but not that they visited by telephone.

[13]Take 1920 as a sample year: Farmers comprised about 30 percent of the male labor force in the United States. Blue-collar workers formed another 48 percent. *At most,* perhaps three-fifths of the remainder, the white-collar workers, could have used a telephone at work freely—which then equals a high guess of 13 percent of all employed men having such access. Put another way, each business telephone had to be "shared" by an average of about eight male workers (or six non-farm, male workers, ten workers of both sexes) And this includes all sorts of "official business only" instruments. At the same time, each residential telephone had to be "shared" by only 2.9 households. In 1930, the business telephone ratio was one per 5.5 male workers and the residential rate was one per 2.4 households. (Data are calculated from U.S. Bureau of the Census 1975:139–140, 783.)

One: Women, especially but not only housewives, typically are more isolated from daily adult contact than men are. Current research shows that women, at least in the child-rearing years, tend more often to lose touch with friends. Such isolation was probably greater in the first half of this century when children were more numerous, fewer women were in the paid labor force, more lived on farms, and travel was more difficult. Thus, telephone visiting was probably the means many women used to attain some of the social interaction their husbands obtained in the workplace and marketplace (see Rakow, 1987: 63, 166).

But if one can "reach out," one can also be reached. Women may have become subject to more demands from kin and friends than when they were more cut off. Some informants complained to Lana Rakow (1987) that the telephone increased their burdens. General observation and claims of women, such as the pleas of farm wives for telephones and good roads, indicate that, on net, increased social contact was nevertheless preferred. Thus, women may have turned to the home telephone more than did men to find that social contact.

This explanation is probably incomplete. The evidence, allusive as it is, points to gender differences in telephone sociability even among men and women with comparable opportunities for adult contact.[14]

Two: Among the gender-typed responsibilities of women is that of social manager. Both men and women commonly expect the latter to issue and respond to social invitations; to organize the preparations for group dinners, outings, church affairs, and so forth; and more generally, to manage the family's social networks—keeping in touch with relatives (including the husbands' kin), exchanging courtesies and token gifts with neighbors, and the like. On a wider scale, women perform similar "socioemotional" tasks in their volunteer work. As Rakow (1987–297) puts it, "telephone talk is work women do to hold together the fabric of the community." Part of women's affinity for the telephone, then, results from the duties they have: their sociability is in service to the household, the extended family, the friendship circle, and the community. (See also di Leanardo, 1984:194ff; Ross, 1983; Kessler and McLeod, 1984; and Leffler, Krannich, and Gillespie, 1984, for examples of women's greater responsibility for and sensitivity to social networks.)

This explanation, too, is incomplete. It implies that telephone conversation is more housework, only another burden. It does not capture the degree of voluntary conversation and the pleasure in conversation suggested by the accounts we have of women and telephony. So a third factor may also be in play.

Three: Women are more comfortable on the telephone than men; and this in turn, because North American women are generally more sociable than North American men. There is considerable evidence in the social-psychological and social networks literatures that, holding constant the opportunities for social contacts, women are more sociable than men, whatever the explanation for that one prefers—constitutional, structural, social, or cultural (see, for example, Fischer and Oliker, 1983; Hoyt and Babchuck, 1983; Kessler and

---

[14]Farm women apparently used the telephone more than did farm men, despite roughly comparable physical isolation. Elderly women today use the telephone more than elderly men do, although both groups are retired (Synge, Rosenthal, and Marshall, 1982) and elderly women have more friends than elderly men do (Fischer and Oliker, 1983). Various testimonials imply that, after working hours, women with jobs outside the home chat on the telephone more than do working men (e.g,, Rakow, 1987).

McLeod, 1984; Bott, 1971; Komarovsky, 1967; Pogrebin, 1987:chs. 13, 14). Given the difference, the telephone fits the modal female style more than it does the modal male style.

A few items in telephone history are consistent with this third contention. A 1930s survey of 27 "typical" Iowa farm families found that women made 60 percent of the calls, including many regarding the farm business (Borman, 1936). Results from a 1940s rural Indiana survey of 166 subscribers explains that pattern in the following way: "Women used the phone most frequently. Many men said they did not like to use the phone, so they had women call for them" (Robertson and Amstutz, 1949:18; see also Rakow, 1987:169–70). A Bell survey suggests the sensitivity of women to the social nuances of telephone conversations. When, in the 1920s, Bell asked a sample of "better-class" subscribers why they did not use long-distance more often, the researchers found that "the feeling seemed general with the *housewives* in these groups that a social conversation cannot be limited to the three-minute initial period without the embarrassment of being somewhat abrupt or discourteous" (Wilson, 1928:51; emphasis added).

These data are, admittedly, crude. But, added to what sociologists know about gender differences in social relations, they lend weight to this explanation: Women developed a greater affinity for the residential telephone than men did, because it was more useful to them in overcoming isolation, in performing their network tasks, and in pursuing an activity that they typically both enjoyed more and were better at than men—sociable interaction.

Implications

The case of the residential telephone presents a more complex picture of gender and technology than appears in most of the literature. One can argue that the telephone, like the stove or washing machine, facilitated women's designated tasks in the home and thereby increased, or at least helped maintain, an oppressive division of labor. More broadly, telephone use may have accentuated or solidified male-female differences in interpersonal relations.

It would be difficult, however, without engaging in some dubious reasoning, to assert that the telephone was another vehicle for the "capitalist-patriarchal order." The reasoning underlying the greater oppression argument tends to be circular, taking this form: There are oppressive tasks women must perform; any change that makes the tasks less oppressive necessarily makes women more able, willing, and likely to perform them and more often; ergo, *any* change—other than removal or "de-gendering" of the task—perpetuates or aggravates the oppression. This deduction can be persuasive in the absence of empirical data. But it is not of much use in understanding actual social change. It is more useful to ask how, within the existing cultural matrix, a technology came to be used and to what ends.

In the current instance, given the extant gender division of labor, it would seem that the telephone made women's work easier. There is little evidence to claim that women performed more (or fewer, for that matter) material tasks in the home because of the telephone. It is reasonable to claim, as did a few women to Lana Rakow, that the telephone made women more vulnerable to requests for their socioemotional labor—to advise, comfort, organize, and so on. Women's tasks in this realm may have grown. But calls go both ways and it is likely that each burdensome call a woman received was matched by at least one help-seeking call a woman made. It is also reasonable to claim that the telephone facilitated work that women were expected to perform anyway. We can say little more without considerably more comparative *evidence*—for example, that in comparable places without telephones, women's duties were more or less onerous.

What is most reasonable to conclude from the evidence, however, is that women also used the telephone, and used it often, to pursue what they *wanted:* sociable conversation. The testimonials and other data suggest that use of the telephone was more often experienced as a pleasure (and more so by women than by men). If so, this is an instance of women "appropriating" a technology to serve their *own* distinctive ends.

There is, of course, the possibility of "false consciousness" on the part of women testifying about the telephone—that it really burdened them more than it eased their burdens, harassed them more than it pleased them, all despite their perceptions. Individual and collective misperceptions are certainly possible. (For example, women may have experienced the purchase of a vacuum cleaner as easing the demands of housecleaning, but not have noticed the upward creep of their standards of cleanliness which may have created more work.) However, such a claim carries a heavy evidentiary burden, since the actors' understandings of their own experience ought to have *prima facie* validity. Simply deducing consequences from a theory of technology is not satisfactory, for plausible deductions can be made in either direction, for more or for less "liberation."

This conclusion implies that we must make careful distinctions among, and even within, technologies. To pursue the point, consider briefly the connection of women's historical experiences to two other technologies that share with the telephone the ability to facilitate sociability.

The few social historians of the *bicycle* seem to agree that many young women used it to shuck Victorian constraints. When mechanics developed a practical "safety bicycle" in the 1890s, middle-class Americans went on a virtual cycling craze. Since riding the contraption in contemporary ladieswear, bustles and all, was difficult, many women adopted risque bloomer outfits and other shape-revealing clothes. (This practice joined with a feminist movement against corsets and for freer garments, as well as an increasing abandonment of Victorian inhibitions elsewhere.) Bicycle outings also allowed young women to lose their chaperons and be alone with their beaus. "More and more women came to regard the bicycle as a freedom machine" (Smith 1972:76). In France, the president of a feminist congress in 1896 toasted the "equalitarian and leveling bicycle" that was about to liberate women (Weber, 1986:203). Of course, this was a "liberation" restricted to younger women. (On bicycles, see, for example, Aronson, 1968, and Smith, 1972; on cultural responses, see, for example, Kern, 1983, and Green, 1983.)

The social history of the *automobile* is more complex. Cowan (1983) and others (for example, Hawkins and Getz, 1986) have argued that common use of the automobile increased housework burdens on women by stimulating new shopping and chauffeuring trips, by undercutting delivery services, neighborhood stores, and other conveniences that had existed for the housebound housewife, and indirectly by expediting suburbanization and its consequent requirement for numerous and long trips.

Granting this point (for the moment—we have little solid evidence), there was also another side to the automobile. Many women reportedly viewed the automobile as a device of personal liberation, especially for rural women. Home economist Christine Fredrick wrote in 1912:

> *Learning to handle the car has wrought my emancipation, my freedom. I am no longer a country bound farmer's wife. . . . The auto is the link which bonds the metropolis to my pastoral existence; which brings me in frequent touch with the entertainment and life of my neighboring small towns—with the joys of bargains, library, and soda-water (quoted by Scharff, 1986).*

Less literate farm wives said much the same when asked about spending scarce funds for automobiles (see the earlier discussion on studies of farm women; also Interrante, 1979; Berger, 1979,65; Wik, 1972:25ff). The theme of ending women's isolation recurs. As in the case of the telephone, we know less about urban women, and urban women were less likely than comparable farm women to drive cars. But there is some evidence that city women, too, enjoyed the personal liberation of the automobile, at least over the alternative, the trolley-car (Scharff, 1986). One expression of the liberation was the boom in family touring that followed mass automobility (Belascoe, 1979; see also Rothman, 1984:294ff).

Perhaps this romance with the automobile turned into a snare. As the automobile became *available* to women, it also become *necessary* to them (for reasons mentioned above); trips were less often pleasant indulgences and more often unavoidable burdens. Still, in many ways and for many years, the automobile, too, seemed to amplify the ability of women to satisfy their own desires.

What the telephone, bicycle, and this facet of the automobile share in common, it seems, is that they are, in part, *technologies of sociability;* they facilitate personal interaction. Women seemed to have similarly grasped other, comparable, turn-of-the-century social changes, and more eagerly than men. They flocked to department stores (Leach, 1984) and to movies (Peiss, 1986), both leaving behind the "domestic sphere" and finding sociability. Women's "affinity" then, for such changes is understandable: women, at least in North America, are the sociable gender.

Women seemed to have taken the telephone and used it for their own ends, as well as their families'. Men's jokes about this affinity are perhaps, at base, simply a defensive acknowledgment of this difference between men and women in personal relations.

References

Andrews, William D. and Deborah Andrews. 1974. "Technology and the housewife in nineteenth-century America." Women's Studies 2:309–328.

Autrim, M. T. 1909. "Outrages of the telephone." Lippincott's Monthly Magazine 84 (July): 125–126.

Arlen, Michael J. 1980. Thirty Seconds. New York. Farrar, Straus & Giroux.

Aronson, S. H. 1968. "The sociology of the bicycle." In M. Truzzi (ed.), Sociology and Everyday life: 293–303. Englewood Cliffs, NJ: Prentice-Hall.

Asmann, Edwin A. 1980. "The telegraph and the telephone: Their development and role in the economic history of the United States: The first century, 1844–1944." Manuscript, Lake Forest College.

Belascoe, W. J. 1979. Americans on the Road: From Autocamp to Motel, 1910–1945. Cambridge, MA: MIT Press.

Bell Canada. 1928. "Selling service on the job." Document #12223:5. Montreal: Bell Canada Historical.

Bennett, Arnold. 1912. "Your United States." Harper's Monthly 125 (July): 191–202.

Bereano, Philip, Christine Bose, and Erik Arnold. 1985. "Kitchen technology and the liberation of women from housework." In W. Faulkner and E. Arnold (eds.), Smothered by Invention. 162–181. London: Pluto Press.

Berger, Michael L. 1979. The Devil Wagon in God's Country: The Automobile and Social Change in Rural America, 1883–1929. Hamden, CT: Archon Books.

Bertho, Catherine. 1981. Telegraphes et Telephones. Paris: Livres de Poche.

Borman, R. R. 1936. "Survey reveals telephone as a money saver on farm." Telephony 111 (11 July): 9–13.

Bose, C., P. L. Bereano, and M. Malloy. 1984. "Household technology and the social construction of housework." Technology and Culture 25 (January): 53–82.

Bott, Elizabeth. 1971. Family and Social Network, 2d ed. New York: Free Press.

Brandon, B., ed. 1981. The Effect of the Demographics of Individual Households on Their Telephone Usage. Cambridge, MA: Ballinger.

Brooks, John. 1976. "Telephone: The First Hundred Years. New York: Harper and Row.

Bureau of Labor Statistics. 1924. "The cost of living in the United States." Bulletin No. 357, U.S. Department of Labor. Washington, DC: U.S. Government Printing Office. (Data file # ICPSR 8299 provided by the Inter-University Consortium for Political and Social Research, Ann Arbor, MI.)

Cowan, Ruth Schwartz. 1976. "The 'industrial revolution' in the home: Household technology and social change in the 29th century." Technology and Culture 17 (January): 1–23.

——. 1979. "From Virginia Due to Virginia Slims: Women and technology in American life." In M. M. Trescott (ed.), Dynamos and Virgins Revisited: 30–44. Metuchen, NJ. Scarecrow Press.

——. 1983. More Work for Mother. New York: Basic Books.

——. 1987. "The consumption junction: A proposal for research strategies in the sociology of technology." In W. E. Bijker, T. P. Huges, and T. Pinch (eds.). The Social Construction of Technology: 261–280. Cambridge. MA: M.I.T. Press.

di Leanardo, Micaela. 1984. The Varieties of Ethnic Experience. Ithaca, NY: Cornell University Press.

Field Research Corporation. 1985. Residence Customer Usage and Demographic Characteristics Study: Summary. Courtesy R. Somer, Pacific Bell.

Fischer, Claude S. 1985. "Studying technology and social life." In M. Castells (ed.), High Technology, Space, and Society: 284–301 Beverly Hills, CA: Sage.

——. 1987a. "The revolution in rural telephony." Journal of Social History 21 (Fall): 5–26.

——. 1987b. "Technology's retreat: the decline of rural telephony, 1920 to 1940." Social Science History 11 (Fall) 295–327.

——. 1983. " 'Touch someone': The telephone industry discovers sociability." Technology and Culture 29 (January): 32–61.

Fischer, Claude S. and Glenn Carroll. 1988. "The diffusion of the telephone and the automobile in the United States, 1902 to 1937." American Journal of Sociology 93 (March): 1153–1178.

Fischer, Claude S. and Stacey Oliker. 1983. "A research note on friendship, gender, and the life cycle." Social Forces 62 (September): 124–133.

Green, Harvey. 1983. The Light of the Home: An Intimate View of the Lives of Victorian Women in America. New York: Pantheon.

Harrell, J. E. 1931. "Residential exchange sales in the New England southern area." Bell System General Commercial Conference on Sales Matters, June. Mf 368B, Illinois Bell Historical, Chicago.

Hawkins, Richard and J. Greg Getz. 1986. "Women and technology: The user's context of the automobile." Paper presented at the American Sociological Association annual meeting in New York.

Horowitz, Daniel. 1985. The Morality of Spending: Attitudes toward the Consumer Society in America, 1875–1940. Baltimore, MD: Johns Hopkins University Press.

Hoyt, D. R. and N. Babchuck. 1983. "Adult kinship networks." Social Forces 62 (September): 84–101.

Interrante, J. 1979. "You can't go to town in a bathtub: Automobile movement and the reorganization of rural American space, 1900–1930." Radical History Review 21 (Fall): 151–168.

Kemp, R. F. 1905. "Telephones in country homes." Telephony 9 (5 May): 432–433.

Kern, S. 1983. The Culture of Time and Space, 1889–1918. Cambridge, MA: Harvard University Press.

Kessler, R. C. and J. D. McLeod. 1984. "Sex differences in vulnerability to undesirable life events." American Sociological Review 49 (October): 620–631.

Kneeland, Hildegarde. 1929. "Is the modern housewife a lady of leisure?" Survey 62 (June): 301–302, 331, 336.

Komarovsky, Mirra. 1967. Blue-collar Marriage. New York: Random House.

Leach, William R. 1984. "Transformations in a culture of consumption: Women and department stores, 1890–1925." Journal of American History 71 (September): 319–342.

Leffler, Ann, Richard S. Krannich, and Dair L. Gillespie. 1984. "When I'm not with the friend I hate, I hate the friend I'm with: Contact, support and hostility networks in community life." Paper presented at the American Sociological Association annual meetings in San Antonio, TX.

MacMeal, H. B. 1934. The Story of Independent Telephony. Chicago: Independent Pioneer Telephone Association.

Maddox, Brenda. 1977 "Women and the switchboard." In I. de S. Pool (ed), The Social Impact of the Telephone: 262–280. Cambridge, MA: MIT Press.

Marchand, Roland. 1985. Advertising the American Dream: Making Way for Modernity, 1920–1940. Berkeley: University of California Press.

Mayer, M. 1977. "The telephone and the uses of time." In I. de S. Pool (ed.), The Social Impact of the Telephone: 225–245. Cambridge, MA: MIT Press.

McGaw, Judith. 1982. "Women and the history of American technology." Signs 7(4): 798–828.

Paine, Robert. 1967. "What is gossip about?" Man 2 (June): 278–285.

Peiss, Kathy. 1986. Cheap Amusements: Working Women and Leisure in Turn-of-the-Century New York. Philadelphia, PA: Temple University Press.

Pogrebin, Letty Cottin. 1987. Among Friends. New York: McGraw Hill.

Printers' Ink. 1910. "Bell encourages shopping by telephone." 70 (19 January).

———. 1933. "Telephone company works with retailers on campaign." 163 (4 May): 41.

Rakow, Lana F. 1987. "Gender, communication, and technology: A case study of women and the telephone." Ph.D. dissertation, Institute of Communications Research, University of Illinois at Urbana-Champaign.

Richardson, Anna Steese. 1930. "Telephone manners: Why not?" Successful Farming (March): 46–47.

Robertson, L. and K. Amstutz. 1949. "Telephone problems in rural Indiana." Bulletin 548 (september), Purdue University Agricultural Experiment Station, Lafayette, Indiana.

Rosher, A. 1968. "Residential telephone usage among the Chicago civic-minded." Master's thesis, Department of History, University of Chicago.

Ross, Ellen. 1983. "Survival networks: Women's neighborhood sharing in London before World War I." History Workshop 15 (Spring): 4–27.

Rothman, Ellen. 1984. Hands and Hearts: A History of Courtship in America. New York: Basic Books.

Rothschild, Joan. 1983. "Technology, housework, and women's liberation: A theoretical analysis." In Joan Rothschild (ed.), Machina Ex Dea: Feminist Perspectives on Technology: 79–93. New York: Pergamon.

Salomon, Ilan. 1986. "Telecommunications and travel relationships: A review." Transportation Research 20A.

Scharff, Virginia A. 1986. "Reinventing the wheel: American women and the automobile, 1910–1930." Paper presented at the Organization of American Historians annual meetings in New York.

Shaw, J. M. 1934. "Buying by telephone at department stores." Bell Telephone Quarterly 13 (July): 267–288.

Sherman, Mary. 1925. "What women want in their homes." Woman's Home Companion 52 (November): 28, 97–98.

Singer, B. D. 1981. Social Functions of the Telephone. Palo Alto, CA: R & E Research Associates.

Smith, R. 1972. A Social History of the Bicycle. New York: McGraw-Hill.

Spacks, Patricia Meyer. 1986. Gossip. Chicago: University of Chicago Press.

Steele, G. O. 1905. "Advertising the telephone." Printers' Ink 51 (12 April): 14–17.

Strasser, Susan. 1982. Never Done: A History of American Housework. New York: Pantheon.

Synge, J., C. J. Rosenthal, and V. W. Marshall. 1982. "Phoning and writing as a means of keeping in touch in the family of later life." paper presented at the Canadian Association on Gerontology annual meetings in Toronto.

Telephony. 1905. "Facts regarding the rural telephone." 9 (5 April) 303.

Thrall, Charles A. 1982. "The conservative use of modern household technology." Technology and Culture 23 (April): 175–194.

U.S. Bureau of the Census. 1910. Special Reports: Telephones: 1907. Washington, DC: Government Printing Office.

——. 1975. Historical Statistics of the United States, 1790–1970. Washington, DC: U.S. Government Printing Office.

U.S. Department of Agriculture. 1915. Social and Labor Needs of Farm Women. Report no. 103. Washington, DC: Government Printing Office.

——. 1944. "The time costs of homemaking—A study of 1500 rural and urban households." Mimeograph, Agricultural Research Administration, Bureau of Human Nutrition and Home Economics.

U.S. Senate. 1909. Report of the Country Life Commission. 60th Congress, 2d Session, Senate Document 705. Washington, DC: Government Printing Office.

Vanek, J. 1978. "Household technology and social status." Technology and Culture 19 (July): 361–375.

Walker, K. E. 1964. "Homemaking still takes time." Journal of Home Economics 61 (October): 621–624.

Ward, Florence E. 1920. "The farm women's problems." U.S. Department of Agriculture Circular 148. Washington, DC: Government Printing Office.

Weber, Eugen. 1986. France: Fin de Siècle. Cambridge, MA: Harvard University Press.

Wik, R. M. 1972. Henry Ford and Grass-Roots America. Ann Arbor: University of Michigan Press.

Wilson, L. B. 1928. "Sales activities." General Commercial Conference, Bell System. In microfilm 368B, Illinois Bell Historial.

Wilson, Margaret Gibbons. 1979. The American Woman in Transition. Westport, CT: Greenwood.

Winner, Langdon. 1977. Autonomous Technology: Technics-Out-Of-Control as a Theme in Political Thought. Cambridge, MA: MIT Press.

Wolfe, L. M. 1979. "Characteristics of persons with and without home telephones." Journal of Marketing Research, August: 421–425.

Discussion Questions

1. Computers might serve the same function today that telephones have in the past. How would you research this proposition? What groups could you study that might benefit from interactions using computers? Would the formation of many different kinds of networks strengthen or weaken the fabric of society? Why?

2. Do you think Fischer's findings point to a factor in the rise of solidarity among women in the women's suffrage and liberation movements? What other new technologies might have contributed? Are there any inventions that may have hindered these movements?

$$C\ h\ a\ p\ t\ e\ r\quad 5$$

Social Groups in a Socially Diverse Society

When Max Weber constructed his model of bureaucracy as an ideal type early in this century, he included "impersonality" as a necessary characteristic. I think you would agree that you want your instructor to assign grades on the basis of your work and not on your appearance or personality. If you feel this isn't done, you become angry and complain that the grade isn't fair.

In her article on black mobility, Sharon Collins examines a specific situation in which impersonality is in question. She concludes that career paths of black executives are not similar to those of their white colleagues. Perhaps using race as a criterion for promotion is not surprising to you, but Collins goes beyond the existence of simple prejudice to analyze specific circumstances for black/white differences in promotion. The explanation centers on three job types: mainstream, racialized, and mixed. The career paths of those in each of the three job categories test "impersonality" as an ideal type by revealing the operations of bureaucracies in the real world.

Black Mobility in White Corporations: Up the Corporate Ladder But Out on a Limb

SHARON M. COLLINS
University of Illinois, Chicago

Spurred in part by threats of federal sanctions, white companies during the 1960s and 1970s incorporated a new echelon of college-educated blacks into previously closed managerial job and business-related professions (Farley 1984; Freeman 1981, 1976a, 1976b; Landry 1987). Indeed, the 1960s witnessed the reversal of a longstanding pattern of declining black-white income ratios with levels of education—and the ratio of black-to-white income rose most rapidly for managers. Employed black men, in particular, were in greater demand for prestigious occupations in the labor market. In 1960, only about 7 percent of non-white male college graduates were managers, compared with 18 percent of college-educated white men (Freeman 1976b). Between 1960 and 1970, the proportion of black male college graduates employed as managers increased almost twofold over the 1960 level (Freeman 1976b). And between 1970 and 1980, the number of black men holding executive, administrative, or managerial jobs increased each year at twice the rate of white men (Farley and Allen 1987).

Yet, even after more than 30 years of social and political pressure to diversify corporate manpower and management teams, the net result is more black managers but negligible gain for black men in the decision-making strongholds of white corporate America (Chicago Urban League 1977; Heidrick and Struggles 1979; Korn/Ferry 1986; 1990; Theodore and Taylor 1991). Despite gains in entry, African-Americans clearly stagnate in their climb up the managerial hierarchy, thereby failing to make inroads into key decision-making positions and in the racial redistribution of power.

Against a backdrop of sustained inequality in corporate job allocation, this paper asks whether constraints to blacks' corporate progress are manufactured in the work process. In the 1960s and 1970s, highly educated blacks experienced less discrimination in access to

Collins, Sharon. Black Mobility in White Corporations: up the Corporate Ladder but out on a Limb. *Social Problems, 44,* 1, 1997, 55–67. By permission of the University of California Press.

61

higher-paying corporate jobs, yet we know little about their careers. Nkomo and Cox (1990) examine macro- and micro-level variables related to job promotion; Kraiger and Ford (1985) focus on discrimination in performance evaluation; and others survey black managers' perceptions of corporate life (Jones 1986; Irons and Moore 1985). The responsibilities and assignments accorded black managers in the post-entry period are a crucial but neglected element for analysis.

This paper explores the problem of race and corporate mobility. It uses a unique data set: in-depth interviews with 76 of the most successful black executives employed in major Chicago-based white corporations in 1986. These black achievers in traditionally closed managerial occupations have had the greatest chance to enter into the higher echelons of organizations in functions tied to profitability. I explore the repercussions of a corporate division of labor on the career development of these managers.

Neoclassical economic theories and social structural explanations of race-based inequality in labor markets often are argued as oppositional insights. That is, human capital theory in economic literature and status attainment theory in sociology presume that economic progress among blacks is a color-blind function of supply-side characteristics such as education, ability, and individual preferences—not race conscious social forces and barriers. The lack of marketable skills, a dependent mentality, inferior education, and even relatively lower IQs are reasons for blacks' inability to gain parity with whites (Herrnstein and Murray 1994; Murray 1984; Smith and Welch 1983; Sowell 1983).

The opposing contention is that individuals' economic attainments are determined by structural aspects of the labor market. This alternate viewpoint attributes people's limited progress to the characteristics of their jobs (Doeringer and Piore 1971; Thurow 1975). Minorities and women, for example, fill occupational niches that are in decline or that do not lead to advancement (Ghiloni 1987; Kanter 1977; Reskin and Roos 1987). Consequently, powerful and prestigious jobs with career growth opportunities—managerial jobs, in particular—are much more likely to be filled by white men. In contrast, insights from my study of black managers in the white private sector cast social structure and human capital as interactive, not as mutually exclusive explanatory schemes.

In this paper, I illustrate how a link between opportunity structure and human capital shaped subjects' abilities to achieve top jobs. In general I view the managerial division of labor as mediating human capital. Therefore, these factors interactively influence blacks' progress in executive arenas. First, I argue that Chicago corporations deployed highly educated black labor out of mainstream positions and into 'racialized' jobs. These are jobs created or reoriented during the 1960s and 1970s to carry out pro-black governmental policies and mediate black-related issues for white-owned companies. Affirmative action, urban affairs, community relations, and purchasing jobs are examples. Next, I show the impact of filling these jobs on executives' upward mobility. Initially, these jobs annointed black job holders with positive status in a company, thus attracting black talent. Over time, however, this structure of opportunity underdeveloped the human capital that corporations value. Consequently, racialized jobs marginalized the job holder's skills and, thus, the job holder. Ultimately, occupants' probability of moving into, competing for, and/or performing in, corporate areas that lead to decision-making positions (that is, general management, sales/marketing, production, finance/accounting, and human resources) was greatly diminished.

The Study

I considered blacks to be "top executives" if: 1) they were employed in a banking institution and had a title of comptroller, trust officer, vice-president (excluding "assistant" vice president), president or chief officer, or 2) they were employed in a non-financial institution as department manager, director, vice president, or chief officer. In the mid-1980s, the respondents in this study held some of the more desirable and prestigious positions in Chicago's major corporations. About two-thirds (52) had the title of director or higher, including three chief officers, 30 vice presidents, and 19 unit directors. (The total includes three people with the title "manager" whose rank within the organization was equivalent to director.) The participants in this study were among the highest-ranking black executives in the country. Five of the executives interviewed were the highest-ranking blacks in corporations nationwide. Almost half (32) were among the highest-ranking black in a company's nationwide management structure.

To locate these managers, first I identified the 52 largest white corporations in Chicago using the *Chicago Reporter's* (1983, 1986) listing of industrials, utilities, retail companies, transportation companies, and banks. Second, I asked knowledgeable informants familiar with the white corporate community in Chicago to identify blacks who met the study criteria. These same informants also identified employees of the targeted companies who might be able to provide names of higher-level black officers. I then used snowball sampling to identify a total of 87 managers. Eleven people were not interviewed because they declined to participate, because of logistical problems, or because they did not meet my criteria. Using resumes respondents forwarded to me before the interview, I explored the characteristics of each executive's job, as well as each respondent's career development and promotional opportunities.

I distinguished two types of jobs held by blacks in white corporations: racialized and mainstream. A job was coded "racialized" when its description indicated an actual and/or symbolic connection to black communities, to black issues, or to civil rights agencies at any level of government. For example, one respondent was hired by the chief executive officer of a major retailer in 1968 specifically to eradicate discriminatory employment practices used in the personnel department. I coded this job "racialized" because it was designed to improve black opportunities in the company at a time when the federal government increasingly was requiring it.

In contrast, jobs in line and support areas that lack racial implications in a company were coded "mainstream." In this category, functions relate to total constituencies, and neither explicit nor implicit connections to blacks could be found in the job description. A vice president and regional sales manager for a *Fortune* 500 company in the manufacturing and retail food industry provides an illustration of a career consisting of mainstream jobs. A *Fortune* 15 East Coast oil company hired this manager as a market researcher in 1961; his job involved marketing only to the total (predominantly white) consumer market not to "special" (predominantly black) markets. He was not assigned to black territories as a salesman nor as a sales manager although, he said, "Those kinds of things even happen now [and once] happened a lot." This manager was not responsible for a predominantly black sales force, nor for sales and marketing to the black community when he managed geographical areas.

In this paper, the "mainstream" is the pipeline of line and support jobs leading to senior executive positions that oversee the strategic planning, human resource/personnel development, or production components of a company. For example, the manager just cited moved up the mainstream sales hierarchy from salesman to sales manager, from zone manager to district manager, from area manager to division manager and, finally, to his current position as a firm officer. Granted, the pipeline narrows as it moves upward, yet the flow of occupants into these jobs fills the executive vice president, senior vice president, group vice president, functional vice president, and corporate specialist slots that comprise company officers. The typical track to top jobs in major corporations is through profit-oriented positions, such as sales, operations, and finance or, to a lesser degree through personnel or public relations (Korn/Ferry 1990).

A Corporate Division of Labor

The corporate division of labor found among Chicago's top black executives is distinctly different than job patterns found among their white peers. In this study, African American executives with mainstream careers in the private sector stand out as the exception, not the rule. Only one-third (25) of the people I interviewed built careers that consisted entirely of mainstream jobs. On the other hand, 12 (16 percent) had one racialized job and about half (39) had two or more racialized jobs. One vice president and company director was a company ombudsman during the 1970s whose task was, he said, to "promote the visibility and good name" of the bank in the black community in Chicago. A second vice president built a career interspersed with black community relations jobs during the late 1960s and 1970s that, he said, "developed a good corporate citizenship image among blacks and . . . work[ed] with . . . local [black] agencies." A third vice president spent part of his tenure in an urban affairs job. He said:

> *After the civil disorders, the riots . . . there was a tremendous movement . . . to have black [representation in the company]. Basically [my] job was to work with the [company] and come up with minority candidates.*

To obtain a rough comparative illustration of black and white executive careers, I conducted an informal survey of top white executives by asking 20 CEOs of major Chicago private sector companies if they ever held affirmative action or urban affairs jobs. (I asked about these jobs specifically because they exemplify racialized jobs.) Only one had (or admitted having) a job in either of these areas. Some CEOs even seemed startled by the question. The CEO that had worked in urban affairs performed different tasks than those performed by my respondents. Although this man represented the company on several city-wide committees to improve race relations, his job, unlike the black executives I interviewed, was a part-time, temporary assignment, not a full-time, permanent position. The results of my informal survey suggest that—among the managerial elite in Chicago— blacks are likely to have held racialized jobs, but whites are not.

Disparate career patterns are not attributable to educational differences. Indeed, African American respondents' educational level closely parallel that of white male senior-level executives in 1986. Ninety-four percent of top executives in *Fortune* 500 companies surveyed by Korn/Ferry (1986) had bachelors' degrees, and 42 percent had graduate degrees. Eighty-nine percent of respondents in my study had at least a bachelor's degree when they entered the private sector. Over one-third (38 percent) earned advanced degrees. Moreover, their level of education is well above the median level of about one year of college for salaried male managers in 1960 and in 1970 (U.S. Bureau of Census 1960, 1973). In addition, slightly more than one-half of the black graduates I interviewed received their college degrees from predominantly white institutions.

Career differences are not extensions of respondents' ports of entry into the private sector. Almost one-half of 45 people who filled affirmative action and urban affairs jobs started in the corporate mainstream with line positions. Therefore, black but not white managerial careers reflect a race conscious interaction with skill and education that tracked black managers into administrative jobs that emerged during the 1960s and 1970s.

The career of one man, who was succeeding in his company but then moved into an urban affairs position exemplifies this interaction between race and career tracking. Between 1964 and 1967 this man rapidly ascended through a series of supervisory and store management slots to become an area supervisor, a middle management position. At 23, his annual salary was more than doubled by a performance-based bonus. Yet, in the midst of this mainstream success (i.e., succeeding in the route typically traveled by the company's top executives), this man was asked to create an urban affairs program. The circumstances that led to this request were relatively straightforward: Civil rights activists had confronted the company with specific demands backed by the threat of a nationwide boycott; and the company viewed blacks as a sizeable proportion of its customer base. The respondent said, "Basically [my] job was to work with the licensee department and [come] up with minority candidates around the country to become [store owners]." After completing a strenuous series of meetings with the company's top executives—which included the head of personnel a senior vice president the head of licensing, the corporate legal council and finally, the company president—he was offered, and he accepted the assignment.

Within this operations-driven corporation, a manager with demonstrated talent for business operations generally would be considered a serious contender for a top-level mainstream position. From this perspective, slotting this man in an urban affairs job appears to be a frivolous use of talent. But in 1968, no other blacks worked at the company's corporate offices (save for one black janitor) and the company was vulnerable to racial protest. Deploying a black middle-level manager, a known commodity, into corporate urban affairs was a rational business decision. Indeed, a white vice president of personnel who worked in a major Chicago firm during the 1960s and 1970s noted that top management often filled newly created affirmative action positions with their best workers. He explained that this strategy signalled to the rank and file workers the seriousness of a company's commitment. Senior corporate managers believed that transferring an experienced black line manager into affirmative action would increase the credibility of this collateral role and enhance its effectiveness.

Black social and political unrest infused black managerial capacities with race-related purposes (Collins 1997). African Americans moved into urban affairs, affirmative action, and other racialized management jobs that required them to interact predominantly with black community organizations and/or to help white companies recruit black labor. A

53-year-old company director, who began his private sector managerial career in operations in a retail company, was deployed to set up the equal employment opportunity function for the company. He recalled that the perquisites accompanying the job were "very attractive (and] that was the place for us [blacks) to be."

Indeed, other occupants of affirmative action and urban affairs jobs who were recruited from mainstream line areas commented that black-oriented jobs appeared to be a route where talented blacks could advance rapidly. Senior-level white management, usually either senior vice presidents or chief executive officers, personally solicited 12 of the 22 recruits (55 percent) from the mainstream. Eleven (50 percent) were given salary increases, more prestigious job tides, and promises of future rewards. Nine people turned down the first attempt at recruitment because they evaluated the job to be a dead end, despite high pay and elevated titles, and were approached a second time by top management. A director of affirmative action and diversity took the job initially because, he said, "I remember the CEO saying, 'we want you to take this beautiful job. It's going to pay you all this money. It's going to make you a star.' "

Racialized Division of Labor and Mobility

What impact did this allocative process have on upward mobility in white corporations? To compare the advancement associated with racialized and mainstream careers, I selected 64 respondents employed in the white private sector at least since 1972 to construct a career typology.[1] Three types of managerial careers—mainstream, mixed, and racialized emerged, based on the jobs that these executives held. Respondents having no racialized jobs in their careers were coded as having mainstream careers (24 of 64). Respondents whose careers incorporated at least one, but not a majority, of racialized jobs were coded as having mixed careers (22 of 64), the careers of those with a majority of racialized jobs were coded as racialized (18 of 64).

Lowered Job Ceilings

By the mid-1980s, racialized respondents had advanced less than respondents in mainstream careers. The top executives (i.e., chief officers and senior vice presidents) spent most of their careers in mainstream areas. There was little difference in the executive job titles associated with mixed and mainstream careers, possibly because the vast majority of mixed careers had only one or two racialized jobs in them.

In contrast, 80 percent of racialized careers terminated with director or manager titles. Only 38 percent of the mainstream careers, and 46 percent of mixed careers terminated with those titles. Not one manager in a racialized career progressed above vice president.

Those who stayed in racialized jobs were ambitious people who saw themselves as doing the best they could, given blacks' historically limited job possibilities in white com-

---

[1]I selected the base year of 1972 because It takes about 15 to 20 years to reach upper management positions In the major companies in the non-financial sector of Chicago (Chicago Urban League 1977).

panies. One equal employment opportunity manager had post-graduate work in physics and engineering. He had been with the company eight years when the employee relations director approached him to set up the company's first affirmative action program. This man accepted the offer because, he said, "I wanted to get into management. That was the first and only opportunity that I felt I was going to get." This executive weighed the job's perquisites against the void in managerial opportunities for blacks in white firms. Racialized managerial positions appeared to be a way to sidestep the career stagnation common among the handful of blacks who previously attained management roles but remained trapped in low-level positions. In the 1970s, such jobs seemed to offer faster mobility, greater freedom and authority, and higher visibility and access to white corporate power brokers than mainstream jobs.

I asked an affirmative action director for a major retail company in Chicago if he ever tried to move back into the mainstream after he took on equal employment opportunity functions. To my surprise he said that he turned down a buyer's job with his first employer. He said, "I was stubborn at that point. No, I didn't want that." Given that buyers were key people in that organization and that the job was a stepping stone to higher-paying positions, his refusal signals the attractiveness of racialized positions in companies in the early 1970s. He said,

> *Remember now, this (equal opportunity) stuff was exciting and there's a trap that you get into. Those of us who are in this kind of area talk about it all the time. It's kind of a golden handcuffs trap. We used to go on the convention circuit around the country . . . The Urban League and the NAACP, promoting our individual corporations. We were visible. We were representing the company. We had big budgets. I mean, you know, you go to every convention. And [you can] get yourself two or three suites and entertain all the delegates. You could spend $15,000 or $20,000 at a convention. I never had that kind of money to spend, to sign a check, so it was very attractive.*

The economic rewards and social status that accompanied racialized positions were unimaginable luxuries to blacks—in this or any employment sector—in the years preceding federal legislation. With the benefit of hindsight, the affirmative action director explained:

> *I believe that had I stayed in operations [I would have] continued to move up and that's where the clout is. But the opportunity just wasn't there [for blacks] when I first started with that company.*

After a slight pause he added, somewhat ruefully, "things changed and it is now."

Only four of 18 managers with racialized careers (22 percent) were the highest ranking black executive in a company's Chicago location. In contrast, 31 of 46 managers who had a majority of mainstream functions in their careers (72 percent) were the highest-ranking black executive in a Chicago company. Acknowledging advancement limitations associated with racialized jobs, respondents alternately described them as "dead end jobs [that had] no power," "nigger jobs," and "money-using" versus "money producing" jobs. The affirmative action director quoted above said that creating and administering the affirmative action function for his company was a misstep in his career.

> *If I had to go back and do it all over again, I would not stay in affirmative action. Them that brings in the dollars is where the most opportunity is. I advise my sons . . . stay out of the staff functions, although those functions are very necessary.*

He went on to name people who took different routes, and who he viewed—somewhat wistfully—as "making it."

Not coincidentally, a manager's position in the corporate division of labor in 1986 coincided with his level of optimism about his future in a company (see Kanter 1977:135). About three-quarters of mainstream (19 of 26) but less than one-quarter of racialized respondents (4 of 20) believed in 1986 that their chances for a promotion or a lateral move leading to promotion in the company were "good" or "very good." Respondents in racialized careers in 1986 reported that they were at the end of their career ladders in white companies. Sixty-five percent (13 of 20) said there would be no additional moves for them in the company, neither lateral nor promotional. Moreover, their pessimism extended to their perceptions of their opportunities for upward mobility on the open job market. The director of affirmative action quoted above summarized this shared perception of future mobility: "ascension for me is over."

The white executive elite I interviewed informally shared the opinion that African-American managers in racialized jobs were "out of the mix," in other words, not in the running for top jobs in a company. The assessment of each group—black and white—is not surprising, because racialized jobs are predominantly support positions, although these jobs can be found in sales and operations areas.[2] White executives, in general, view support functions as one of the worst routes to top jobs in a company (Korn/Perry 1990). Nkomo and Cox (1990) indicate line positions play a highly significant positive role in individuals' promotion success. Support jobs are less desirable than line jobs because they lack influence and have shorter and more limited chains of career opportunities (Kanter 1977). I suggest further that the chain of opportunity becomes even shorter when linked to a job with racial purposes. These jobs not only impose relatively lower career ceilings, they underdevelop the talents and skills that corporations value, and therefore marginalize the job holder.

Limited Skill Development

Pressures placed on companies by federal government legislation and by protests in urban black communities made racialized jobs valuable to companies. In placating blacks and buffering corporations from racial turmoil, racial jobs were highly unstructured; employees handled new and unpredictable contingencies. More than 80 percent of first racialized jobs were created when the respondents filled them. Ultimately, however, this managerial divi-

---

[2]Sales functions involved helping white corporations orient products' positive images to black consumers. People in operations took on racialized functions when managing a predominantly black workforce and mediating black-white relationships in racially volatile employment settings.

sion of labor undermined the development of black human capital. As job content evolved, racialized jobs became routine work centered on a narrow set of administrative tasks extracted from generalist personnel functions. One manager noted that his job in the 1970s involved recruiting blacks, but not whites, into a company. Another mentioned the job was essentially "[black] number counting." A third man said the company promoted him and increased his salary because he was serving a function. He admitted he was aware, even then, that his future in the company might be limited:

> *You have a little stepladder . . . a logical progression (of personnel functions] you have to go through if you are to ever become a personnel director. I wasn't doing any of that. As far as I could see, the company wanted black folks to be my only responsibility.*

The narrowness of the jobs' routines limited—not broadened—these people's development of knowledge and skills. An executive for a clothing manufacturer and retailer made this clear when he summarized his experience:

> *[The company] sent me to Chicago for a week long workshop on affirmative action. In that one week I learned all I needed to know about affirmative action, and I haven't learned much since. It's the kind of field that nothing, well a few laws might change, but the concept doesn't. You don't branch out. There's nothing, oh, now how can I explain it? There's not a lot of specialties . . . in affirmative action. You deal with 6 or 7 basic laws, or regulations, and . . . once you know those there's not an awful lot more to learn. I'm serious about it. Since 1965 or 1972, 1 don't think I've learned very much more.*

Racialized managers in the 1960s and 1970s initially were rewarded with mobility in their companies. Ultimately, however, they required little or no company investment for job preparation and training. This racialized structure of mobility, therefore, created and solidified career ceilings through a cumulative work experience. Although managers' status elevated when their departments, titles, and salaries grew, respondents weren't trained in other areas. When I asked managers for job descriptions associated with various promotions, one affirmative action manager in a segregated career dismissed the question, indicating that he was "essentially doing the same thing" in each affirmative action job, although the scope of each job and his title and grade-level changed. His report distinctly contrasts with those of respondents who were promoted in mainstream personnel. In the case of personnel executives, at least six distinct components of job experience were clearly delineated—including employee relations, employment, compensation and benefits, and labor relations.

In contrast, people who ascended racialized career ladders became more specialized and increasingly secluded from generalist management areas. One manager summarized the gulf between mainstream and racialized personnel in the following way:

> *If you stay in affirmative action, when you go looking for a job you're going to be seen as the affirmative action person. And personnel jobs are bigger than that.*

Narrowly defined racialized jobs rely on interpersonal skills and external relationships without building administrative skills and internal support networks important to advancement. For example, a manager in a manufacturing company described his urban affairs job as if he were an ambassador-at-large:

> *I just moved about. Traveled. Everything was coming out of the community and I was there. I'd make 10, sometimes 12, meetings [in the black community] a day.*

An executive in the food industry described his affirmative action job in a strikingly similar way:

> *I spent most of my time in the [black] community trying to . . . let people know that there were jobs and positions available in this company. I did a lot of speaking with community groups.*

An executive in a communications firm said, "Mostly I worked with local community agencies to get the word out that there were opportunities [in the company]."

A director of urban affairs linked his company with black civil rights and social service organizations and represented it in black-dominated settings. This college-educated man moved out of sales and became skilled at brokering the interest of his company, successfully "absorbing" the tensions between white companies and urban black constituencies. He said that in 1971:

> *[My role was to] make [the company] look good. I did what they needed done to look good in the community. They utilized me in that fashion. For eleven years I was just their spook who sat by the door, and I understood that. Certainly I was, and I charged them well for it.*

Marginalized Job Holders

The structure of upward mobility became restrictive so that success in segregated areas prolonged these managers' career segregation. Prolonged career segregation, in turn, further undermined these executives' value in mainstream corporate functions. Promoting respondents in place created and solidified career barriers by conferring information about respondents' abilities. That is, racialized human capital became a factor in marginalizing respondents by limiting their value in mainstream corporate functions. People in segregated careers faced two alternatives for enhancing their chances for upward mobility: (1) to laterally move into an entirely different corporate area associated with mainstream planning, production, or human resources administration, or (2) to move laterally to the mainstream component of the racialized area (e.g., from community relations to public relations). People who specialized in affirmative action, community relations, and other race-related jobs were stymied in both routes by real or perceived limits to their usefulness in mainstream fields.

When an affirmative action manager (and one-time comptroller) tried to re-enter the corporate mainstream, she found she was locked into her racialized niche at each turn. She said:

I tried to negotiate myself out [of affirmative action]. There didn't seem to be a lot of . . . future. I wanted to try to get back into merchandising at that point. Or go back into comptrolling or to go somewhere else in personnel. You know nothing ever came out of it. I even took a special class . . . to get accreditation in personnel as a personnel generalist. Which I completed. [It] had absolutely no effect on me going anywhere. . . .It got to where the [job] level and the salary level to go and change fields is too high . . . to [be] able to sell me to someone else. The likelihood of me going outside of [affirmative action] at this point is pretty well zero.

The trade-off to rising in companies in racialized jobs that required specialized skills and external networks was that managers became cut off from the internal networks and skill-building that would enable them to move into, and then move up in, the corporation's job mainstream.

A community relations manager for a major electronics corporation—when noting that his company's commitment to urban affairs programs for blacks began to decrease notice-ably in the 1980s—also illustrates this trade-off. Observing, as he put it, the "handwriting on the wall," he made multiple attempts to move out of his dissolving niche in the company and into a mainstream production area. He first attempted to get into production, and next into general administrative services. Describing these attempts he said:

I was just not able to make that break. I talked to [people] in various divisions that I was interested in, and I got the lip service that they would keep [me] in mind if something opened up. As it happened, that just did not develop. I can never remember being approached by anyone. Nothing [happened]—that I can really hang [onto] as an offer. People would ask, "have you ever run a profit and loss operation?"

Finally, he described himself as taking "hat in hand" and approaching senior management in 1982 to request duties he knew to be available in a general administrative area. He said:

Frankly, this was an attempt to seize an opportunity. This time I went and I asked for a [new assignment). We had some retirement within the company and some reorganization. I saw an opportunity to help myself. The urban affairs was shrink-ing. A number of jobs we created [in urban affairs] were completely eliminated. It just happened that the opportunity (to pick up administrative services) was there. It had a significant dollar budget and profit and loss opportunity . . . it was con-crete and useful So I asked for it.

Yet he was only temporarily successful in his attempt to exchange urban affairs for a more stable assignment in administrative services. One year later he was invited to resign from the company because of poor performance.

The story told by a second urban affairs manager—who tried a move to warehouse distribution in a retail company—reveals similar constraints. This manager was a depart-ment director, a position that was targeted to be cut from the company. This manager also discovered that the trade-off for rising in a company in urban affairs was an inability to shift into any mainstream corporate function. Here is his assessment:

> *I was too old to do what you had to do to compete. . . . I was competing with 21 and 22 year olds to get into the system. They couldn't charge [my salary] to a store and have me doing the same thing the others [were] doing [for much less money].' You need the ground level experience. When I should have gotten it, I was busy running an affirmative action department.*

Indeed, from a practical standpoint, retraining this individual would not likely reap a long-term benefit because of his age. Consequently, I asked this manager why he didn't move laterally into mainstream public relations, an area (apparently) he was more qualified to pursue. He responded:

> *I thought about it very seriously. I wondered where I was going with the system. It came up quite often. I talked about it when I first accepted this job. And at the end. They told me, "We don't know. We'll have to get back to you." They never did.*

That his superiors never got back to him "at the end" may reflect the fact that the organization needed him precisely where he was placed. Or, it may result from the fact that he lacked a skill base and/or his superiors perceived that his skills differed from those managers who had moved up the ladder in generalized public relations. The latter point is highlighted by the comments of a manager who failed in his attempt to transfer into compensation and benefits—precisely because his past concentration in affirmative action made him underqualified for the job. He explained:

> *I moved over . . . as director. Now, mind you, I'm going from a corporate [affirmative action] job . . . to . . . compensation and benefits. I told the chairman of the company I didn't have any experience in that field. I might not be his man.*

In short, because of limited skills and career "track records," people who were concentrated in racialized roles lacked the human capital to compete in mainstream company areas. The same skills that once made them valuable now constrained them.

Discussion

Rather than viewing human capital and structure as mutually exclusive explanatory variables, these interviews illustrate that the organization of managerial job assignments and job allocation create human capital deficits. Human capital and the structure of management occupations are not independent phenomena; they interact to mediate labor market outcomes. In the case of black managers, human capital explains the existence of a supply of black labor that companies could draw from when confronted with governmental anti-bias pressures in the 1960s and 1970s. Yet, although human capital was a necessary ingredient for entry and initial job attainments, it does not sufficiently explain who competes for and succeeds in attaining organization power. For black managers, the structure of opportunities associated with the managerial assignments looms large as an additional explanatory variable. The relationship between human capital is circular: A race-based system of job allocation creates a deficit in on-the-job training and experience, and this structurally imposed deficit, in turn, leads to human capital deficits that create barriers to black advancement.

The talent and training that these managers initially brought to their occupations were filtered through a peripheral system of jobs and cumulative work experience. As respondents moved into—and then up through—racialized management assignments, they were locked out from mainstream management jobs. The devaluation of their abilities eventually constrained their progress in executive arenas.

The observations derived from this study have several implications. The first concerns the level of analysis. Studies that rely only on aggregate level data cannot explain black progress, or the lack of progress, without a supplementary closer look at the jobs African Americans hold. This study shows that individual skill and talent is embedded in, and brought forth by, a sequence of assignments in an ongoing work process. Both Althauser (1975:143) and Freeman (1976b:146) have commented on this. Althauser suggests the need to focus on characteristics of the jobs black men hold, just as attention is now given to the job holders' characteristics. Freeman further notes that the degree to which blacks are in token (i.e., black-related) jobs, the significance of blacks' gains may be overstated. More recently, Bielby and Baron (1984, 1986) show that analyses that use detailed occupational categories reveal more occupational segregation. Yet, there are few case studies on black professional and managerial careers.

The second implication concerns the more abstract problem of how inequality is manufactured. To the extent that blacks occupy jobs cut off from core company goals, they are held back from core skill development. The interaction between an individual and the work s/he does can evolve so that a worker matures or evolves in such a way that the worker is taken out of the running. When viewed through the lens of my analysis, the often noted—but rarely explored—high concentration of blacks in corporate support implies a process of deskilling highly educated blacks through the absence of on-the-job profit-centered work experiences. How such a concentration occurred is a critical research question regarding the status of blacks in white collar occupations. In this study, the black managerial vanguard entering the white private sector was eased out of the running for top executive jobs via racialized careers because of a mix of corporate pressure, career naivete, and black's perceptions of race-related corporate barriers (Collins 1997).

Human capital and structural explanations of what influences black achievement generally correspond to functionalist and conflict perspectives in sociology. By extension, therefore, findings from this study are nested in a broad paradigm of inequality. Using a conflict perspective, career construction can be viewed as part of a process of social closure to defend the existing advantage of white managers (see Tomaskovic-Devey 1993). This idea is similar to Reskin and Roos's (1987) proposal that occupational sex segregation is best understood within the broader conceptual framework of status hierarchies. The corporate role in the allocation of jobs—and the assessment of their value—was not a function of objective or impersonal supply characteristics, but of a race-conscious employment discrimination. It is not clear that the subsequent deskilling of a black cohort depressed their wages, as Braverman (1974) suggested. Rather, this deskilling served a more pressing purpose. The problem for white corporate elites was how to incorporate protected groups of minorities while minimizing their impact on organizational culture and structure. The creation and allocation of racialized jobs was an efficient way to meet both goals. These jobs appeased governmental legislation and black demands for more economic resources, while reducing the threat of increased competition for managerial power in organizations along racial lines. Initially, racialized jobs had attractive characteristics that suggested they were important to a company—faster mobility, greater freedom, and high visibility to white power brokers, but over time, racialized functions became routinized and devalued. Ultimately, the peculiar evolution during the 1960s and 1970s of careers documented in this study diminished the black executive pool in Chicago corporations that could compete to manage mainstream units in the 1980s and beyond. Consequently, many respondents over the last three decades did not—and could not—blossom into black executives in powerful decision making roles.

References

Braverman, Harry. 1974. Labor and Monopoly Capital: The Degradation of Work in the Twentieth Century. Albany: State University of New York Press.

Chicago Reporter. 1983. Annual Corporate Survey. December:2–6.

———. 1986. Annual Corporate Survey. January: 7–10.

Chicago Urban League. 1977. Blacks In Policy-Making Positions in Chicago. Chicago: Chicago Urban League.

Collins, Sharon M. 1997. Black Corporate Executives: The Making and Breaking of a Black Middle Class. Philadelphia: Temple University Press.

Doeinger, Peter B., and Michael J. Piore. 1971. Internal Labor Markets and Manpower Analysis. Lexington, Mass.: D.C. Heath.

Farley, Reynolds. 1984. Blacks and Whites: Narrowing the Gap? Cambridge: Harvard University Press.

Farley, Reynolds, and Walter R. Allen. 1997. The Color Line and the Quality of Life in America. New York: Russell Sage.

Freeman, Richard. 1976a. The Black Elite. New York: McGraw-Hill.

———. 1976b. The Over-Educated American. New York: Academic Press.

———. 1981. "Black economic progress after 1964: Who has gained and why." In Studies in Labor Markets. ed. S. Rosen. 247–295. Chicago: University of Chicago Press.

Ghiloni, Beth W. 1987. "The velvet ghetto: Women, power, and the corporation." in Power Elites and Organizations, eds. G. William Domhoff and Thomas R. Dye, 21–36. Newbury Park, Calif.: Sage.

Heidrick and Struggles, Inc. 1979. Chief Personnel Executives Look at Blacks in Business. New York: Heidrick and Struggles, Inc.

Herrnstein. Richard J., and Charles Murray. 1994. The Bell Curve: Intelligence and Class Structure in American Life. New York: Free Press.

Irons, Edward, and Gilbert W. Moore. 1985. Black Managers in the Banking Industry. New York: Praeger.

Jones, Edward W. 1986. "Black Managers: The dream deferred." Harvard Business Review (May–June):84–89.

Kanter, Rosabeth Moss. 1977. Men and Women of the Corporation. New York: Basic Books.

Korn/Ferry. 1986. Korn/Ferry Internationals' Executive Profile: A Survey of Corporate Leaders in the Eighties. New York: Korn/Ferry International.

———. 1990. Korn/Ferry Internationals' Executive Profile: A Decade of Change in Corporate Leadership. New York: Korn/Ferry International.

Kraiger, Kurt, and J. Kevin Ford. 1985. "A meta-analysis of ratee race effects in performance ratings." Journal of Applied Psychology 70:56–63.

Landry, Bart. 1987. The New Black Middle Class. Berkeley, Calif.: University of California Press.

Murray, Charles. 1984. Losing Ground: American Social Policy 1950–1980. New York: Basic Books.

Nkomo, Stella M., and Taylor Cox, Jr. 1990. "Factors affecting the upward mobility of black managers in private sector organizations." The Review of Black Political Economy 78:40–57.

Reskin, Barbara F. 1990. Job Queues, Gender Queues: Explaining Women's Inroads into Male Occupations. Philadelphia: Temple University Press.

Reskin, Barbara F., and Patricia Roos. 1987. "Status hierarchies and sex segregation." In ingredients for Women's Employment Policy, eds., Christine Bose and Glenna Spite, 71–81. Albany: State University of New York Press.

Smith, James P., and Finis R. Welch. 1983. "Longer trends in black/white economic status and recent effects of affirmative action." Paper prepared for Social Science Research Council conference at the National Opinion Research Center, Chicago.

National Opinion Research Center, Chicago. 1986. Closing the Gap: Forty Years of Economic Progress for Blacks. Santa Monica, Calif.: Rand Corporation.

Sowell, Thomas. 1983. "The Economics and Politics of Race." Transcript from "The Firing Line" program. Taped in New York City on November 1983 and telecast later by PBS.

Theodore, Nikolas C., and D. Garth Taylor. 1991. The Geography of Opportunity: The Status of African Americans in the Chicago Area League.

Thurow, Lester. 1975. Generating Inequality. New York: Basic Books.

Tomaskovic-Devey, Donald. 1993. Gender and Racial Inequality at Work: The Sources and Consequences of Job Segregation. Ithaca: N.Y.: ILR Press.

U.S. Bureau of Census. 1960. Occupational Characteristics. Series PC(2)-7A. Washington, D.C.: The Bureau of Census.

———. 1973. Occupational Characteristics. Series PC(2)-7A. Washington, D.C.: The Bureau of Census.

U.S. Department of Labor. 1990. Report on the Glass Ceiling Initiative. Washington, D.C.: U.S. Department of Labor.

Discussion Questions

1. Imagine someone working as a clerk for Wendy's or Radio Shack entering the company's management training program. Do you think she or he would have the same career opportunities in the company as someone who is hired directly into management? Would it benefit the company to promote equally, or are there reasons for treating job tracks differently? Besides using interviews as Collins did, how else might you test this relationship between job entry and career paths?

2. To what degree do you think the informal structure of the bureaucracies studied by Collins contributed to the career paths she found? Would white executives in a black corporation experience exclusion from the informal structure? If so, would this limit their mobility within the organization?

Chapter **6**

Deviance and Social Control

Have you ever watched the evening news and wondered why the lead story was important enough to be covered first? Or perhaps you have watched the country respond to the coverage of a hurricane or other disaster, and then observed a more damaging event ignored a week later. In this article, Fishman suggests that the media produce responses to events by the way they cover them. Focusing specifically on deviance, the author argues that the media actually create crime waves through their coverage.

But how is this possible? Fishman studied a "crime wave against the elderly," in New York City in 1976, concluding that newspapers and television stations "created" it through methods they used to investigate and report crimes. Does this mean those reporting the news intentionally manipulate it for their own purposes? Not really. There seems to be a process that begins with news themes being identified (such as crime against the elderly) and then progresses to a point at which an ideology is created and accepted by both the news media and the public. If anyone purposefully creates crime waves, Fishman argues, it is often politicians or the police.

Crime Waves as Ideology*

MARK FISHMAN
Brooklyn College, C.U.N.Y.

When we speak of a crime wave, we are talking about a kind of social awareness of crime, crime brought to public consciousness. It is something to be remarked upon at the corner grocery store, complained about in a community meeting, and denounced at the mayor's press conference. One cannot be mugged by a crime wave, but one can be scared. And one can put more police on the streets and enact new laws on the basis of fear. Crime waves may be "things of the mind," but they have real consequences.

Crime waves are prime candidates for ideology. This study analyzes a specific crime wave that occurred in New York City in late 1976. This case both illustrates and informs my analysis that the crime waves which periodically appear in the press are constructs of the mass media and contribute to an ideological conception of crime in America.[1]

My use of the term ideology follows Dorothy Smith (1972). All knowledge is knowledge from some point of view, resulting from the use of procedures for knowing a part of the world. Ideological accounts arise from "procedures which people use as a means *not to know*" (1972:3, emphasis mine). Routine news gathering and editing involve "procedures not to know." The business of news is embedded in a configuration of institutions. These include a community of news organizations from which journalists derive a sense of "what's news now," and governmental agencies upon which journalists depend for their raw

Fishman, Mark. Crime Waves as Ideologies. *Social Problems, 25,* 5, June 1978, 531–543. By permission of the University of California Press.

*This is a revised version of a paper presented at the 1977 Annual Meeting of the Society for the Study of Social Problems. I wish to acknowledge Ronald Vandor and David Lester, whose many hours of research assistance made this paper possible, Pamela Fishman, who helped clarify much of my thinking about crime news, and Malcolm Spector and Gaye Tuchman for their helpful comments on an earlier draft.

[1]This paper focuses on the generation of crime waves, not their effects. Thus, I infer that media crime waves contribute to existing images and fears of crime in society. To substantiate this inference would require a study of crime wave effects with a different method from that used here. There is, however, research indicating that people's fears and images of crime derive, in large part, from the news media. See, for example, Davis (1952:330) and Biderman, et al. (1967:128).

materials. Through their interactions and reliance on official sources, news organizations both invoke and reproduce prevailing conceptions of "serious crime."

Crimes Against the Elderly

In late 1976, New York City experienced a major crime wave. The city's three daily newspapers and five local television stations reported a surge of violence against elderly people. The crime wave lasted approximately seven weeks, eventually receiving national television and newspaper coverage.

One consequence of this was the public definition of a new type of crime.[2] "Crimes against the elderly" became a typical crime with typical victims, offenders, and circumstances. Reported muggers, murderers, and rapists of the elderly were usually black or hispanic youths with long juvenile records. They came from ghetto neighborhoods near enclaves of elderly whites who, for various reasons (usually poverty), had not fled the inner city. Using this scenario, journalists reported incident after brutal incident throughout November and December 1976.

The outcry against these crimes was immediate. The Mayor of New York City, who was preparing to run for re-election, criticized the juvenile justice system and the criminal courts. The New York City Police Department gave its Senior Citizens Robbery Unit (S.C.R.U.) manpower to extend plain-clothes operations. Camera crews from local news stations filmed S.C.R.U. officers dressed as old people and arresting muggers. Local police precincts held community meetings to advise the elderly how to protect themselves. New York State legislators introduced bills to make juvenile records available to a judge at the time of sentencing, to deny sixteen to nineteen year olds juvenile status if they victimized an old person, and to mandate prison sentences for crimes of violence against the aged. These proposals were passed in both the State Senate and Assembly, but were eventually vetoed by the Governor on August 19, 1977—nine months after the crime wave had ended.

A May 1977 Harris poll suggested the crime wave also had a nation-wide effect on people's fear of crime. Moreover, it had an effect on the crime categories which the Harris organization used in its surveys; this poll included a new type of crime, crimes against the elderly, not previously present in Harris polls. Harris found that sixty percent of his respondents felt that assaults against elderly people in their home areas had been going up, and that fifty percent of those age fifty or older said they were more uneasy on the streets than they had been one year ago.[3]

---

[2]While the New York City crime wave represents the first widely publicized formulation of "crimes against the elderly," the issue was not first defined by the New York media. Fredric DuBow (personal communication) has pointed out that the law enforcement establishment had formulated crimes again elderly as a new type of crime at least two years prior to the crime wave: Since 1974 it was an important funding theme of L.E.A.A.; in 1975 it was the subject of a major conference; and in February 1976 *Police Chief* devoted a special issue to it.

These earlier law enforcement formulations probably led to the creation of the New York Police Department's Senior Citizens Robbery Unit (S.C.R.U.) well before the city's crime wave. As we shall see, S.C.R.U. played a crucial role in directing media attention to crimes against the elderly in the first stages of the crime wave. Thus, it seems that early "professional formulations" led to the establishment of a specialized agency which, in turn, enabled the media publicly to formulate a category for crimes against the elderly.

[3]Reported in the *New York Post,* May 9, 1977.

It is doubtful that there really was a crime wave or any unusual surge of violence against elderly people. No one really knows, least of all the journalists who reported the crime wave. The police statistics from the N.Y.P.D. do not show a crime wave.[4] In fact, for one type of crime, homicide, the police showed a nineteen percent *drop* over the previous year's rate of elderly people murdered. This is significant because the news media began their reporting with coverage of several gruesome murders. (Twenty-eight percent of the stories reported by the three media organizations I surveyed were stories about homicides. In contrast, the police reported that homicides made up less than one percent of crimes against the elderly in 1976.)

For other types of crime with elderly victims police statistics showed an increase over the previous year. Crime victimization, however, rose for all age categories in 1976. In some cases, the increases were greater for elderly victims, in others less. Robbery was up ten percent in the general population, nineteen percent for the elderly. Grand larceny was up twenty-nine percent for the general population, twenty-five percent for the elderly. In short, police statistics substantiate only that there was a continuing increase in victimization of the elderly (as well as of the general population), not that old people were singled out, as never before. Moreover, the homicide rate contradicts the media presentation of a crime wave.

This paper, however, is not a study in the disparity between police statistics and crime news. Prior studies of crime news and crime waves (Davis, 1952; Roshier, 1973), as well as anecdotal reports (Steffens, 1931:285–291), have shown the irony of crime waves: although the public is alarmed and politicians respond to media reports of a dramatic increase in crime, such "waves" have no basis in police statistics. This study goes beyond sociological irony to examine *how and why news organizations construct crime waves*. Crime waves are taken to be waves of coverage of some topic in crime. Crime waves as *media waves* may or may not be related to something happening "on the streets" or in the police crime rates. Studying crime waves means studying processes in the mass media.

Method

I collected two kinds of data. First, two student researchers and I conducted participant observation from November 1976 to April 1977 on a New York City local television station, WAVE (a pseudonym). One student was a full-time WAVE journalist who worked as a news writer, program producer, and assignment editor. We focused on how the assignment editor assembled the daily news program by deciding what major stories would be covered for the day and assigning reporters and camera crews to these stories. In addition, we conducted interviews with journalists from WAVE and the New York *Daily News*.

Second, we kept a record of all news relating to crimes against the elderly reported from September 1976 through February 1977 in two newspapers, the New York *Daily News* and the *New York Post,* and on WAVE, which aired a one hour newscast in the evening. This enabled us to "locate" the New York crime wave, to determine when it began and ended,

[4]Thus far I have been unable to obtain a complete, month-by-month set of 1976 N.Y.P.D. crime rates. Therefore, for all but the homicide rate, the figures described below are tentative, based on partial rates for 1976.

and to determine the kind of coverage crimes against the elderly received before, during, and after the crime wave period.

The Crime Wave: A View From the Outside

Over the six-month period of observation the *News,* the *Post,* and WAVE presented eighty-nine stories of crimes against the elderly. Fifty-six stories or sixty-three percent occurred during the crime wave period. The weekly frequencies of news stories from all three media are shown in Figure 6.1. This graph clearly indicates a wave of media reporting that began in the last week of October and trailed off by the second week of December. It shows a sharp, swift rise in coverage for the first two weeks, then a slow, uneven decline for the remaining five weeks.

Examining the individual patterns of coverage for each news organization reveals that prior to the crime wave each organization was reporting approximately one story of crime

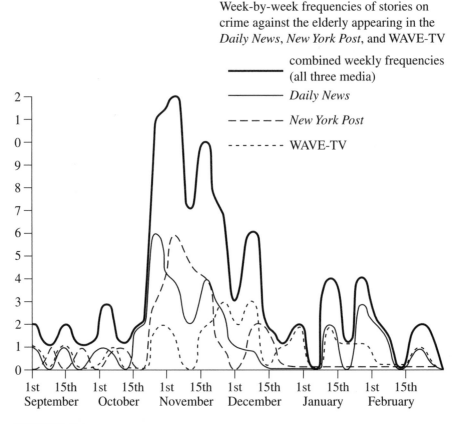

Week-by-week frequencies of stories on crime against the elderly appearing in the *Daily News, New York Post,* and WAVE-TV

———— combined weekly frequencies (all three media)

———— *Daily News*

— — — — *New York Post*

- - - - - - - WAVE-TV

FIGURE 6.1

against the elderly every other week. After the wave, coverage in all three media was sporadic, but heavier than coverage during the prewave period, indicating that the media appear to have been sensitized to the topic.

The three individual crime waves in the *News,* the *Post,* and WAVE show that the marked increase in coverage did not coincide in all three media. The *News* had a sudden increase in the third week of October; WAVE and the *Post* did not increase their coverage until the fourth week of October. Further, in this fourth week the two "latecomers" began their increase *simultaneously.* Prior to their increased coverage, the *Post* and WAVE did not parallel each other. It was only after the *News* began reporting a wave that the others developed a synchronous pattern. This trend suggests that the other media simultaneously responded to the *Daily News'* portrayal of a wave of violence against the elderly.

All three media show different crime wave profiles. WAVE steeply increased coverage to a single peak, then had an equally steep decline (seventeen days rising and sixteen days falling). In contrast, the *Daily News* and the *Post* show bimodal curves. In the *News* there was a swift initial rise (ten days), from which coverage subsided slowly, then it turned upward to a second peak (lower than the first), and finally declined.

The unevenness of the *Daily News's* wave was echoed in the *Post.* The *Post* participated less actively in the crime wave than did the *News* or WAVE. We might even say that the *Post* did not show a crime wave, except that the period of its heaviest coverage coincided with the crime wave period in the other media. Moreover, the *Post's* pre- and postwave patterns were similar to the other media, and during the crime wave it showed a bimodal wave which paralleled that of the *Daily News.* Thus, the *Post's* wave seems to have been a weak reflection of the *Daily News's* curve.

How can we explain these bimodal patterns? The likely reason why the *News* and *Post* reduced their coverage after the first peaks involves a major news event coinciding with this drop: the 1976 Presidential Election of November 2. The elections seem to have crowded out crimes against the elderly from the newspapers, but not from local TV news, since stations like WAVE were not trying to compete with network coverage of the Presidential race. Thus, during the slow news period after the elections, the *News* and *Post* seemed to have "rediscovered" the crime wave, which was still present in local TV news.

In other words, it seems the *News'* and the *Post's* second peak was a response to the continuing crime wave in the television media (assuming other TV stations behaved like WAVE). Just as the initial appearance of the crime wave in the *Daily News* seems to have spurred increased coverage by the *Post* and WAVE, so the continuing coverage of the crime wave on television seems to have "re-awakened" interest in the topic by the *Daily News* and the *Post.* Thus, *the behavior of each news organization during the crime wave seems to have been in response to the other media.*

Seeing Themes in Crime: A View From the Inside

How do individual crimes come to be seen as a crime wave? The answer is found in the methods by which news is organized. News workers make crime waves by seeing "themes" in the news. Crime waves are little more than the continued and heavy coverage of numerous occurrences which journalists report as a single topic (for example, "crimes against the elderly").

News themes are various: "everything Jimmy Carter did today," "the taxi cab strike," "Vietnam," "the disintegrating American family," or "labor disputes." A news theme is a unifying concept. It presents a specific news event, or a number of such events, in terms of some broader concept. For example, the mugging of an eighty-two-year-old Bronx woman can be reported "the latest instance of the continuing trend in crimes against the elderly." A news theme allows journalists to cast an incident as an *instance* of something.

The Glasgow Media Group (1976:355) provides an interesting example of thematized news events from one British television newscast:

> *The week had its share of unrest. Trouble in Glasgow with striking dustmen and ambulance controllers, short time in the car industry, no Sunday Mirror or Sunday People today and a fair amount of general trouble in Fleet Street and a continuing rumble over the matter of two builders pickets jailed for conspiracy.*

As the authors point out, disparate incidents are reported together under the single theme of "unrest." Calling these things "unrest" imposes order on the events reported. Audience members are meant to see the events as unified, as instances of a single theme.

Themes give news shows and newspapers a presentational order. Items are presented in groups organized around a theme. Some themes are related to others, making it possible for groups of news stories to be placed near each other. For instance, during the crime wave against the elderly, the first ten minutes of a sixty-minute news program at WAVE was organized around interrelated themes:

1. Police apprehend three youngsters who allegedly mugged an elderly Queens couple.
2. Police and senior citizens meet at a Queens precinct to discuss fighting crimes against the elderly.
3. A feature report on the Senior Citizens Robbery Unit.
4. Police seize guns and drugs intended for warring gangs in the Bronx.
5. Two members of a youth gang are arrested for robbing someone at knife point.
6. R.O.T.C. cadet charged in the stabbing death of another cadet.
7. New York State audit finds the city police have been mishandling $9.1 million of federal funds.
8. New York City and the police union are still working on a new contract, at the same time that some layed-off firemen and subway cops will be rehired.

First, there are small groups of stories, each containing a theme that the stories in the group share in common (the first three stories are about "crimes against the elderly" and the next three about "youth crime"). Second, groups of stories are placed next to other groups, since the different themes of each group share common features (the group of crimes against the elderly and the group of youth crimes both can be seen to be about youthful perpetrators and police responses to them).

Journalists do not create themes merely to show an audience the appearance of order. News themes are very useful in newswork itself. In particular, editors selecting and organizing the day's stories need themes.[5] Every day, news editors face a glut of "raw materials" (wire service reports, press releases, police crime dispatches) out of which they must fashion relatively few news stories. This task involves a selection process which operates somewhat differently in television and newspaper newsrooms. The essentials of the process are the same: individual news items are identified and sorted according to possible themes.

The chances that any event or incident will be reported increase once it has been associated with a current theme in the news. Crime incidents are rarely reported unless news workers see them related to a past or emerging trend in criminality or law enforcement. A brief description of how the assignment editor at WAVE developed the first segment of the news show just cited illustrates this point. The assignment editor determined the top stories for the day when he noticed that several previously unrelated stories were all part of the same current newsworthy theme: crimes against the elderly. And the discovery of this theme was no coincidence: that day's program was in the midst of the crime wave period.

The assignment editor did not begin his day knowing that crime news, and, in particular, that crimes against the elderly, would receive top billing in the evening's news show. When he started work at 8:45 AM he already knew of two stories that he would most likely cover:[6] One was a feature report on the Senior Citizens Robbery Unit fighting crimes against the elderly. This feature, which eventually ran as the third story in the evening newscast, had been taped days before; it was part of a continuing series on S.C.R.U. the station had been airing for the past few weeks. The second story was a feature report on a "food fair" that afternoon in Manhattan. The editor planned to send a reporter and camera crew to cover it, but also wanted to line up, as he put it, "some better stories" for the day.

Ten minutes after he arrived in the newsroom the assignment editor began scanning his news sources for lead stories. He sifted through reams of wire service news that had collected overnight under the wire machines; he scanned the police dispatches of the previous night's and that morning's crime incidents (about ten or twelve) received through a teletype called "the police wire." He also looked to other news media for story ideas: he read the *Daily News* and *New York Times* and he listened to an all-news radio station.

In the *Daily News* he found a small story about rehiring firemen and Transit Authority police who had been laid off. He thought this would be a good story because "this indicates things may be turning around in the city." This incident became newsworthy when the assignment editor could see it as part of a current newsworthy theme (New York's fiscal crisis).

Still, the assignment editor despaired that he had "no real news," that this was "a slow news day." However, around ten AM two things happened. First, when scanning the police crime dispatches, the assignment editor found that in the 113th precinct in Queens an elderly couple had been mugged, and that one perpetrator was wounded by police. As he

---

[5]The editor's use of news themes is part of the more general tendency of newsworkers to code and categorize news events in order to "routinize their unexpectedness." See Tuchman, 1973.

[6]The assignment editor started with these two stories because his superior in the newsroom had suggested that they be covered.

was clipping this dispatch, he heard over the all-news radio that the 112th precinct in Queens, very close to where the mugging occurred, was holding a crime prevention meeting with senior citizens. He now knew what his lead stories for the day would be, and he knew what he had to do to line them up:

1. He would send a reporter out to the 113th precinct to find, and get on film, whatever he could about the mugging (interviews with police, perhaps with some witnesses or with the victims themselves; and, if he was lucky, film of any suspects that were apprehended).

2. Then the reporter could go over to the nearby 112th precinct to film the police meeting with senior citizens.

3. These two reports would be followed by the pre-taped feature on S.C.R.U.

4. The story on rehiring firemen and Transit police, as well as a few other brief wire service reports relevant to crime which might come in during the rest of the day, would all follow the above three lead stories in some as yet undetermined order. The story on the "food fair" would be placed further back in the show.

Each story, seen independently, might not have merited attention. But seen together, all of them were made newsworthy by the perception of a common theme. The editor's "discovery" of the theme of crime against the elderly made the day's news come together. He knew how to assign a schedule to his reporter and camera crew; and he knew pretty much what the day's news was going to be.

The selection of news on the basis of themes is one component in the ideological production of crime news. It constitutes a "procedure not to know." This procedure requires that an incident be stripped of the actual context of its occurrence so that it may be relocated in a new, symbolic context: the news theme. Because newsworthiness is based on themes, the attention devoted to an event may exceed its importance, relevance, or timeliness were these qualities determined with reference to some theory of society. In place of any such theoretical understanding of the phenomena they report, newsworkers make incidents meaningful only as *instances of themes*—themes which are generated within the news production process. Thus, something becomes a "serious type of crime" on the basis of what is going on inside newsrooms, not outside them.

From Crime Themes to Crime Waves

Crime themes are potential crime waves. A news organization cannot make a crime wave without the collaboration of other media reporting the same crime theme. Crime waves emerge out of an interaction among news organizations.

The Indefinite Overlapping Character of New Judgments

All newsworkers depend on other media organizations for their sense of "what's news today." For example, the WAVE assignment editor began his day by reading the morning papers, the *Daily News* and *The New York Times,* and by listening to an all-news radio station. He later read the *New York Post* and watched when other TV stations aired their news. This editor told me that he did not mind using "anything, any source of news. I'm not proud. I'll steal any source of news."

In reality, stories were not stolen wholesale; rather, the other news media provided an important pool of ideas for story assignments. The noon and evening TV news shows rarely were used for this purpose because, by the time these shows were aired, most of the editor's news was set. The news on other stations mainly confirmed the assignment editor's news judgments, since his planned 10 PM news was, with few exceptions, identical to what his competitors were broadcasting. It seems his competitors were doing just what he was doing: reading the *Times* and the *News,* listening to the all-news radio, and taking stories from the same news sources (wire services, police news dispatches, and press releases).[7]

News judgments continuously overlap in space and time. Editors of afternoon and evening media look for, and are oriented by, the news in the morning media. Editors of the morning media derive their sense of news from afternoon and evening media. Since these media may be in different regions and different cities, news judgments spread throughout an indefinite expanse of territory. The wire services and a few nationally read newspapers, *The New York Times* and *Washington Post,* increase the diffusion of news judgments throughout the U.S.

Moreover, this overlap provides a continuity of news judgments. A specific incident or theme presented in the morning will be covered in the evening, perhaps with fresh incidents, more details, a new development or a "local angle" on the story. The process may repeat itself the next day, reproducing the theme of the previous evening.

The Crime Wave Dynamic

When journalists notice each other reporting the same crime theme, it becomes entrenched in a community of media organizations. Reporters and editors will know that "this kind of crime is news." To use Sack's (1972:333) term, journalists have established a "consistency rule": *every crime incident that can be seen as an instance of the theme, will be seen and reported as such.* The rule is used to identify the newsworthiness of certain crimes. Reporters and editors will know, for example, that a certain incident is "another one of those crimes against the elderly" and not just an incident that can be categorized in a variety of ways.

Each use of the consistency rule reestablishes the rule. Any use of the principle invites readers or viewers of the news, including other journalists, to use the same principle. In order to recognize a crime incident as an instance of a theme, readers or viewers must use the same consistency rule which was used to produce that news.

Journalists who have not yet seen a particular crime theme learn to see it simply by watching their competition. They are able, using the consistency rule, to report the same crime theme their competition taught them to see. At this point, when a crime theme is beginning to spread through more and more media organizations, the "reality" of the theme is confirmed for the media organizations who first reported it. They now see others using the theme. Moreover, as the theme persists, news organizations already using the theme will

---

[7]While my example of overlapping news judgments is drawn from a local television station, the same phenomenon occurs both on newspapers and national network news (Epstein, 1973:150).

not hesitate to report new instances, because they confirm a past news judgment that "this thing really is a type of crime happening now." Thus, each use of the theme confirm and justifies its prior uses.

If it continues long enough, the process constitutes a crime wave dynamic. All crime waves begin as simple themes but by means of this dynamic can swell into waves. Crime themes constantly appear in the media and few reach the proportions of full-scale crime waves. After all, it only takes one editor with a little imagination to introduce a new theme into the news. Why is it that few crime themes go beyond a few days of coverage by one or two news organizations?

Clearly, something more than the crime wave dynamic is necessary for a theme to grow into a wave: *There must be a continuous supply of crime incidents that can be seen as instances of a theme.* Journalists may be primed to report a wave of crime incidents, but they also must know of enough incidents to report the wave. (During the period of my research, New York City journalists had been frustrated in reporting an expected "mafia war." This theme never persisted long for lack of enough incidents. Thus, "mafia war" was a hungry crime theme, starved of enough incidents to make it the crime wave it could have become.) The supply of incidents is crucial in determining the growth of crime waves. What are journalists' sources of crime news?

Perpetrators of crime could be a source, but news workers rarely learn of crimes directly from offenders. The primary source is law enforcement agencies.[8] In the newsroom of WAVE, journalists first learned of crime incidents through three sources:[9] the "police wire," the police radio, and other news organizations (wire service reports, the all-news radio station, and the *Daily News*). The first two of these were direct links to the city police. Crime news is really police news. Thus, *the media's supply of crime incidents is a function of the crime reporting practices of law enforcement agencies.* This reliance on law enforcement agencies constitutes another component of the ideological production of crime news. News workers will not know what the police do not routinely detect or transmit to them. What journalists do know of crime is formulated for them by law enforcement agencies.

The Pool of Potential Crime Waves

The police supply news organizations with an assortment of crime incidents every day. For media organizations in towns and small cities this assortment often consists of *all* crimes known to the police in a twenty-four-hour period. But in large urban areas there are far too many crimes known to the police for any reporter to know them all. Therefore, urban journalists depend on the police to provide a "summary" of these incidents.

In New York City, the daily summary is known as the "police wire." All the city's major media have a teletype that receives crime dispatches from the N.Y.P.D.'s Office of Public

---

[8]The only exception that comes to mind is the coverage of mafia news by specialized reporters on large New York publications: *The New York Times,* the New York *Daily News,* the *New York Post* the *Wall Street Journal,* and *Newsday.*

[9]There was an occasional fourth source: phone calls from the police.

Information. In one day, this police wire types out anywhere from twelve to twenty-five messages. The crime items appearing over the police wire constitute a "crime wave pool": a collection of crime incidents known to the media and having the potential of being seen as certain crime themes. Crime themes steadily supplied with instances over the police wire can become crime waves.

While journalists may invent crime themes (I suspect the police suggest and encourage many of them), a crime wave needs enough incidents on the police wire to support it. The police have power both to veto and promote the media's construction of crime waves. The collection of crime incidents the police provide to news organizations may systematically preclude certain themes from becoming waves (the veto power). Moreover, the same collection of incidents may contain enough crime items of a certain type to allow only a restricted class of crime themes to become crime waves (the enabling power).

For three ten-day periods from mid-February to the end of March 1977, a copy of all crime dispatches of the police wire was kept. Over this thirty-day period, 468 individual dispatches (averaging 15.6 per day) were received. Of these, I ignored ninety-seven (21%) which the police and journalists did not consider crime items. (They were mostly traffic advisories and non-suspicious fires.)

The remaining 371 crime dispatches reveal that the police wire provides journalists with a heavy and steady diet of "street crimes." Two thirds (246 items or 66.3%) of the crime items consisted of: a) robberies and burglaries (eight-five items or twenty-three percent of all crime items), b) unspecified shootings and stabbings (156 items or forty-two percent) and c) a sprinkling of other assaults (five items or one percent—mostly rapes).

The remaining one-third of the police wire consisted of a variety of incidents: thirteen bombings; nine police suspended or arrested; six demonstrations requiring police action; five hostage situations; four raids for gambling, pornography, and drugs; three people run over by subway trains; one arson; and one hit-and-run. In addition, this third contained incidents which, I assume, the police considered "strange" and consequently of interest to the media (for example, a bus stolen, the theft of a large amount of poisons, a man threatening to set himself on fire, a person crushed by an elevator, and the discovery of a disembodied head.)

The first thing worth noting about the police wire is what it does *not* contain: incidents of price-fixing, consumer fraud, sub-standard housing, unhealthy food, environmental pollution, political bribery and corruption, and the like. None appear in this pool of crime incidents from which crime waves arise, yet all of these may occur enough to constitute a crime wave if the media were to have routine access to knowledge of their occurrence.

One reason why these do not appear over the police wire is that agencies other than the city police enforce the laws governing these kinds of crime. Because police manpower is devoted to street crimes, it is street crime reports that the police wire carries. If journalists are to report other kinds of crime, they must draw on other sources (usually the wire services and other media organizations) which provide instances of such crime only sporadically.

Moreover, in the police wire one is unable to find a number of very common crimes which local police *do* know about, but consider "uninteresting" and, thus, not worth transmitting to the media.[10] These included what journalists told me were "too common" to be news: everything from bicycle theft, liquor store stick-ups and rapes, to wife beating, child molesting and other "family matters" not resulting in homicide or hospitalization.

It is likely that a large number of the street crimes reported over the police wire were, in fact, family disputes, crimes against women, and racial conflict. But it was difficult to tell this from the information in the crime dispatches. This is particularly true of the large number of shootings and stabbings, which reporters tended to ignore.

Any descriptive features in a crime dispatch provide important clues to newsworkers looking for themes in crime. From reading the police wire, I was struck by the lack of detail. Victims, if they were identified at all, and if they were persons not businesses, were identified by sex and age. When more was told, they were described as: 1) "elderly" (for homicides and robberies), 2) policemen (for any assaults), or 3) banks (for robberies). Perpetrators (and in the police wire these were always persons, not businesses) were usually identified by sex and a specific age. When more was said, it was almost always in connection with a "youth gang" or the offender's youth. Victim-offender relationships were rarely mentioned. It was quite difficult to identify cases where the victim and offender knew each other. Thus the police wire gives one the impression most crimes occur between strangers. Finally, the location of a crime was usually provided in terms of a specific address or intersection. But a *type* of location was mentioned only when it could be said the incident occurred in a public or semi-public place, for example, a street, a subway, a schoolyard, or an apartment hallway.

Thus, the kinds of crime items and the descriptions of them in the police wire support only special sorts of crime themes that journalists may report. Crime in public places, crimes between strangers, and crime specific to age are themes that the police wire can and does provide numerous instances of. "Crimes against the elderly" is one theme that has already blossomed into a crime wave with the help of the police wire. But other themes such as "youth gang crime," "subway crime," and "school yard crime," have an excellent chance of becoming new crime waves.

Apparently, the police who transmit crime dispatches to the media select incidents that they think will interest journalists. This criterion of selectivity has two consequences, both keeping the present image of "serious crime" from changing in the news. First, when the police perceive that the media are interested in a certain type of crime (for example, crimes against the elderly), they include instances of it in the police wire whenever they can. Thus, the police bolster emerging crime waves as long as those waves pertain to crimes the police routinely detect (that is, street crime). Second, the police decide what the media are interested in on the basis of what the media have reported before.

The police-supplied incidents that make up the media's crime wave pool all support prevailing notions of "serious crime." The crime wave pool leads the media to reproduce a common image that "real crime" is crime on the streets, crime occurring between strangers, crime which brutalizes the weak and defenseless, and crime perpetrated by vicious youths. Such crimes exist, but this imagery becomes *the only reality of crime* which people will take

---

[10]There were some exceptions. A handful of common crimes did appear over the police wire (e.g., four rapes in a thirty day observation period). The journalists I observed could not explain why these were there, and they ignored them.

seriously because it is the only reality impressed upon them in the media. And it is the only reality newsworkers are able to report continuously as themes in crime, and, periodically, as full-scale crime waves.

The Role of Authorities

I have described the crime wave pool as if it were only composed of crime incidents. This description is only partially true. During the initial phase of crime waves, media organizations mostly report crime incidents as instances of their theme-becoming-a-wave. But as soon as a crime theme looks like it is catching on and becoming a wave, journalists have another kind of news to report: the responses of politicians, police, and other officials.

The first signs of New York's crime wave against the elderly appeared in the last week of October 1976, when the city's media began reporting incidents of crime against old people. There was widespread coverage of three incidents: the murder of two aged sisters in their Bronx apartment, the rape-murder of an eighty-five-year-old Manhattan woman, and the release on fifty dollars bail of a youth who beat an elderly person. After this third incident, the first official response appeared: Mayor Beame called a news conference and, with the Police Commissioner at his side, he vowed to make the city safe for old people by beefing up the police's Senior Citizens Robbery Unit and by working for reforms in the criminal justice system. From this point on, "crimes against the elderly" became a favorite topic for political rhetoric and proposed reforms.

Starting from the very first week of the crime wave, the media could report both crimes against the elderly *and* stories of what the authorities were saying and doing about it. The entire wave was bolstered throughout its seven week course by coverage of official statements, possible reforms of the criminal justice system, legislative debate and action, the formation of new police programs, and community conferences on the problem. These kinds of stories made up thirty-five percent of the crime-wave-related news published during the period.

Officials and authorities were willing to assume from the outset that the crime wave represented something real or, at least, they were unwilling to express any doubts in public. Thus, by making public statements and taking official action on the basis of this assumption, authorities made the wave look even more real. And they guaranteed that the wave would go on for some time. As official responses to "the problem" trailed off in mid-December, so did the number of crime incidents known to the media from the police wire and other police sources. The wave finally died.

It is clear that officials with a stake in "doing something" about crime, have power over crime waves. Whether or not they inspire crime waves, they can attempt to redirect the focus of coverage of a crime wave already being reported. Nowhere is this clearer than in the first four weeks of *Daily News* coverage of the wave of crimes against the elderly. *News* headlines during the first week emphasized "the problem," citing instance after instance. But in the next three weeks the stories (starting with the Mayor's first press conference) shifted focus to "what is being done about the problem."

Politicians and police use their news-making power to channel the coverage of social problems into a definite direction (Molotch and Lester, 1974): news of the problem becomes news of how the system is working to remedy the situation. Authorities may also use their newsmaking powers to stop certain crime themes from becoming crime waves. There is tentative data indicating that another crime theme, "crimes on the subways," was stopped from becoming a full-scale crime wave by the New York City Transit Authority.

In the third week of February 1977, the *Daily News,* the *New York Post,* and WAVE all suddenly increased their coverage of murders and muggings in subways. In the middle of that week the Police Chief of the Transit Authority told a *Daily News* reporter there was no crime wave and, soon thereafter, three senior Transit officials called a news conference to assert that the subways were safer than the city streets. From that point on, coverage of subway crime steadily decreased to its pre-wave level.

If an unwanted crime wave should arise, officials can use their newsmaking powers to deny the wave's existence or to redirect crime coverage into a "safe" direction. There is some evidence, however, that crimes against the elderly was not an "unwanted crime wave"—at least for some officials in the New York City Police Department.

The *Daily News* reporter who wrote the feature articles which turned out to be the beginning of the crime wave, told me that he received "considerable help" from the Senior Citizens Robbery Unit, whose job it was to catch muggers and murderers of the elderly (and the same unit that the Mayor expanded early in the crime wave). On October seventh, the reporter first wrote a story on two crimes with elderly victims that appeared over the police wire on the same day. This story was published October 8, two weeks before the wave. At that time, a *Daily News* editor thought it would be a good idea for the reporter to do a series of feature stories on "this kind of crime." (Such features had shown up periodically in other media organizations before.)

While he was first researching these feature stories, the reporter was in frequent contact with S.C.R.U. This police unit let him know they felt beleaguered, under-staffed, and that they were fighting a battle that deserved more attention. (According to the reporter, "They proselytized a lot.") After he had written his feature stories, police from S.C.R.U. began calling him whenever they knew of a mugging or murder of an elderly person. This enabled the reporter to follow up his series with reports of specific crime incidents. Finally, it was S.C.R.U. which first told the reporter about the youth who was let out on fifty dollars bail after beating an elderly person. All major media in New York quickly picked up this story after the *News* reported it. At that point, the crime wave had begun.

I do not want to assert that from this brief history of one crime wave all waves are inspired by the police or politicians. It is not that simple. The crime wave against the elderly in New York seems to have resulted from a mixture of happenstance and police assistance. The history of this crime wave, however, does show that officials can and do use their positions to nurture fledgling crime themes first identified by journalists. Equally, they may use their position to deny the reality of crime waves.

Summary and Conclusions

Crime waves begin as crime themes that journalists perceive in the process of organizing and selecting news to be presented to a public. Because journalists depend on one another for their sense of "what's news," a crime theme can spread throughout a community of news organizations. As each news organization sees the theme presented by other organizations, they learn to use the theme and present it in their news.

But for this crime wave dynamic to occur, journalists must be able to associate a crime theme with a continuous supply of incidents that can be seen as instances of the theme. Media organizations know of crime almost exclusively through law enforcement agencies. The media's major source of supply for crime incidents in New York City is the N.Y.P.D.'s police wire. Crime dispatches over this wire are largely reports of street crimes: robberies, burglaries, shootings, stabbings, and other assaults. These constitute a pool of potential crime waves, excluding the possibility of certain themes. Non-street crime themes, if they were to receive massive publicity as crime waves, might challenge prevailing notions of "serious crime" in this society.

Moreover, once crime themes receive heavy coverage in the media, authorities can use their power to make news in an attempt to augment, modify, or deny a burgeoning crime wave. Thus, official sources not only control the supply of raw materials upon which crime news is based, but also the growth of crime waves.

While this study has dealt with the generation of crime waves, the news-making processes it reveals have broad implications. News plays a crucial role in formulating public issues and events, and in directing their subsequent course. Just as the interplay between local politics and local media organizations brought about New York City's crime wave, so the interplay between national elites and national media organizations may well have given rise to a number of social issues now widely accepted as mixtures in the recent American political scene.

Consider Watergate. As a few investigative reporters persisted in digging up news about the illegal activities of the Nixon administration, national elites competed among one another to halt, support, or redefine the growing Watergate news theme. Eventually, special prosecutors and Congressional committees were formed; that is, a bureaucratic apparatus was set up which began to feed the media with fresh instances of the Watergate theme. Once Nixon was deposed, this apparatus was dismantled, and so was the Watergate "news wave."

Watergate, the Bert Lance affair, the "death" of political activism of the 1960's, and many other accepted political "realities" may have been produced by the same ideological machinery that underlies crime waves.

References

Biderman, Albert, Louise Johnson, Jennie McIntyre, and Adrianne Weir. 1967. "Report on a pilot study in the District of Columbia on victimization and attitudes toward law enforcement." Washington, D.C.: U.S. Government Printing Office.

Davis, F. James. 1952. "Crime news in Colorado newspapers." American Journal of Sociology 57:325–30.

Epstein, Edward Jay. 1973. News From Nowhere. New York: Random House.

Glasgow Media Group. 1976. "Bad news." Theory and Society 3:339–63.

Molotch, Harvey and Marilyn Lester. 1974. "News as purposive behavior: the strategic use of routine events, accidents, and scandals." American Sociological Review 39:101–12.

Roshier, Bob. 1973. "The selection of crime news in the press." Pp. 28–39 in S. Cohen and J. Young (eds.), The Manufacture of News. Beverly Hills: Sage.

Sacks, Harvey. 1972. "On the analyzability of stories by children." Pp. 325–45 in J. Gumperz and D. Hymes (eds.) Directions in Sociolinguistics. New York: Holt, Rinehart and Winston.

Smith, Dorothy. 1972. "The ideological practice of Sociology." Unpublished paper, Department of Sociology, University of British Columbia.

Steffens, Lincoln. 1931. The Autobiography of Lincoln Steffens. New York: Harcourt Brace.

Tuchman, Gaye. 1973. "Making news by doing work: routinizing the unexpected." American Journal of Sociology 79:110–31.

Discussion Questions

1. It was reported in 1997 that the rates of all kinds of crimes declined throughout the United States. Do you think this was a theme picked up by the media and emphasized until it became an ideology? Who, if anyone, might intentionally push this theme to benefit some cause? Politicians? The police? The FBI? If so, what would they have to gain?

2. Watch your local news for several nights. Which stories dealt with crime or other deviance? Did any specific themes emerge from them? Which specific stories might be used to create a crime wave? What might be the process through which this could happen? Who would the crime wave ideology benefit?

$$Chapter \quad 7$$

Social Stratification in Global Perspective

As you have no doubt discovered in reading the chapter in your textbook on social stratification, this article by Davis and Moore stating the functionalist position on why stratification is universal in every culture is classic. On the surface, the answer given is fairly simple: because it is functional for the society. The argument addressing how it is functional is more complex, however. It begins with the existence of necessary roles in a society and attempts to show that unequal distribution of scarce resources—wealth, prestige, power, and privilege—is required to fill the roles. The main premise of the article is the basic functionalist approach to social arrangements in a society: They exist because they are necessary for the maintenance of the society.

The second article containing Melvin Tumin's response is also classic. Tumin considers each of Davis's and Moore's arguments and attempts to refute them. While he proposes no new unified theory of social stratification, Tumin does suggest eight testable hypotheses to gauge the validity of the functionalist arguments.

Were Davis and Moore convinced by Tumin's arguments? Of course not. They responded with a comment in which they refused to yield a single point!

Some Principles of Stratification

KINGSLEY DAVIS   WILBERT E. MOORE

In a previous paper some concepts for handling the phenomena of social inequality were presented.[1] In the present paper a further step in stratification theory is undertaken—an attempt to show the relationship between stratification and the rest of the social order.[2] Starting from the proposition that no society is "classless," or unstratified, an effort is made to explain, in functional terms, the universal necessity which calls forth stratification in any social system. Next, an attempt is made to explain the roughly uniform distribution of prestige as between the major types of positions in every society. Since, however, there occur between one society and another great differences in the degree and kind of stratification, some attention is also given to the varieties of social inequality and the variable factors that give rise to them.

Clearly, the present task requires two different lines of analysis—one to understand the universal, the other to understand the variable features of stratification. Naturally each line of inquiry aids the other and is indispensable, and in the treatment that follows the two will be interwoven, although, because of space limitations, the emphasis will be on the universals.

Throughout, it will be necessary to keep in mind one thing—namely, that the discussion relates to the system of positions, not to the individuals occupying those positions. It is one thing to ask why different positions carry different degrees of prestige, and quite another to ask how certain individuals get into those positions. Although, as the argument will try to show, both questions are related, it is essential to keep them separate in our thinking. Most of the literature on stratification has tried to answer the second question (particularly with regard to the case or difficulty of mobility between strata) without tackling the first.

Davis, Kingsley and Wilbert Moore. Some Principles of Stratification. *American Sociological Review, 10,* April, 1945: 242–49. Reprinted by permission of the American Sociological Association and the authors.

[1]Kingsley Davis, "A Conceptual Analysis of Stratification," *American Sociological Review,* 7:309–321, June, 1942.

[2]The writers regret (and beg indulgence) that the present essay, a condensation of a longer study, covers so much in such short space that adequate evidence and qualification cannot be given and that as a result what is actually very tentative is presented in an unfortunately dogmatic manner.

The first question, however, is logically prior and, in the case of any particular individual or group, factually prior.

The Functional Necessity of Stratification

Curiously, however, the main functional necessity explaining the universal presence of stratification is precisely the requirement faced by any society of placing and motivating individuals in the social structure. As a functioning mechanism a society must somehow distribute its members in social positions and induce them to perform the duties of these positions. It must thus concern itself with motivation at two different levels: to instill in the proper individuals the desire to fill certain positions, and, once in these positions, the desire to perform the duties attached to them. Even though the social order may be relatively static in form, there is a continuous process of metabolism as new individuals are born into it, shift with age, and die off. Their absorption into the positional system must somehow be arranged and motivated. This is true whether the system is competitive or non-competitive. A competitive system gives greater importance to the motivation to achieve positions, whereas a non-competitive system gives perhaps greater importance to the motivation to perform the duties of the positions; but in any system both types of motivation are required.

If the duties associated with the various positions were all equally pleasant to the human organism, all equally important to societal survival, and all equally in need of the same ability or talent, it would make no difference who got into which positions, and the problem of social placement would be greatly reduced. But actually it does make a great deal of difference who gets into which positions, not only because some positions are inherently more agreeable than others, but also because some require special talents or training and some are functionally more important than others. Also, it is essential that the duties of the positions be performed with the diligence that their importance requires. Inevitably, then, a society must have, first, some kind of rewards that it can use as inducements, and, second, some way of distributing these rewards differentially according to positions. The rewards and their distribution become a part of the social order, and thus give rise to stratification.

One may ask what kind of rewards a society has at its disposal in distributing its personnel and securing essential services. It has, first of all, the things that contribute to sustenance and comfort. It has, second, the things that contribute to humor and diversion. And it has, finally, the things that contribute to self respect and ego expansion. The last, because of the peculiarly social character of the self, is largely a function of the opinion of others, but it nonetheless ranks in importance with the first two. In any social system all three kinds of rewards must be dispensed differentially according to positions.

In a sense the rewards are "built into" the position. They consist in the "rights" associated with the position, plus what may be called its accompaniments or perquisites. Often the rights, and sometimes the accompaniments, are functionally related to the duties of the position. (Rights as viewed by the incumbent are usually duties as viewed by other members of the community.) However, there may be a host of subsidiary rights and perquisites that are not essential to the function of the position and have only an indirect and symbolic connection with its duties, but which still may be of considerable importance in inducing people to seek the positions and fulfill the essential duties.

If the rights and perquisites of different positions in a society must be unequal, then the society must be stratified, because that is precisely what stratification means. Social inequality is thus an unconsciously evolved device by which societies insure that the most important positions are conscientiously filled by the most qualified persons. Hence every society, no matter how simple or complex, must differentiate persons in terms of both prestige and esteem, and must therefore possess a certain amount of institutionalized inequality.

It does not follow that the amount or type of inequality need be the same in all societies. This is largely a function of factors that will be discussed presently.

The Two Determinants of Positional Rank

Granting the general function that inequality subserves, one can specify the two factors that determine the relative rank of different positions. In general those positions convey the best reward, and hence have the highest rank, which (*a*) have the greatest importance for the society and (*b*) require the greatest training or talent. The first factor concerns function and is a matter of relative significance; the second concerns means and is a matter of scarcity.

Differential Functional Importance

Actually a society does not need to reward positions in proportion to their functional importance. It merely needs to give sufficient reward to them to insure that they will be filled competently. In other words, it must see that less essential positions do not compete successfully with more essential ones. If a position is easily filled, it need not be heavily rewarded, even though important. On the other hand, if it is important but hard to fill, the reward must be high enough to get it filled anyway. Functional importance is therefore a necessary but not a sufficient cause of high rank being assigned to a position.[3]

Differential Scarcity of Personnel

Practically all positions, no matter how acquired, require some form of skill or capacity for performance. This is implicit in the very notion of position, which implies that the incumbent must, by virtue of his incumbency, accomplish certain things.

---

[3]Unfortunately, functional importance is difficult to establish. To use the position's prestige to establish it, as is often unconsciously done, constitutes circular reasoning from our point of view. There are, however, two independent clues: (*a*) the degree to which a position is functionally unique, there being no other positions that can perform the same function satisfactorily; (*b*) the degree to which other positions are dependent on the one in question. Both clues are best exemplified in organized systems of positions built around one major function. Thus, in most complex societies the religious, political, economic, and educational functions are handled by distinct structures not easily interchangeable. In addition, each structure possesses many different positions, some clearly dependent on, if not subordinate to, others. In sum, when an institutional nucleus becomes differentiated around one main function, and at the same time organizes a large portion of the population into its relationships, the *key* positions in it are of the highest functional importance. The absence of such specialization does not prove functional unimportance, for the whole society may be relatively unspecialized; but it is safe to assume that the more important functions receive the first and clearest structural differentiation.

There are, ultimately, only two ways in which a person's qualifications come about: through inherent capacity or through training. Obviously, in concrete activities both are always necessary, but from a practical standpoint the scarcity may lie primarily in one or the other, as well as in both. Some positions require innate talents of such high degree that the persons who fill them are bound to be rare. In many cases, however, talent is fairly abundant in the population but the training process is so long, costly, and elaborate that relatively few can qualify. Modern medicine, for example, is within the mental capacity of most individuals, but a medical education is so burdensome and expensive that virtually none would undertake it if the position of the M.D. did not carry a reward commensurate with the sacrifice.

If the talents required for a position are abundant and the training easy, the method of acquiring the position may have little to do with its duties. There may be, in fact, a virtually accidental relationship. But if the skills required are scarce by reason of the rarity of talent or the costliness of training, the position, if functionally important, must have an attractive power that will draw the necessary skills in competition with other positions. This means, in effect, that the position must be high in the social scale—must command great prestige, high salary, ample leisure, and the like,

How Variations Are to Be Understood

In so far as there is a difference between one system of stratification and another, it is attributable to whatever factors affect the two determinants of differential reward—namely, functional importance and scarcity of personnel. Positions important in one society may not be important in another, because the conditions faced by the societies, or their degree of internal development, may be different. The same conditions, in turn, may affect the question of scarcity; for in some societies the stage of development, or the external situation, may wholly obviate the necessity of certain kinds of skill or talent. Any particular system of stratification, then, can be understood as a product of the special conditions affecting the two aforementioned grounds of differential reward.

Major Societal Functions and Stratification

Religion

The reason why religion is necessary is apparently to be found in the fact that human society achieves its unity primarily through the possession by its members of certain ultimate values and ends in common. Although these values and ends are subjective, they influence behavior, and their integration enables the society to operate as a system. Derived neither from inherited nor from external nature, they have evolved as a part of culture by communication and moral pressure. They must, however, appear to the members of the society to have some reality, and it is the role of religious belief and ritual to supply and reinforce this appearance of reality. Through belief and ritual the common ends and values are connected with an imaginary world symbolized by concrete sacred objects, which world in turn is related in a meaningful way to the facts and trials of the individual's life. Through the worship of the sacred objects and the beings they symbolize, and the acceptance of super-natural prescriptions that are at the same time codes of behavior, a powerful control over human conduct is exercised, guiding it along lines sustaining the institutional structure and conforming to the ultimate ends and values.

If this conception of the role of religion is true, one can understand why in every known society the religious activities tend to be under the charge of particular persons, who tend thereby to enjoy greater rewards than the ordinary societal member. Certain of the rewards and special privileges may attach to only the highest religious functionaries, but others usually apply, if such exists, to the entire sacerdotal class.

Moreover, there is a peculiar relation between the duties of the religious official and the special privileges he enjoys. If the supernatural world governs the destinies of men more ultimately than does the real world, its earthly representative, the person through whom one may communicate with the supernatural, must be a powerful individual. He is a keeper of sacred tradition, a skilled performer of the ritual, and an interpreter of lore and myth. He is in such close contact with the gods that he is viewed as possessing some of their character-istics. He is, in short, a bit sacred, and hence free from some of the more vulgar necessities and controls.

It is no accident, therefore, that religious functionaries have been associated with the very highest positions of power, as in theocratic regimes. Indeed, looking at it from this point of view, one may wonder why it is that they do not get *entire* control over their soci-eties. The factors that prevent this are worthy of note.

In the first place, the amount of technical competence necessary for the performance of religious duties is small. Scientific or artistic capacity is not required. Anyone can set himself up as enjoying an intimate relation with deities, and nobody can successfully dis-pute him. Therefore, the factor of scarcity of personnel does not operate in the technical sense.

One may assert, on the other hand, that religious ritual is often elaborate and religious lore abstruse, and that priestly ministrations require tact, if not intelligence. This is true, but the technical requirements of the profession are for the most part adventitious, not related to the end in the same way that science is related to air travel. The priest can never be free from competition, since the criteria of whether or not one has genuine contact with the supernatural are never strictly clear. It is this competition that debases the priestly position below what might be expected at first glance. That is why priestly prestige is highest in those societies where membership in the profession is rigidly controlled by the priestly guild itself. That is why, in part at least, elaborate devices are utilized to stress the identi-fication of the person with his office—spectacular costume, abnormal conduct, special diet, segregated residence, celibacy, conspicuous leisure, and the like. In fact, the priest is always in danger of becoming somewhat discredited—as happens in a secularized society—because in a world of stubborn fact, ritual and sacred knowledge alone will not grow crops or build houses. Furthermore, unless he is protected by a professional guild, the priest's identification with the supernatural tends to preclude his acquisition of abundant worldly goods.

As between one society and another it seems that the highest general position awarded the priest occurs in the medieval type of social order. Here there is enough economic pro-duction to afford a surplus, which can be used to support a numerous and highly organized priesthood; and yet the populace is unlettered and therefore credulous to a high degree. Perhaps the most extreme example is to be found in the Buddhism of Tibet, but others are encountered in the Catholicism of feudal Europe, the Inca regime of Peru, the Brahminism of India, and the Mayan priesthood of Yucatan. On the other hand, if the society is so crude as to have no surplus and little differentiation, so that every priest must be also a cultivator or hunter, the separation of the priestly status from the others has hardly gone far enough for priestly prestige to mean much. When the priest actually has high prestige under these circumstances, it is because he also performs other important functions (usually political and medical).

In in extremely advanced society built on scientific technology, the priesthood tends to lose status, because sacred tradition and supernaturalism drop into the background. The ultimate values and common ends of the society tend to be expressed in less anthropomorphic ways, by officials who occupy fundamentally political, economic, or educational rather than religious positions. Nevertheless, it is easily possible for intellectuals to exaggerate the degree to which priesthood in a presumably secular milieu has lost prestige. When the matter is closely examined the urban proletariat, as well as the rural citizenry, proves to be surprisingly god-fearing and priest-ridden. No society has become so completely secularized as to liquidate entirely the belief in transcendental ends and supernatural entities. Even in a secularized society some system must exist for the integration of ultimate values, for their ritualistic expression, and for the emotional adjustments required by disappointment, death, and disaster.

Government

Like religion, government plays a unique and indispensable part in society. But in contrast to religion, which provides integration in terms of sentiments, belief, and rituals, it organizes the society in terms of law and authority. Furthermore, it orients the society to the actual rather than the unseen world.

The main functions of government are, internally, the ultimate enforcement of norms, the final arbitration of conflicting interests, and the over-all planning and direction of society; and externally, the handling of war and diplomacy. To carry out these functions it acts as the agent of the entire people, enjoys a monopoly of force, and controls all individuals within its territory.

Political action, by definition, implies authority. An official can command because he has authority, and the citizen must obey because he is subject to that authority. For this reason stratification is inherent in the nature of political relationships.

So clear is the power embodied in political position that political inequality is sometimes thought to comprise all inequality. But it can be shown that there are other bases of stratification, that the following controls operate in practice to keep political power from becoming complete: (*a*) The fact that the actual holders of political office, and especially those determining top policy must necessarily be few in number compared to the total population. (*b*) The fact that the rulers represent the interest of the group rather than of themselves, and are therefore restricted in their behavior by rules and mores designed to enforce this limitation of interest. (*c*) The fact that the holder of political office has his authority by virtue of his office and nothing else, and therefore any special knowledge, talent, or capacity he may claim is purely incidental, so that he often has to depend upon others for technical assistance.

In view of these limiting factors, it is not strange that the rulers often have less power and prestige than a literal enumeration of their formal rights would lead one to expect.

Wealth, Property, and Labor

Every position that secures for its incumbent a livelihood is, by definition, economically rewarded. For this reason there is an economic aspect to those positions (e.g., political and religious) the main function of which is not economic. It therefore becomes convenient for the society to use unequal economic returns as a principal means of controlling the entrance of persons into positions and stimulating the performance of their duties. The amount of the economic return therefore becomes one of the main indices of social status.

It should be stressed, however, that a position does not bring power and prestige *because* it draws a high income. Rather, it draws a high income because it is functionally important and the available personnel is for one reason or another scarce. It is therefore superficial and erroneous to regard high income as the cause of a man's power and prestige, just as it is erroneous to think that a man's fever is the cause of his disease.[4]

The economic source of power and prestige is not income primarily, but the ownership of capital goods (including patents, good will, and professional reputation). Such ownership should be distinguished from the possession of consumers' goods, which is an index rather than a cause of social standing. In other words, the ownership of producers' goods is, properly speaking, a source of income like other positions, the income itself remaining an index. Even in situations where social values are widely commercialized and earnings are the readiest method of judging social position, income does not confer prestige on a position so much as it induces people to compete for the position. It is true that a man who has a high income as a result of one position may find this money helpful in climbing into another position as well, but this again reflects the effect of his initial, economically advantageous status, which exercises its influence through the medium of money.

In a system of private property in productive enterprise, an income above what an individual spends can give rise to possession of capital wealth. Presumably such possession is a reward for the proper management of one's finances originally and of the productive enterprise later. But as social differentiation becomes highly advanced and yet the institution of inheritance persists, the phenomenon of pure ownership, and reward for pure ownership, emerges. In such a case it is difficult to prove that the position is functionally important or that the scarcity involved is anything other than extrinsic and accidental. It is for this reason, doubtless, that the institution of private property in productive goods becomes more subject to criticism as social development proceeds toward industrialization. It is only this pure, that is, strictly legal and functionless ownership, however, that is open to attack; for some form of active ownership, whether private or public, is indispensable.

---

[4]The symbolic rather than intrinsic role of income in social stratification has been succinctly summarized by Talcott Parsons, "An Analytical Approach to the Theory of Social Stratification," *American Journal of Sociology.* 45:841–862, May, 1940.

One kind of ownership of production goods consists in rights over the labor of others. The most extremely concentrated and exclusive of such rights are found in slavery, but the essential principle remains in serfdom, peonage, encomienda, and indenture. Naturally this kind of ownership has the greatest significance for stratification, because it necessarily entails an unequal relationship.

But property in capital goods inevitably introduces a compulsive element even into the nominally free contractual relationship. Indeed, in some respects the authority of the contractual employer is greater than that of the feudal landlord, inasmuch as the latter is more limited by traditional reciprocities. Even the classical economics recognized that competitors would fare unequally, but it did not pursue this fact to its necessary conclusion that, however it might be acquired, unequal control of goods and services must give unequal advantage to the parties to a contract.

Technical Knowledge

The function of finding means to single goals, without any concern with the choice between goals, is the exclusively technical sphere. The explanation of why positions requiring great technical skill receive fairly high rewards is easy to see, for it is the simplest case of the rewards being so distributed as to draw talent and motivate training. Why they seldom if ever receive the highest rewards is also clear: the importance of technical knowledge from a societal point of view is never so great as the integration of goals, which takes place on the religious, political, and economic levels. Since the technological level is concerned solely with means, a purely technical position must ultimately be subordinate to other positions that are religious, political, or economic in character.

Nevertheless, the distinction between expert and layman in any social order is fundamental, and cannot be entirely reduced to other terms. Methods of recruitment, as well as of reward, sometimes lead to the erroneous interpretation that technical positions are economically determined. Actually, however, the acquisition of knowledge and skill cannot be accomplished by purchase, although the opportunity to learn may be. The control of the avenues of training may inhere as a sort of property right in certain families or classes, giving them power and prestige in consequence. Such a situation adds an artificial scarcity to the natural scarcity of skills and talents. On the other hand, it is possible for an opposite situation to arise. The rewards of technical position may be so great that a condition of excess supply is created, leading to at least temporary devaluation of the rewards. Thus "unemployment in the learned professions" may result in a debasement of the prestige of those positions. Such adjustments and readjustments are constantly occurring in changing societies; and it is always well to bear in mind that the efficiency of a stratified structure may be affected by the modes of recruitment for positions. The social order itself, however, sets limits to the inflation or deflation of the prestige of experts: an over-supply tends to debase the rewards and discourage recruitment or produce revolution, whereas an under-supply tends to increase the rewards or weaken the society in competition with other societies.

Particular systems of stratification show a wide range with respect to the exact position of technically competent persons. This range is perhaps most evident in the degree of specialization. Extreme division of labor tends to create many specialists without high prestige since the training is short and the required native capacity relatively small. On the other hand it also tends to accentuate the high position of the true experts—scientists, engineers, and administrators—by increasing their authority relatively to other function-ally important positions. But the idea of a technocratic social order or a government or priesthood of engineers or social scientists neglects the limitations of knowledge and skills as a basic for performing special functions. To the extent that the social structure is truly specialized the prestige of the technical person must also be circumscribed.

Variation in Stratified Systems

The generalized principles of stratification here suggested form a necessary preliminary to a consideration of types of stratified systems, because it is in terms of the principles that the types must be described. This can be seen by trying to delineate types according to certain modes of variation. For instance, some of the most important modes (together with the po-lar types in terms of them) seem to be as follows:

1. The Degree of Specialization

The degree of specialization affects the fineness and multiplicity of the gradations in power and prestige. It also influences the extent to which particular functions may be emphasized in the invidious system, since a given function cannot receive much emphasis in the hierarchy until it has achieved structural separation from the other functions. Finally, the amount of specialization influences the bases of selection. Polar types: *Specialized, Unspecialized.*

2. The Nature of the Functional Emphasis

In general when emphasis is put on sacred matters, a rigidity is introduced that tends to limit specialization and hence the development of technology. In addition, a brake is placed on social mobility, and on the development of bureaucracy. When the preoccupa-tion with the sacred is withdrawn, leaving greater scope for purely secular preoccupations, a great development, and rise in status, of economic and technological positions seemingly takes place. Curiously, a concomitant rise in political position is not likely, because it has usually been allied with the religious and stands to gain little by the decline of the latter. It is also possible for a society to emphasize family functions—as in relatively undiffer-entiated societies where high mortality requires high fertility and kinship forms the main basis of social organization. Main types: *Familistic, Authoritarian* (*Theocratic* or sacred, and *Totalitarian* or secular), *Capitalistic.*

3. The Magnitude of Invidious Indifferences

What may be called the amount of social distance between positions, taking into account the entire scale, is something that should lend itself to quantitative measurement. Consid-erable differences apparently exist between different societies in this regard, and also be-tween parts of the same society. Polar types: *Equalitarian, Inequalitarian.*

4. The Degree of Opportunity

The familiar question of the amount of mobility is different from the question of the comparative equality or inequality of rewards posed above, because the two criteria may vary independently up to a point. For instance, the tremendous divergences in monetary income in the United States are far greater than those found in primitive societies, yet the equality of opportunity to move from one rung to the other in the social scale may also be greater in the United States than in a hereditary tribal kingdom. Polar types: *Mobile* (open), *Immobile,* (closed).

5. The Degree of Stratum Solidarity

Again, the degree of "class solidarity" (or the presence of specific organizations to promote class interests) may vary to some extent independently of the other criteria, and hence is an important principle in classifying systems of stratification. Polar types: *Class organized, Class unorganized.*

External Conditions

What state any particular system of stratification is in with reference to each of these modes of variation depends on two things: (*a*) its state with reference to the other ranges of variation, and (*b*) the conditions outside the system of stratification which nevertheless influence that system. Among the latter are the following:

1. The Stage of Cultural Development

As the cultural heritage grows, increased specialization becomes necessary, which in turn contributes to the enhancement of mobility, a decline of stratum solidarity, and a change of functional emphasis.

2. Situation with Respect to Other Societies

The presence or absence of open conflict with other societies, of free trade relations or cultural diffusion, all influence the class structure to some extent. A chronic state of warfare tends to place emphasis upon the military functions, especially when the opponents are more or less equal. Free trade, on the other hand, strengthens the hand of the trader at the expense of the warrior and priest. Free movement of ideas generally has an equalitarian effect. Migration and conquest create special circumstances.

3. Size of the Society

A small society limits the degree to which functional specialization can go, the degree of segregation of different strata, and the magnitude of inequality.

Composite Types

Much of the literature on stratification has attempted to classify concrete systems into a certain number of types. This task is deceptively simple, however, and should come at the end of an analysis of elements and principles, rather than at the beginning. If the preceding discussion has any validity it indicates that there are a number of modes of variation between different systems, and that any one system is a composite of the society's status with reference to all these modes of variation. The danger of trying to classify whole societies under such rubrics as *caste, feudal,* or *open class* is that one or two criteria are selected and others ignored, the result being an unsatisfactory solution to the problem posed. The present discussion has been offered as a possible approach to the more systematic classification of composite types.

Some Principles of Stratification
A Critical Analysis[1]

MELVIN M. TUMIN

The fact of social inequality in human society is marked by its ubiquity and its antiquity. Every known society, past and present, distributes its scarce and demanded goods and services unequally. And there are attached to the positions which command unequal amounts of such goods and services certain highly morally toned evaluations of their importance for the society.

The ubiquity and the antiquity of such inequality has given rise to the assumption that there must be something both inevitable and positively functional about such social arrangements.

Clearly, the truth or falsity of such an assumption is a strategic question for any general theory of social organization. It is therefore most curious that the basic premises and implications of the assumption have only been most casually explored by American sociologists.

The most systematic treatment is to be found in the well-known article by Kingsley Davis and Wilbert Moore, entitled "Some Principles of Stratification."[2] More than twelve years have passed since its publication, and though it is one of the very few treatments of

Tumin, Melvin M. Some Principles of Stratification: A Critical Analysis. *American Sociological Review, 18,* 4, 1953, 387–393. By permission of the American Sociological Association.

[1]The writer has had the benefit of a most helpful criticism of the main portions of this paper by Professor W. J. Goode of Columbia University. In addition, he has had the opportunity to expose this paper to criticism by the Staff Seminar of the Sociology Section at Princeton. In deference to a possible rejoinder by Professors Moore and Davis, the writer has not revised the paper to meet the criticisms which Moore has already offered personally.

[2]*American Sociological Review,* X (April, 1945), pp. 242–249. An earlier article by Kingsley Davis, entitled, "A Conceptual Analysis of Stratification," *American Sociological Review,* VII (June, 1942). pp. 309–321, is devoted primarily to setting forth a vocabulary for stratification analysis. A still earlier article by Talcott Parsons, "An Analytical Approach to the Theory of Social Stratification," *American Journal of Sociology,* XLV November, 1940), pp. 849–862, approaches the problem in terms of why "differential ranking is considered a really fundamental phenomenon of social systems and what are the respects in which such ranking is important." The principal line of integration asserted by Parsons is with the fact of the normative orientation of any society. Certain crucial lines of connection are left unexplained, however, in this article, and in the Davis and Moore article of 1945 only some of these lines are made explicit.

stratification on a high level of generalization, it is difficult to locate a single systematic analysis of its reasoning. It will be the principal concern of this paper to present the beginnings of such an analysis.

The central argument advanced by Davis and Moore can be stated in a number of sequential propositions, as follows:

1) Certain positions in any society are functionally more important than others, and require special skills for their performance.

2) Only a limited number of individuals in any society have the talents which can be trained into the skills appropriate to these positions.

3) The conversion of talents into skills involves a period during which sacrifices of one kind or are made by those undergoing the training.

4) In order to induce the talented persons to undergo these sacrifices and acquire the training, their future positions must carry an inducement value in the form of differential, i.e., privileged and disproportionate access to the scarce and desired reward which the society has to offer.[3]

5) These scarce and desired goods consist of the rights and perquisites attached to, or built into, the positions, and can be classified into those things which contribute to *a*) sustenance and comfort, *b*) humor and diversion, *c*) self-respect and ego expansion.

6) This differential access to the basic rewards of the society has as a consequence the differentiation of the prestige and esteem which various strata acquire. This may be said, along with the rights and perquisites, to constitute institutionalized social inequality, i.e. stratification.

7) Therefore, social inequality among different strata in the amounts of scarce and desired goods, and the amounts of prestige and esteem which they receive, is both positively functional and inevitable in any society.

Let us take these propositions and examine them *seriatim*.[4]

1. CERTAIN POSITIONS IN ANY SOCIETY ARE MORE FUNCTIONALLY IMPORTANT THAN OTHERS AND REQUIRE SPECIAL SKILLS FOR THEIR PERFORMANCE

The key term here is "functionally important." The functionalist theory of social organization is by no means clear and explicit about this term. The minimum common referent is to something known as the "survival value" of a social structure.[5] This concept immedi-

---

[3]The "scarcity and demand" qualities of goods and services are never explicitly mentioned by Davis and Moore. But it seems to the writer that the argument makes no sense unless the goods and services are so characterized. For if rewards are to function as differential inducements they must not only be differentially distributed but they must be both scarce and demanded as well. Neither the scarcity of an item by itself nor the fact of its being in demand is sufficient to allow it to function as a differential inducement in a system of unequal rewards. Leprosy is scarce and oxygen is highly demanded.

[4]The arguments to be advanced here are condensed versions of a much longer analysis entitled, *An Essay on Social Stratification*. Perforce, all the reasoning necessary to support some of the contentions cannot be offered within the space limits of this article.

[5]Davis and Moore are explicitly aware of the difficulties involved here and suggest two "independent clues" other than survival value. See footnote 1 on p. 48 of their article.

ately involves a number of perplexing questions. Among these are: *a*) the issue of minimum vs. maximum survival, and the possible empirical referents which can be given to those terms; *b*) whether such a proposition is a useless tautology since any *status quo* at any given moment is nothing more and nothing less than everything present in the *status quo*. In these terms, all acts and structures must be judged positively functional in that they constitute essential portions of the *status quo; c*) what kind of calculus of functionality exists which will enable us, at this point in our development, to add and subtract long and short range consequences, with their mixed qualities, and arrive at some summative judgment regarding the rating an act or structure should receive on a scale of greater or lesser functionality? At best, we tend to make primarily intuitive judgments. Often enough, these judgments involve the use of value-laden criteria, or, at least, criteria which are chosen in preference to others not for any sociologically systematic reasons but by reason of certain implicit value preferences.

Thus, to judge that the engineers in a factory are functionally more important to the factory than the unskilled workmen involves a notion regarding the dispensability of the unskilled workmen, or their replaceability, relative to that of the engineers. But this is not a process of choice with infinite time dimensions. For at some point along the line one must face the problem of adequate motivation for *all* workers at all levels of skill in the factory. In the long run, *some* labor force of unskilled workmen is as important and as indispensable to the factory as *some* labor force of engineers. Often enough, the labor force situation is such that this fact is brought home sharply to the entrepreneur in the short run rather than in the long run.

Moreover, the judgment as to the relative indispensability and replaceability of a particular segment of skills in the population involves a prior judgment about the bargaining-power of that segment. But this power is itself a culturally shaped *consequence* of the existing system of rating, rather than something inevitable in the nature of social organization. At least the contrary of this has never been demonstrated, but only assumed.

A generalized theory of social stratification must recognize that the prevailing system of inducements and rewards is only one of many variants in the whole range of possible systems of motivation which, at least theoretically, are capable of working in human society. It is quite conceivable, of course, that a system of norms could be institutionalized in which the idea of threatening withdrawal of services, except under the most extreme circumstances, would be considered as absolute moral anathema. In such a case, the whole notion of relative functionality, as advanced by Davis and Moore, would have to be radically revised.

2. ONLY A LIMITED NUMBER OF INDIVIDUALS IN ANY SOCIETY HAVE THE TALENTS WHICH CAN BE TRAINED INTO THE SKILLS APPROPRIATE TO THESE POSITIONS (I.E., THE MORE FUNCTIONALLY IMPORTANT POSITIONS)

The truth of this proposition depends at least in part on the truth of proposition 1 above. It is, therefore, subject to all the limitations indicated above. But for the moment, let us assume the validity of the first proposition and concentrate on the question of the rarity of appropriate talent.

If all that is meant is that in every society there is a *range* of talent, and that some members of any society are by nature more talented than others, no sensible contradiction can be offered, but a question must be raised here regarding the amount of sound knowledge present in any society concerning the presence of talent in the population.

For, in every society there is some demonstrable ignorance regarding the amount of talent present in the population. *And the more rigidly stratified a society is, the less chance does that society have of discovering any new facts about the talents of its members.* Smoothly working and stable systems of stratification, wherever found, tend to build-in obstacles to the further exploration of the range of available talent. This is especially true in those societies where the opportunity to discover talent in any one generation varies with the differential resources of the parent generation. Where, for instance, access to education depends upon the wealth of one's parents, and where wealth is differentially distributed, large segments of the population are likely to be deprived of the chance even to *discover* what are their talents.

Whether or not differential rewards and opportunities are functional in any one generation, it is clear that if those differentials are allowed to be socially inherited by the next generation, then, the stratification system is specifically dysfunctional for the discovery of talents in the next generation. In this fashion, systems of social stratification tend to limit the chances available to maximize the efficiency of discovery, recruitment and training of "functionally important talent."[6]

Additionally, the unequal distribution of rewards in one generation tends to result in the unequal distribution of motivation in the succeeding generation. Since motivation to succeed is clearly an important element in the entire process of education, the unequal distribution of motivation tends to set limits on the possible extensions of the educational system, and hence, upon the efficient recruitment and training of the widest body of skills available in the population.[7]

Lastly, in this context, it may be asserted that there is some noticeable tendency for elites to restrict further access to their privileged positions, once they have sufficient power to enforce such restrictions. This is especially true in a culture where it is possible for an elite to contrive a high demand and a proportionately higher reward for its work by restricting the numbers of the elite available to do the work. The recruitment and training of doctors in modern United States is at least partly a case in point.

Here, then, are three ways, among others which could be cited, in which stratification systems, once operative, tend to reduce the survival value of a society by limiting the search, recruitment and training of functionally important personnel far more sharply than the facts of available talent would appear to justify. It is only when there is genuinely equal access to recruitment and training for all potentially talented persons that differential rewards can conceivably be justified as functional. And stratification systems are apparently *inherently antagonistic* to the development of such full equality of opportunity.

3. THE CONVERSION OF TALENTS INTO SKILLS INVOLVES A TRAINING PERIOD DURING WHICH SACRIFICES OF ONE KIND OR ANOTHER ARE MADE BY THOSE UNDERGOING THE TRAINING

---

[6]Davis and Moore state this point briefly on p. 51 but do not elaborate it.

[7]In the United States, for instance, we are only now becoming aware of the amount of productivity we, as a society, lose by allocating inferior opportunities and rewards, and hence, inferior motivation, to our Negro population. The actual amount of loss is difficult to specify precisely. Some rough estimate can be made, however, on the assumption that there is present in the Negro population about the same range of talent that is found in the White population.

Davis and Moore introduce here a concept, "sacrifice," which comes closer than any of the rest of their vocabulary of analysis to being a direct reflection of the rationalizations, offered by the more fortunate members of a society, of the rightness of their occupancy of privileged positions. It is the least critically thought-out concept in the repertoire, and can also be shown to be least supported by the actual facts.

In our present society, for example, what are the sacrifices which talented persons undergo in the training period? The possibly serious losses involve the surrender of earning power and the cost of the training. The latter is generally borne by the parents of the talented youth undergoing training, and not by the trainees themselves. But this cost tends to be paid out of income which the parents were able to earn generally by virtue of *their* privileged positions in the hierarchy of stratification. That is to say, the parents' ability to pay for the training of their children is part of the differential *reward* they, the parents, received for their privileged positions in the society. And to charge this sum up against sacrifices made by the youth is falsely to perpetrate a bill or a debt already paid by the society to the parents.

So far as the sacrifice of earning power by the trainees themselves is concerned, the loss may be measured relative to what they might have earned had they gone into the labor market instead of into advanced training for the "important" skills. There are several ways to judge this. One way is to take all the average earnings of ace peers who did go into the labor market for a period equal to the average length of the training period. The total income, so calculated, roughly equals an amount which the elite can, on the average, earn back in the first decade of professional work, over and above the earnings of his age peers who are not trained. Ten years is probably the maximum amount needed to equalize the differential.[8] There remains, on the average, twenty years of work during each of which the skilled person then goes on to earn far more than his unskilled age peers. And, what is often forgotten, there is then still another ten or fifteen year period during which the skilled person continues to work and earn when his unskilled age peer is either totally or partially out of the labor market by virtue of the attrition of his strength and capabilities.

One might say that the first ten years of differential pay is perhaps justified, in order to regain for the trained person what he lost during his training period. But it is difficult to imagine what would justify continuing such differential rewards beyond that period.

Another and probably sounder way to measure how much is lost during the training period is to compare the per capita income available to the trainee with the per capita income of the age peer on the untrained labor market during the so-called sacrificial period. If one takes into account the earlier marriage of untrained persons, and the earlier acquisition of family dependents, it is highly dubious that the per capita income of the wage worker is significantly larger than that of the trainee. Even assuming, for the moment, that there is a difference, the amount is by no means sufficient to justify a lifetime of continuing differentials.

What tends to be completely overlooked, in addition, are the psychic and spiritual rewards which are available to the elite trainees by comparison with their age peers in the labor force. There is, first, the much higher prestige enjoyed by the college student and

[8]These are only very rough estimates, of course, and it is certain that there is considerable income variation within the so-called elite group, so that the proposition holds only relatively more or less.

the professional-school student as compared with persons in shops and offices. There is, second, the extremely highly valued privilege of having greater opportunity for self-development. There is, third, all, the psychic gain involved in being allowed to delay the assumption of adult responsibilities such as earning a living and supporting a family. There is, fourth, the access to leisure and freedom of a kind not likely to be experienced by the persons already at work.

If these are never taken into account as rewards of the training period it is not because they are not concretely present, but because the emphasis in American concepts of reward is almost exclusively placed on the material returns of positions. The emphases on enjoyment, entertainment, ego enhancement, prestige and esteem are introduced only when the differentials in those which accrue to the skilled positions need to be justified. If these other rewards were taken into account, it would be much more difficult to demonstrate that the training period, as presently operative, is really sacrificial. Indeed, it might turn out to be the case that even at this point in their careers, the elite trainees were being differentially rewarded relative to their age peers in the labor force.

All of the foregoing concerns the quality of the training period under our present system of motivation and rewards. Whatever may turn out to be the factual case about the present system—and the factual case is moot—the more important theoretical question concerns the assumption that the training period under *any* system must be sacrificial.

There seem to be no good theoretical grounds for insisting on this assumption. For, while under any system certain costs will be involved in training persons for skilled positions, these costs could easily be assumed by the society-at-large. Under these circumstances, there would be no need to compensate anyone in terms of differential rewards once the skilled positions were staffed. In short, there would be no need or justification for stratifying social positions on *these* grounds.

4. IN ORDER TO INDUCE THE TALENTED PERSON'S TO UNDERGO THESE SACRIFICES AND ACQUIRE THE TRAINING, THEIR FUTURE POSITIONS MUST CARRY AN INDUCEMENT VALUE IN THE FORM OF DIFFERENTIAL, I.E., PRIVILEGED AND DISPROPORTIONATE ACCESS TO THE SCARCE AND DESIRED REWARDS WHICH THE SOCIETY HAS TO OFFER

Let us assume, for the purposes of the discussion, that the training period is sacrificial and the talent is rare in every conceivable human society. There is still the basic problem as to whether the allocation of differential rewards in scarce and desired goods and services is the only or the most efficient way of recruiting the appropriate talent to these positions.

For there are a number of alternative motivational schemes whose efficiency and adequacy ought at least to be considered in this context. What can be said, for instance, on behalf of the motivation which De Man called "joy in work," Veblen termed "instinct for workmanship" and which we latterly, have come to identify as "intrinsic work satisfaction"? Or to what extent could the motivation of "social duty" be institutionalized in such a fashion that self interest and social interest come closely to coincide? Or, how much prospective confidence can be placed in the possibilities of institutionalizing "social service" as a widespread motivation for seeking one's appropriate position and fulfilling it conscientiously?

Are not these types of motivations, we may ask, likely to prove most appropriate for precisely the "most functionally important positions?" Especially in a mass industrial society, where the vast majority of positions become standardized and routinized, it is the skilled jobs which are likely to retain most of the quality of "intrinsic job satisfaction" and be most readily identifiable as socially serviceable. Is it indeed impossible then to build these motivations into the socialization pattern to which we expose our talented youth?

To deny that such motivations could be institutionalized would be to overclaim our present knowledge. In part, also, such a claim would seem to derive from an assumption that what has not been institutionalized yet in human affairs is incapable of institutionalization. Admittedly, historical experience affords us evidence we cannot afford to ignore. But such evidence cannot legitimately be used to deny absolutely the possibility of heretofore untried alternatives. Social innovation is as important a feature of human societies as social stability.

On the basis of these observations, it seems that Davis and Moore have stated the case much too strongly when they insist that a "functionally important position" which requires skills that are scarce, "must command great prestige, high salary, ample leisure, and the like," if the appropriate talents are to be attracted to the position. Here, clearly, the authors are postulating the unavoidability of very specific types of rewards and, by implication, denying the possibility of others.

5. THESE SCARCE AND DESIRED GOODS CONSIST OF RIGHTS AND PERQUISITES ATTACHED TO, OR BUILT INTO, THE POSITIONS AND CAN BE CLASSIFIED INTO THOSE THINGS WHICH CONTRIBUTE TO A) SUSTENANCE AND COMFORT; B) HUMOR AND DIVERSION; C) SELF RESPECT AND EGO EXPANSION

6. THIS DIFFERENTIAL ACCESS TO THE BASIC REWARDS OF THE SOCIETY HAS AS A CONSEQUENCE THE DIFFERENTIATION OF THE PRESTIGE AND ESTEEM WHICH VARIOUS STRATA ACQUIRE. THIS MAY BE SAID, ALONG WITH THE RIGHTS AND PERQUISITES, TO CONSTITUTE INSTITUTIONALIZED SOCIAL INEQUALITY, I.E., STRATIFICATION

With the classification of the rewards offered by Davis and Moore there need be little argument. Some question must be raised, however, as to whether any reward system, built into a general stratification system, must allocate equal amounts of all three types of reward in order to function effectively, or whether one type of reward may be emphasized to the virtual neglect of others. This raises the further question regarding which type of emphasis is likely to prove most effective as a differential inducer. Nothing in the known facts about human motivation impels us to favor one type of reward over the other, or to insist that all three types of reward must be built into the positions in comparable amounts if the position is to have an inducement value.

It is well known, of course, that societies differ considerably in the kinds of rewards they emphasize in their efforts to maintain a reasonable balance between responsibility and reward. There are, for instance, numerous societies in which the conspicuous display of differential economic advantage is considered extremely bad taste. In short, our present knowledge commends to us the possibility of considerable plasticity in the way in which different types of rewards can be structured into a functioning society. This is to say, it cannot yet be demonstrated that it is *unavoidable* that differential prestige and esteem shall accrue to positions which command differential rewards in power and property.

What does seem to be unavoidable is that differential prestige shall be given to those in any society who conform to the normative order as against those who deviate from that order in a way judged immoral and detrimental. On the assumption that the continuity of a society depends on the continuity and stability of its normative order, some such distinction between conformists and deviants seems inescapable.

It also seems to be unavoidable that in any society, no matter how literate its tradition, the older, wiser and more experienced individuals who are charged with the enculturation and socialization of the young must have more power than the young, on the assumption that the task of effective socialization demands such differential power.

But this differentiation in prestige between the conformist and the deviant is by no means the same distinction as that between strata of individuals each of which operates *within* the normative order, and is composed of adults. The *latter* distinction, in the form of differentiated rewards and prestige between social strata is what Davis and Moore, and most sociologists, consider the structure of a stratification system. The *former* distinctions have nothing necessarily to do with the workings of such a system nor with the efficiency of motivation and recruitment of functionally important personnel.

Nor does the differentiation of power between young and old necessarily create differentially valued strata. For no society rates its young as less morally worthy than its older persons, no matter how much differential power the older ones may temporarily enjoy.

7. THEREFORE, SOCIAL INEQUALITY AMONG DIFFERENT STRATA IN THE AMOUNTS OF SCARCE AND DESIRED GOODS, AND THE AMOUNTS OF PRESTIGE AND ESTEEM WHICH THEY RECEIVE, IS BOTH POSITIVELY FUNCTIONAL AND INEVITABLE IN ANY SOCIETY

If the objections which have heretofore been raised are taken as reasonable, then it may be stated that the only items which any society *must* distribute unequally are the power and property necessary for the performance of different tasks. If such differential power and property are viewed by all as commensurate with the differential responsibilities, and if they are culturally defined as *resources* and not as rewards, then, no differentials in prestige and esteem need follow.

Historically, the evidence seems to be that every time power and property are distributed unequally, no matter what the cultural definition, prestige and esteem differentiations have tended to result as well. Historically, however, no systematic effort has ever been made, under propitious circumstances, to develop the tradition that each man is as socially worthy as all other men so long as he performs his appropriate tasks conscientiously. While such a tradition seems utterly utopian, no known facts in psychological or social science have yet demonstrated its impossibility or its dysfunctionality for the continuity of a society. The achievement of a full institutionalization of such a tradition seems far too remote to contemplate. Some successive approximations at such a tradition, however, are not out of the range of prospective social innovation.

What, then, of the "positive functionality" of social stratification? Are there other, negative, functions of institutionalized social inequality which can be identified, if only tentatively? Some such dysfunctions of stratification have already been suggested in the body of this paper. Along with others they may now be stated, in the form of provisional assertions, as follows:

1. Social stratification systems function to limit the possibility of discovery of the full range of talent available in a society. This results from the fact of unequal access to appropriate motivation, channels of recruitment and centers of training.

2. In foreshortening the range of available talent, social stratification systems function to set limits upon the possibility of expanding the productive resources of the society, at least relative to what might be the case under conditions of greater equality of opportunity.

3. Social stratification systems function to provide the elite with the political power necessary to procure acceptance and dominance of an ideology which rationalizes the *status quo,* whatever it may be, as "logical," "natural" and "morally right." In this manner, social stratification systems function as essentially conservative influences in the societies in which they are found.

4. Social stratification systems function to distribute favorable self-images unequally throughout a population. To the extent that such favorable self-images are requisite to the development of the creative potential inherent in men, to that extent stratification systems function to limit the development of this creative potential.

5. To the extent that inequalities in social rewards cannot be made fully acceptable to the less privileged in a society, social stratification systems function to encourage hostility, suspicion and distrust among the various segments of a society and thus to limit the possibilities of extensive social integration.

6. To the extent that the sense of significant membership in a society depends on one's place on the prestige ladder of the society, social stratification systems function to distribute unequally the sense of significant membership in the population.

7. To the extent that loyalty to a society depends on a sense of significant membership in the society, social stratification systems function to distribute loyalty unequally in the population.

8. To the extent that participation and apathy depend upon the sense of significant membership in the society, social stratification systems function to distribute the motivation to participate unequally in a population.

Each of the eight foregoing propositions contains implicit hypotheses regarding the consequences of unequal distribution of rewards in a society in accordance with some notion of the functional importance of various positions. These are empirical hypotheses, subject to test. They are offered here only as exemplary of the kinds of consequences of social stratification which are not often taken into account in dealing with the problem. They should also serve to reinforce the doubt that social inequality is a device which is uniformly functional for the role of guaranteeing that the most important tasks in a society will be performed conscientiously by the most competent persons.

The obviously mixed character of the functions of social inequality should come as no surprise to anyone. If sociology is sophisticated in any sense, it is certainly with regard to its awareness of the mixed nature of any social arrangement, when the observer takes into account long as well as short range consequences and latent as well as manifest dimensions.

Summary

In this paper, an effort has been made to raise questions regarding the inevitability and positive functionality of stratification, or institutionalized social inequality in rewards, allocated in accordance with some notion of the greater and lesser functional importance of various positions. The possible alternative meanings of the concept "functional importance" has been shown to be one difficulty. The question of the scarcity or abundance of available talent has been indicated as a principal source of possible variation. The extent to which the period of training for skilled positions may reasonably be viewed as sacrificial has been called into question. The possibility has been suggested that very different types of motivational schemes might conceivably be made to function. The separability of differentials in power and property considered as resources appropriate to a task from such differentials considered as rewards for the performance of a task has also been suggested. It has also been maintained that differentials in prestige and esteem do not necessarily follow upon differentials in power and property when the latter are considered as appropriate resources rather than rewards. Finally, some negative functions, or dysfunctions, of institutionalized social inequality have been tentatively identified, revealing the mixed character of the outcome of social stratification, and casting doubt on the contention that

Social inequality is thus an unconsciously evolved device by which societies insure that the most important positions are conscientiously filled by the most qualified persons.[9]

Discussion Questions

1. Choose someone who is willing to debate whether social stratification is functional for society, one of you supporting Davis's and Moore's arguments and the other adhering to Tumin's objections. See which you think is the stronger position. After you finish, step out of your roles as debaters and see if you can come to some consensus on the merits of the two positions.

2. Write on a piece of paper one-word answers to these questions: (1) Is social stratification in the United States inevitable? (2) Is the U.S. system of social stratification fair? After you and others have revealed your answers, discuss the reasons you feel as you do. Why is it inevitable, or why does it exist if it isn't inevitable? Are parts of the system fairer than other parts? If the system is unfair, what changes would make it more fair?

[9]Davis and Moore, *op. cit.,* p. 243.

Chapter 8

Social Class in the United States

Every year a few sociologists have the privilege of delivering presidential addresses to national or regional organizations. They normally use the opportunity to paint a sort of broad mural of some sociological concern. Marvin Olsen grasped such an opportunity in 1990 by addressing inequalities in wealth in the United States. Specifically, Olsen discusses the much debated question of whether continual economic growth will result in reducing inequality. In other words, does everyone share equally in a nation's prosperity?

In an attempt to answer this question, Olsen looks at patterns of economic growth and the distribution of wealth in the United States over a period of almost four decades. As the economy grew, what happened to the incomes of people in various levels of income distribution from 1950 to 1987? The answer may surprise you.

On the basis of patterns from the recent past, it may be possible to project income distribution for the future, especially if there are limits to continual economic growth. Olson suggest three possible models that predict what the future will hold for you as you enter a career at a particular occupational level.

The Affluent Prosper While
Everyone Else Struggles*

MARVIN E. OLSEN
Michigan State University

Since at least the fifteenth century, when the western world began to move beyond feudal political economies and theologically dominated cultural beliefs, economic growth resulting in steadily increasing incomes and wealth has been viewed as an unquestioned benefit of "modernization" (Wallerstein 1980). The viewpoint is as pervasive in 1990 as it probably has been for the past 500 years—if not more so. Every increase in the Gross National Product of the United States and other western nations is hailed as an unmitigated blessing, on the assumption that as national wealth expands most people—although certainly not everyone—are potentially able to enjoy a higher material standard of living and a more satisfying lifestyle.

For sociologists, that optimistic perspective was bolstered immensely by the theoretical argument proposed by Gerhard Lenski in his 1966 book *Power and Privilege.* Lenski argued quite convincingly that although socioeconomic inequality tended to increase steadily as humanity moved from foraging to horticultural to agrarian societies, that historical trend began to level off with the emergence of industrial societies. He also maintained that as modern nations reached full industrialization, socioeconomic inequality began to decline for the first time in recorded history. Consequently, not only were most people in these societies better off than ever before, they were finally escaping from the age-old tendency for the rich to become richer and the poor to become poorer. That optimistic perspective has been further strengthened by the image of the coming post-industrial society, as portrayed by Daniel Bell (1973) and many others. In that vision of the future, most—if not all—of the population would no longer have to be concerned about economic survival and would enjoy the seemingly endless benefits of a fully automated and highly productive economy. Consequently, it would only be a matter of time until virtually all socioeconomic inequality was eliminated forever.

Olsen, Marvin E. The Affluent Prosper while Everyone Else Struggles. *Sociological Focus* 23 (2), May 1990, 73–87. © 1990 The North Central Sociological Association.

Regrettably, the real world rarely follows the rosy predictions of optimistic sociologists. As we move into the 1990s and look forward to the twenty-first century, it is time to take a hard, realistic look at what has actually been happening to socioeconomic inequality at the height of industrialization in the United States, as well as what may become reality in the coming century. Is there any basis for expecting that socioeconomic inequality will decline further, or has the latter half of the twentieth century been only a temporary anomaly in the relentless historical trend toward ever-increasing class inequality?

One of the first writers to address this topic was Paul Blumberg, in his 1980 book *Inequality in an Age of Decline.* Since then, a number of other writers have dealt with it (Blackburn and Bloom 1985, Bluestone and Boyden 1988; Committee on Ways and Means of the U.S. House of Representatives 1989; Smith 1986-87; Tilly 1986). All of those works have presented empirical evidence suggesting that somewhere around 1970 socioeconomic inequality ceased to decline in the United States, and since then then has been inching upward again. In particular, several of those studies have indicated that in addition to the poor becoming poorer, the size and economic condition of the middle class have recently begun to decline. If this is true, it could have momentous consequences for American society in many realms of social life.

My objectives in this paper are threefold. First, to examine a wider range of indicators of national income in the United States since 1970 than were employed in those previous studies, to determine the validity of their thesis of a recent turnaround in socioeconomic inequality. Second, to sketch several alternative models of contemporary and future trends in socioeconomic inequality. Third, to offer some speculative predictions about inequality in the 1990s and the twenty-first century. My empirical analysis is limited to the period between 1970, when that turnaround apparently began, and 1987, the last year for which national income data are presently available. All of the data cited here were taken from the 1989 or earlier editions of the Statistical Abstract of the United States (U.S. Bureau of the Census). This analysis is limited to the United States since I only had access to detailed income data for this country. Further research will have to ascertain whether other highly industrialized nations are also displaying the U.S. pattern.

The National Economy

Before examining income levels and distributions, let us briefly review what has happened to the U.S. economy since 1970. All monetary figures in this and subsequent analyses are standardized in two ways. (1) They are reported on a per capita or per living unit basis, to take account of the growth in the U.S. population from 205 to 244 million people between 1970 and 1987. (2) They are all expressed in real 1987 dollars, to take account of the fact that inflation had reduced the value of a 1970 dollar to 37 cents in 1987, so that a 1970 dollar was equivalent to $2.70 in 1987.

The U.S. economy grew steadily between 1970 and 1987 (U.S. Bureau of the Census 1989:424). The Gross National Product (GNP) per capita rose from $13.4 thousand to $18.4 thousand, which was an increase of 39 percent (or an average of 2.3 percent per year). Personal income per capita—which is the GNP minus capital expenditures, corporate profits, and indirect corporate taxes, plus transfer payments to individuals and families—rose from \$11.0 to \$15.5 thousand, or 41 percent. And disposable income per capita—which is personal income less all federal (but not state and local) taxes—rose from \$9.5 to \$13.1 thousand, or 38 percent. In short, there was roughly 40 percent more aggregate wealth per capita in the United States in 1987 than in 1970.

This national economic growth was due partly to a small increase in the proportion of the population that was gainfully employed, which rose from 58 percent in 1970 to 62 percent in 1987. Virtually all of that increase resulted from employment of women, which rose from 41 percent to 53 percent (U.S. Bureau of the Census 1989:385). A second explanation of this national economic growth lies in the fact that the total productivity of the business sector of the economy increased by 66 percent during that same period (U.S. Bureau of the Census 1989:403).

Another aspect of the U.S. economy that is relevant to this analysis is the ratio of labor costs to output per hour of paid employment. In the business sector, that ratio grew by 61 percent. The compensation received by private-sector employees thus increased considerably more rapidly than did their productivity (U.S. Bureau of the Census 1989:403). This factor, combined with the overall growth in the GNP per capita, should have resulted in considerably higher incomes for most individuals and families in 1987 than in 1970. Let us now examine actual income figures to see if that did occur.

Income Levels

The indicators of personal income per capita and disposable income per capita are both aggregate measures derived from the GNP, and hence do not tell us how much income individuals and families actually received. Although both of those aggregate measures increased by about 40 percent in real dollars, that may not have occurred among people's actual incomes. For data on incomes received by individuals and families, we must turn to national surveys conducted annually by the Census Bureau. Those income data are reported in two different ways: for living units and for individuals.

Let us look first at living units. These data are reported in terms of both households and families. A household is one or more persons who occupy a single dwelling unit, so that it includes single persons and unmarried cohabiting couples, as well as families. A family is defined as two or more people who are related by marriage or birth.

Median household income in the United States was \$25.6 thousand in real 1987 dollars in 1970. By 1980, it had dropped slightly to \$24.4 thousand. In 1987, it was back up to \$26.0 thousand (U.S. Bureau of the Census 1989:440). In other words, median household income was virtually the same in 1987 as in 1970, having increased by only 1.6 percent.

To put changes in median family incomes in perspective, let us go back momentarily to 1950. Between then and 1970, the median family income in this society almost doubled in real dollars. The rate of increase was 97 percent during those earlier two decades, with a somewhat higher rate of increase during the 1960s than the 1950s. That economic boom largely ended around 1970, however. In that year, the median family income (again expressed in 1987 dollars) was \$28.9 thousand; in 1980 it remained at \$29.0 thousand, and by 1987 it had risen slightly to \$30.9 thousand (U.S. Bureau of the Census, 1989: 445). In other words, family incomes remained essentially constant during the 1970s but did grow by 6.6 percent between 1980 and 1987. Thus the typical family was slightly better off financially in 1987 than in 1970, but the spectacular rise in the standard of living that occurred during the 1950s and 1960s did not continue past about 1970.

Median income figures are also available for different kinds of families, so that we can determine which kinds of families fared better or worse than average between 1970 and 1987. (1) All families that contained a married couple saw their median income increase from $30.8 to $34.7 thousand, which was a 12.7 percent rise. (2) Those married couple families in which the wife was not employed, however, saw their median income drop from $27.2 to $24.8 thousand, for an 8.8 percent decline. (3) Those married couple families in which both spouses were employed, in contrast, saw their median income rise from $35.9 to $40.4 thousand, which was a 12.5 percent increase. (4) Among single-adult families headed by a man, these figures were $26.3 thousand in 1970 but only $24.8 thousand in 1987, for a decline of 5.7 percent. (5) Among single-adult families headed by a woman, the corresponding figures were $14.9 and $14.6 thousand, for a decline of 2.0 percent.

These figures tell us that the overall rise in median family income between 1970 and 1987 was due entirely to greater earnings among two-income families. Not only were more women becoming employed—employment of married women rose from 41 percent in 1970 to 56 percent in 1987 (U.S. Bureau of the Census, 1989:385)—but their incomes appear to have increased at a greater rate than inflation. Among all families with only one wage-earner—regardless of whether they contained two or only one adult—the median income declined between 1970 and 1987.

Finally, households consisting of a single individual show two interesting income trends during this period. Among single men, the median income grew from $13.2 to $15.8 thousand, which was a rise of 34.8 percent. Single women also raised their median income, from $7.3 to $8.1 thousand, but this was only an 11.0 percent rise. Single persons were therefore a second type of household—in addition to two-income families—that did experience rising real incomes between 1970 and 1987. It must be noted, however, that single men received more than twice as much income as single women in 1987, and that this gender income gap among single people has been widening in recent years.

Let us now examine income figures for employed individuals, without considering their family status. Among all employed persons age 15 and older, the median income was $12.8 thousand in both 1970 and 1987, representing no change in income (U.S. Bureau of the Census, 1989:449). The mean weekly earnings of these people—which omit weeks in which they were not employed—declined from $325 to $313, or 3.6 percent, during that period. If we distinguish between full- and part-time workers, we discover that people who worked full-time did experience an increase of 7.8 percent in their median incomes, from $20.5 to $22.1 thousand. In contrast, part-time workers saw their median income drop by about 10 percent, although exact figures are not available for them.

Overall, median incomes for all households, families, and individuals did not change greatly between 1970 and 1987. While some categories of people did experience slight increases in real incomes, other categories of people suffered small declines during that period. And quite clearly, no category of people enjoyed the spectacular rise in real incomes that most people experienced during the 1950s and 1960s.

Nevertheless, both personal income per capita and disposable income per capita rose by about 40 percent between 1970 and 1987. Who received all that additional income that was flowing to the American public? To answer that question, we must examine the distributions of income among various segments of the population.

Income Distributions

The most common way of analyzing the income distribution within a population is by income levels, which can be done in terms of either dollar levels or income quartiles.

Let us look first at distributions by dollar levels. Since these are absolute figures, they enable us to determine how the income distribution has changed relative to levels of living such as affluence and poverty. For this analysis, incomes are arbitrarily divided into four broad categories (1) under $10,000, which can loosely be called the Poverty Level; (2) from $10,000 to $24,999, which can be called the Marginal Level; (3) from $25,000 to $49,999, which might be called the Comfortable Level; and (4) $50,000 and over, which is called the Affluent Level.

The proportions of all *households* at each of those four income levels in 1970 and 1987 and the rates of change during that period are given in the top panel of Table 8.1 (U.S. Bureau of the Census 1989:440). The proportion of all *families* at each of those four income levels at those two points in time and the rates of change for them are given in the bottom panel of the table.

In general, both sets of data tell us that income was more unevenly distributed in 1987 than in 1970. The proportion of Poverty Level dwelling units increased slightly or remained the same (depending on the type of unit). At the two middle levels of Marginal and Comfortable dwelling units, the proportions decreased somewhat. At the Affluent Level, meanwhile, the proportion of dwelling units increased sharply. With the exception of people living in poverty, therefore, there was an upward shift in real incomes among about 85 percent of the population. And considerably more families and households were living rather affluently. That upward income shift among large numbers of people may seem commendable. However, it does indicate a widening income gap between the bulk of the population and those left behind in poverty. As William Wilson (1987) has elaborately demonstrated, the "underclass" is still with us and is not declining in size.

The major limitation of income distributions based on dollar levels is that they do not tell us how various segments of the population are faring on a relative basis. To answer such

TABLE 8.1   Proportions of Households and Families at Four Income Levels in 1970 and 1987, and Rates of Change During That Period

Household Income Level	% in 1970	% in 1987	% Change
Poverty	18.4	18.4	0
Marginal	30.6	29.8	−2.3
Comfortable	38.3	33.3	−13.1
Affluent	12.8	18.5	+44.5

Family Income Level	% in 1970	% in 1987	% Change
Poverty	11.1	11.7	+5.4
Marginal	30.3	27.8	−8.3
Comfortable	43.2	37.7	−12.7
Affluent	15.4	22.9	+48.7

questions as "Is the middle class gaining or losing income relative to other classes?" we must examine income distributions based on income quintiles. In this case, the reported figures are not proportions of households or families with specific incomes, but rather the proportion of all income going to families within each 20 percent of income recipients (quintile distributions are not reported for households. Those data (and also data for the top five percent of all families) are reported in Table 8.2, together with the rates of change during that period (U.S. Bureau of the Census 1974:392; 1989:446).

These figures demonstrate clearly that income became more unequally distributed between 1970 and 1987 in the United States. Moreover, they indicate a greater trend toward inequality than did the distribution based on dollar levels. The lower three income quintiles or 60 percent of all families—received smaller proportions of the total U.S. income in 1987 than in 1970. The lowest quintile of families—which receives only about one-twentieth of all income—experienced a decline of 4.2 percent. The second quintile—which receives only slightly more than one-tenth of all income—declined by 11.5 percent. The third quintile—which receives nearly its "fair share" of all income—declined by 5.1 percent.

In contrast, the higher two income quintiles received larger proportions of the total U.S. income in 1987 than in 1970. For the fourth quintile—which receives slightly more than its "fair share" of all income—that increase was a miniscule 0.8 percent. However, the highest quintile—which receives more than 40 percent of all family income—increased its proportion of this total income by 6.8 percent. (To be in this quintile, a family had to have a total income of slightly more than $50,000 in 1987.) And the top five percent of all families increased its share by 9.0 percent. In sum, the majority of American families received a smaller slice of the total income pie in 1987 than in 1970, while the more affluent twenty percent of them—and especially the richest five percent of them—received significantly larger slices of that income pie. The affluent prospered while most other people struggled financially.

Further confirmation of the above generalizations concerning shifts in income distributions, in both absolute and relative terms, comes from a study conducted in 1989 by the Committee on Ways and Means of the U.S. House of Representatives. That study, which compared 1973 with 1987, incorporated several refinements in measurement procedures. For instance, it examined all households rather than just families; it defined income levels and quintiles relative to the official poverty line; and it adjusted the data to take account of

TABLE 8.2 Proportions of Total Income Received by Family Income Quintiles in 1970 and 1987, and also by the Top Five Percent of All Families, and Rates of Change During That Period

Family Income Quintiles	% of Total Income in 1970	% of Total Income in 1987	% Change
Lowest 20% of all families	5.4	4.6	−4.2
Second 20% of all families	12.2	10.8	−11.5
Third 20% of all families	17.8	16.9	−5.1
Fourth 20% of all families	23.9	24.1	+0.8
Highest 20% of all families	40.9	43.7	+6.8
Top 5% of all families	15.5	16.9	+9.0

the number of persons in the household. The consequence of those measurement refinements was to demonstrate even greater increases in income inequality than were seen in the data reported above.

The House study found that the proportion of total income received by the bottom quintile of all families declined by 21.8 percent between 1973 and 1987; the second quintile experienced a 10.1 percent decline; and the third quintile declined by 2.3 percent. In contrast, the fourth quintile increased its proportion of all income by 2.1 percent, while the proportion for the highest quintile increased by 6.0 percent (Committee, 1989:987). These findings indicate that regardless of the methodological procedures used to measure income distributions, we cannot escape the conclusion that during the 1970s and 1980s the poor became poorer and people with middle-level incomes experienced some financial decline, while at the same time the affluent fifth of the population enjoyed a moderate increase in real incomes—both absolutely and relative to all others.

Since all of the preceding analyses indicate that people with the lowest income suffered a serious decline in real income during the 1970s and 1980s, let us look briefly at figures for families falling below the government's official poverty line. And since that poverty line is widely acknowledged to be inadequate to sustain any family on a permanent basis, let us also look at figures for families falling below 125 percent of the poverty line, which represents the absolute minimum amount of income that can sustain a family permanently. The percentages of both families and individuals that fell below both of these poverty lines in 1970 and 1987 are given in Table 8.3 (U.S. Bureau of the Census 1989:453, 455).

Regardless of the measure used—either families or individuals, and either the official poverty line or 125 percent of it—the conclusion is the same. All four measures indicate that the proportion of the population living in poverty increased between 1970 and 1987. Moreover, that increase was larger in reference to the official poverty line than for 125 percent of that line, which tells us that abject poverty increased more rapidly than did survivable poverty. Quite clearly, the United States did nothing to eliminate poverty between 1970 and 1987, but rather let it grow.

From these various analyses of shifts in income distributions, we now have a partial answer to the question of who received the additional income that has flowed into American society since 1970. Most of that money went to already affluent families and households with incomes over $50,000, who constitute roughly the top one-fifth of the income distrib-

TABLE 8.3   Families and Individuals Below the Official Poverty Line and 125 Percent of that Line in 1970 and 1987, and Rates of Change During That Period

People in Poverty	% in 1970	% in 1987	% Change
Families below the poverty line	10.1	10.8	+6.9
Families below 125% of the poverty line	14.4	14.5	+0.7
Individuals below the poverty line	12.6	13.5	+7.1
Individuals below 125% of the poverty line	17.6	18.1	+2.8

ution. And within that affluent category, the top one-twentieth of families and households received an especially disproportional share of that money. At the same time, the bottom three-fifths of families and households received less real income in 1987 than they did in 1970, and a greater proportion of families and individuals were living in poverty.

What these trends mean, in essence, is that the middle income class in American society has been shrinking for the past two decades (Blackburn and Bloom 1985; Rose 1986; Tilly 1986). Some of those previously middle-class people have climbed into the affluent class, but a large proportion of them have fallen into the marginal or poverty income classes.

As a final brief step in this analysis of income distributions, let us examine that distribution in terms of people's occupational status. The U.S. Census divides all occupations into the following eight broad categories: professional and technical persons, managers and administrators, sales workers, clerical workers, skilled craftspersons, semiskilled operatives, service workers, and unskilled laborers. Median family incomes of full-time employed workers in those occupational categories are shown in Table 8.4 (U.S. Bureau of the Census 1977:370; 1989:406).

These data tell much the same story we have already seen, but with one new piece of information. Not all higher-status people had income gains between 1970 and 1987. The occupational category of professional and technical people retained the same median income throughout this period. (The diversity of this category may, however, be masking income gains by higher-status professionals and income losses by lower-status semiprofessionals and technicians.) The only occupational category that increased its median family income during this period was administrators and managers, whose real income rose by 7.6 percent. All other occupational categories, meanwhile, had lower median incomes in 1987 than in 1970. The largest declines occurred among service workers and laborers, both of which fell more than 16 percent. Income inequality has clearly widened between the top and bottom of the occupational status hierarchy. Once again, we see that "To those who have shall be given."

TABLE 8.4   Median Family Income by Occupational Status in 1970 and 1987, and Rates of Change During That Period

Occupational Status	Median Family Income in 1970	Median Family Income in 1987	% Change
Professional and Technical	$28,600	$28,600	0
Managerial and Administrative	$26,200	$28,200	+7.6
Sales	$20,800	$19,400	–6.7
Clerical	$20,300	$18,400	–9.4
Skilled Craft	$20,800	$19,400	–6.7
Semiskilled Operative	$17,400	$16,300	–6.3
Service	$15,800	$13,200	–16.5
Labor	$15,500	$13,700	–16.6

Alternative Inequality Trend Models

The United States has never seriously attempted to redistribute income or wealth to promote greater economic equality, as have the Scandinavian countries. Instead, we have always relied on economic growth to provide an ever-increasing financial pie to be distributed among the population. With the exception of the depression years of the 1930s, this strategy worked quite well until about 1970. As long as the majority of people were experiencing steadily rising real incomes and steadily improving standards of living, no one was greatly concerned that the overall distribution of income had not changed significantly for over 50 years.

Unfortunately, not all of the people managed to get a foothold on this "prosperity escalator." In the 1960s we belatedly "rediscovered" that poverty still persisted in the midst of plenty. We then made a great political show of declaring a War on Poverty through vast governmental programs. The proportion of the population below the official poverty line did decline from 22 percent in 1960 to 12 percent in 1970, while those below 125 percent of the poverty line dropped from 31 to 18 percent. We have since discovered, however, that most of that decline in poverty was due to the booming economic growth of the national economy during the 1960s, not to the War on Poverty.

Meanwhile, during that decade everyone else was enjoying economic prosperity and expanding affluence, as John Kenneth Galbraith's (1958, 1967) writings eloquently informed us. This optimistic reliance on economic growth to resolve—at least eventually—the age-old problem of economic inequality was reflected in Gerhard Lenski's (1966) stratification theory and popularized by Daniel Beu's (1960) book *The End of Ideology,* as well as much of the other sociological literature of that time.

Regrettably, there were two serious flaws in that optimistic perspective: it was both misleading and invalid. It was misleading because it confused improved levels of living with greater equality. Inequality is always a relative matter. No matter how well off one may be financially, if many other people are much better off, inequality still exists. Mature industrialism has markedly raised the standard of living of approximately 85 percent of the population since 1950, but it has done nothing to reduce income or wealth inequality in this society. Instead, we have simply relied on constant economic growth to avoid the unpleasant task of redistributing income and wealth and thus reducing economic inequality.

The optimistic argument is invalid because it rests on the assumption that steady economic growth will continue indefinitely. As long as the economy continued to expand, proponents of this perspective could insist that what really counted for most people was their actual level of living, not their relative status in an abstract income distribution. As long as they were living fairly comfortably and could look forward to even more income in the future, why should they care if other people were making five or even ten times as much money as they were?

In recent years, however, increasing numbers of social scientists have begun to cast serious doubts on the validity of the economic growth scenario for the future. There now appear to be several inescapable ecological, economic, and social limits to economic growth through perpetual industrial expansion. That literature, initiated by the Club of

Rome's "limits to growth" study (Meadows et al. 1970), is now vast, and cannot be reviewed here. If we are willing to agree that there is at least some validity to the limits to growth thesis, however, we are led to the inevitable conclusion that when economic growth can no longer be relied on to raise the standards of living of most people more-or-less continually, socioeconomic inequality will either remain unchanged or may likely increase unless a society adopts programs to redistribute income and wealth.

Paul Blumberg's book *Inequality in an Age of Decline* (1980) attempted to peer into the future and discern what might happen to socioeconomic inequality in the United States and other industrial nations as their economies cease to grow. He presented three alternative future models of socioeconomic inequality that I want to sketch and expand. The first model, which he called Class Convergence, represents the thinking of the traditional optimists. He gave only one version of this model, but I want to add a slightly different version. As depicted below, his Class Convergence model consisted of three horizontal lines, representing three different socioeconomic status levels—roughly "high," "medium," and "low"—through time. At the left side of his diagram, which might represent roughly 1960, those three lines are rather far apart. Over time, the top and bottom lines converge toward the middle line, indicating that the bulk of the population will come to enjoy a comfortable middle-class standard of living sometime in the future. I call this version the Comfortable Class Convergence model.

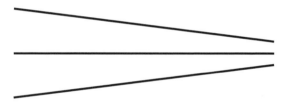

My alternative version of this model, which I think more accurately reflects the vision of writers such as Lenski and Bell, depicts all three lines steadily rising from left to right. However, the middle and bottom lines rise more sharply than the top line. Future socioeconomic convergence thus occurs at the level of economic affluence rather than just comfort. Consequently, I call this the Affluent Class Convergence model.

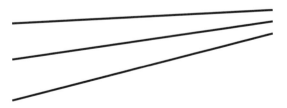

Blumberg did an excellent job of demonstrating that neither form of that convergence model is applicable to the United States at the present time, and will not likely be relevant in the near future. All the data presented in this paper support his contention.

Blumberg's second model depicts the "sustainable society" scenario that has been described by Dennis Pirages (1977) and numerous other writers. In this diagram, which Blumberg called the Class Stability model, the three lines remain parallel and equally far apart through time. Socioeconomic inequality remains unchanged, neither increasing nor decreasing. Although this is not an optimistic view of the future, it is not terribly pessimistic either, and it is certainly a real possibility.

Blumberg's analysis led him to conclude, however, that a third model is most probable in the near future. In this diagram, which he called the Class Divergence model, the top line remains level, the middle line declines somewhat, and the bottom line falls sharply. Thus socioeconomic inequality increases through time, as both the middle class and the poor suffer declining incomes.

As presented by Blumberg, this model depicts only "one-way" class divergence, since there is no upward line, only two downward lines. I want to suggest, however, that a more likely form of this Class Divergence model which is suggested by the results of this and all other recent studies of income trends—would depict "two-way" socioeconomic divergence, in which there were both upward and downward lines. Moreover, there are two possible versions of this alternative form of the divergence model.

Affluence/Poverty Divergence   Affluence/Mass Divergence

In both of these versions, the top line rises moderately rather than remaining level, as in Blumberg's model. Affluence continues to increase for the top portion of the population. In the first version of this model, which I call the Affluence/Poverty Divergence scenario, the middle line remains essentially level while the bottom line declines markedly. Socioeconomic inequality thus widens as the affluent become richer and the poor become poorer. The bulk of the population at the middle level, meanwhile, continues to enjoy a moderately comfortable standard of living. In the second version of the model, which I call the Affluence/Mass Divergence scenario, the middle line declines somewhat and the bottom line drops steeply. Thus the bulk of the population experiences increasing economic hardships, while people at the bottom of the income distribution suffer severe deprivation.

The results of this study indicate that the Affluent/Poverty Divergence version best describes what has been happening in the United States during the past two decades. While the affluent one-fifth of the population has prospered, the majority of the people have had to struggle to maintain their standard of living because their real incomes have either remained level or declined slightly. To the extent that the majority of families has thus far maintained economic stability and not experienced a declining standard of living, this appears to have been primarily the result of three factors: wives obtaining paid employment, changes in the federal tax structure, and families increasing their personal debt.

We have already seen that the only category of families who actually raised their median income between 1970 and 1987 were those in which both spouses were employed. Let us briefly examine the other two factors that have enabled many middle-level families to maintain their accustomed standards of living.

Recent changes in the federal tax structure have benefited principally the top income quintile of families, and to a lesser extent the fourth and third quintiles. A just-released study by the Congressional Budget Office (*Detroit Free Press* 1990) shows that between 1980 and 1990 the federal tax rate declined by 5.5 percent for the highest income quintile of American families, in addition to the real income increases they experienced during this decade. The tax rate for the fourth quintile of families, meanwhile, dropped by 2.2 percent, in addition to their small gain in real incomes. As a result, this 40 percent of the population had considerably more disposable income in 1990 than in 1980. The tax rate for the third income quintile increased 1.2 percent, but this was less than the amount that their real incomes rose during the 1980s, so that they also gained some purchasing power. (Although the real median income of this quintile declined slightly between 1970 and 1987, this latter study found that it rose slightly between 1980 and 1990.) In contrast, the federal tax rate for the second income quintile rose somewhat more than its median income, and the rate for the bottom quintile increased significantly while its real income declined. Consequently, recent changes in the federal tax structure have further diminished the purchasing power of the bottom 40 percent of the population.

Throughout the 1970s and 1980s, meanwhile, the amount of personal debt in this country has steadily risen. Many people have been going further and further into debt in order to maintain their standard of living. Consumer debts (all debts except real property mortgages) increased by 52 percent between 1970 and 1987, from $1,850 per capita (in 1987 dollars) to $2,810 per capita (U.S. Bureau of the Census 1989:499). Mortgage debts, meanwhile, rose by a staggering 500 percent, from $6,680 per capita to $40,620 per capita—largely, of course, because of rapidly escalating house prices. Total personal debt therefore went up from $8,530 to $43,430 per capita, for an increase of over 500 percent. Quite clearly, credit purchasing has been a major strategy used by most Americans to maintain their standard of living in the past two decades.

Sometime in the near future, however, these financial coping strategies will cease to be effective for most people. When nearly all wives are employed, when people have spent their tax savings, and when they have exhausted their lines of credit, a harsh day of financial reckoning will eventually occur. The likely outcome will be that the middle and working classes will begin experiencing a decline in their standard of living. At that point, the Affluent/Mass Divergence scenario will become reality, as a majority of the population begins riding a downward financial escalator. Meanwhile, in both versions of this alternative divergence model, poverty steadily increases.

Future Speculations

Any of the scenarios depicted by these various models of socioeconomic inequality could possibly become reality sometime in the near future. But which one is most likely to occur? The answer to that question depends not on projections of current trends, but on public policy decisions and the programs initiated by those policies.

If we want greater socioeconomic equality—at least at the comfortable, if not the affluent level—the United States government will have to adopt a wide variety of policies and programs designed to redistribute income and wealth, rather than relying on economic growth to keep people satisfied. William Wilson (1987) has advocated several of these public actions that are imperative if we are to eventually eliminate the truly disadvantaged of all races: a broad national economic plan, a full-employment policy, a massive job training program, and extensive child care facilities. If we also want to maintain the economic viability of the middle class, I would add to Wilson's list a number of policies and programs that would recognize the right of all citizens to as much free education as they wish and can utilize, total health care for all people, complete legal assistance, and adequate housing for everyone. I would also propose a guaranteed minimal income plan for all households, in place of most existing welfare programs, similar to the Family Assistance Plan proposed by Presidents Johnson and Nixon but never adopted. Sadly, I seriously doubt if most of these policies and programs will be accepted in the foreseeable future.

The Class Stability model, in which the present structure of socioeconomic inequality continues into the future with little alteration, strikes me as quite unlikely. The contemporary world is changing far too rapidly for any socioeconomic patterns to continue unchanged for very long.

The most likely scenario for the 1990s and beyond, I fear, is some form of the socioeconomic divergence model. And on the basis of the data reported in this paper, I expect that the Affluent/Mass Divergence model will be the closest to reality. In that case, the United States—and probably many other highly industrialized nations—would experience increasing class bifurcation. Both the upper class of national and local elites—who are extremely powerful and wealthy, and the upper-middle or affluent class—consisting of 20 to 25 percent of the population—will likely continue to do quite well, riding the crest of the economy as it moves from an industrial to an information base. Composed of college-educated professionals, administrators, technicians, financial manipulators, and other holders of privileged socioeconomic statuses, the affluent class will continue to see its income, wealth, and standard of living improve steadily if not spectacularly.

The middle half of the population will not be so fortunate, however. This large "middle mass" of white- and blue-collar people is composed primarily of those with a high school education and perhaps a year or two of college or technical training, who are employed as low-level clerical and sales persons, and skilled or semiskilled workers. During at least the next decade or two, they will likely find it increasingly difficult to find steady employment at a pay rate adequate to maintain a comfortable standard of living. They will therefore go deeper and deeper into debt as they struggle to maintain their past level of living, or else experience a declining standard of living. In either case, the gap between the minority of privileged "haves" and the large majority of increasingly disadvantaged "have-nots" could become a virtually unbridgeable gulf. The bottom 20 to 25 percent of the population, meanwhile, will have few or no opportunities to escape from economic deprivation, severe poverty, or dependence on public welfare.

If you believe, as I do, that severe class bifurcations—with its extremes of wealth and affluence coupled with financial hardships and grinding poverty—is harmful for any society, this is indeed a bleak vision of the future. It would also be a politically explosive situation. Many members of the "sinking mass" of middle- and working-class people would likely become highly resentful and angry, turn their frustration and wrath on vulnerable scapegoats such as racial and ethnic minorities, and support politicians who promised simple and quick solutions to their problems. Eventually, if the situation continued to worsen, the society could become ripe for either the emergence of an authoritarian political demigod or a political revolution.

Fortunately, future scenarios are not predictions, but only possibilities. If we—as sociologists and citizens—believe that increasing socioeconomic divergence and class bifurcation is pragmatically unwise and/or ethically intolerable, we face a massive challenge in the years ahead. We, and all others who share our values, must begin taking actions now to avoid this scenario and to create a society—and eventually a world—in which socioeconomic inequality is reduced and all people are able to enjoy a comfortable standard of living. In an era of shrinking natural resources and other ecological and economic limits, this will be a most demanding task. Nevertheless, it could be accomplished, as the Scandinavian countries have already largely demonstrated. Can the United States and the other highly industrialized nations of the world rise to the challenge confronting us?

References

Bell, Daniel. 1960. *The End of Ideology.* Glencoe: The Free Press.

———. 1973. *The Coming of Post-Industrial Society.* New York. Basic Books.

Blackburn, McKinley L., and David E. Bloom. 1985. "What is Happening to the Middle Class?" *American Demographics* 17:19–25.

Bluestone, Barry. and Frank I. Boyden. 1988. *The Great U-Turn: Corporate Restructuring and the Polarization of America.* New York: Basic Books.

Blumberg, Paul. 1980. *Inequality in an Age of Decline.* New York: Oxford University Press.

Committee on Ways and Means. U.S. House of Representatives. 1989. *Background Material and Data on Programs Within the Jurisdiction of the Committee on Ways and Means.* Washington. D.C.: U.S. Government Printing Office.

Detroit Free Press. 1990. "Tax Bite Stings Poor the Worst." February 19:1.

Galbraith, John Kenneth. 1958. *The Affluent Society.* Boston: Houghton Mifflin Co.

———. 1967. *The New Industrial State.* Boston: Houghton Mifflin Co.

Lenski, Gerhard. 1966. *Power and Privilege: A Theory of Social Stratification.* New York: McGraw-Hill Book Co.

Meadows, Donella, H., Dennis L. Meadows, Jorgen Randers, and William W. Behrens III. 1972. *The Limits to Growth.* London: Earth Island Ltd.

Pirages, Dennis Clark, ed. 1977. *The Sustainable Society.* New York: Praeger Publishers.

Smith, James D. 1986-87. "Wealth in America." *Institute of Social Research Newsletter* (Winter):3.

Tilly, Chris. 1986. "The U-Turn on Equality: The Puzzle of Middle Class Decline." *Dollars and Sense* 116:11–13.

U.S. Bureau of the Census. 1989 and earlier. *Statistical Abstract of the United States.* Washington, D.C.: U.S. Government Printing Office.

Wallerstein, Immanuel. 1980. *The Modern World-System II.* New York: Academic Press.

Wilson, William J. 1987. *The Truly Disadvantaged: The Inner City, the Underclass, and Public Policy.* Chicago: The University of Chicago Press.

Discussion Questions

1. Considering the occupation you intend to enter, what do you think may happen to your income if the economy continues to grow for the rest of your life? What will happen if the economy stays level or declines? In each case, do you think the gap between your income and the higher incomes of others will grow, or will you see greater inequality? What about the gap between your income and the lower incomes of other individuals?

2. Olsen suggests that there are two aspects of income levels. One is the issue of whether people at each level will gain income over time. The other involves how much the distance between income levels will change. In other words, will there be more equality or inequality of income for the whole society? Which of these questions do you think is more important to you as an individual? Why? Is one more important for the health of U.S. society as a whole? What do you think will happen in the United States if people from the middle class and below decline in income, in addition to finding a growing gap between them and those at the top?

C h a p t e r **9**

Inequalities of Race and Ethnicity

What kind of America is emerging out of the relationship between African Americans and white America?

As you no doubt know, this is a question being asked, and commented on, by many people in many sectors of the nation, both black and white. One sociologist, Lewis Killian, has been studying race relations since the early 1960s. In this article, he looks back 30 years to the hopes and dreams of equality that were held by many at a time of protest, of a war on poverty, and of the passage of the first major civil rights bill in 100 years. It was a time of both hope and optimism that prejudice and discrimination could be eliminated and equality could be realized.

What has happened to that dream? Killian argues that these and other aspects of race relations have stagnated or declined. He quotes the preface of a major report on African Americans in the United States: "We also describe the continuance of conditions of poverty, segregation, discrimination, and social fragmentation of the most serious proportions."

Accepting this description as accurate, Killian suggests that the underlying cause is a gap between the attitudes and commitment of U.S. whites. Although the principle of racial equality seems to be largely accepted by white Americans, they are unwilling to support governmental policies that could bring it about. Accepting this to be a true description, Killian sees little hope of positive change in the future. What do you think?

Race Relations and the Nineties
Where Are the Dreams of the Sixties?*

LEWIS M. KILLIAN
The University of West Florida

One of the most inspiring events of the 1960s occurred on August 28, 1963, when Martin Luther King, Jr., stood on the steps of the Lincoln Memorial and declared, "I have a dream my four little children will one day live in a nation where they will not be judged by the color of their skin but by the content of their character. I have a dream today!" (1986:219). This was an era of brave, optimistic dreams. Those dreams began to take shape ten years before King's memorable speech, as the school desegregation decision of 1954 gave rise to brave hopes in the hearts of segregated, downtrodden blacks. The concept "a revolution of rising expectations" well described their situation. Victories over white southern resistance in Montgomery, Tallahassee, Little Rock, and New Orleans provided black Americans and their white allies with a sense of empowerment. The sit-ins of the early sixties, still non-violent, still interracial, showed that the Movement could not be suppressed. As King said in his address, "Nineteen sixty-three is not an end, but a beginning. And those who hope that the Negro needed to blow off steam and will now be content will have a rude awakening if the nation returns to business as usual" (1986:219). Yet as we stand on the brink of the nineties the dreams have dimmed and the nation has indeed returned to business as usual. In his last presidential address to SCLC, in 1968, King urged again, "Let us be dissatisfied until men and women, however black they may be, will be judged on the basis of the content of their character and not on the basis of the color of their skin" (1986:251). How sorely pained he would be were he to witness the state of ethnic relations today!

A Succession of Dreams

The Civil Rights vision formulated by King and his lieutenants was the first of a series of dreams. It was symbolized by its famous slogan, "black and white together."

Killian, Lewis. Race Relations in the Nineties: Where Are the Dreams of the Sixties? *Social Forces, 69,* 1, September 1990, 1–13. By permission of The University of North Carolina Press.

Before the tragic end of his career King did place greater and greater emphasis on economic equality, particularly as he saw segregation diminishing while black unemployment and poverty persisted. He called for full employment, a guaranteed annual income, redistribution of wealth, and skepticism toward the capitalistic economy. "A true revolution of values," he declared, "will soon look uneasily on the glaring contrast of poverty and wealth" (1986:241).

During the height of the Civil Rights Movement the courage of the workers and the vicious violence of the white southern resistance engendered a national orgy of guilt and fear that provided the catalyst for the passage of the Civil Rights Act of 1964 and the Voting Rights Act the next year. The basic economic changes required if laws mandating desegregation and equal opportunity were to have more than a minimal effect had not come about, however. Moreover, the urban insurrections, brought to the forefront of the news by the Watts riot of 1965, awakened the nation to the fact that blacks were still far from content. King's dream of a revolution fueled by love and fought with nonviolence faded in the smoke of ghetto fires. The competing dream of Black Power dominated the last half of the decade.

The Black Power Dream

The vision of black power as the way out of inequality and stigmatization had deep roots in black history in the United States. Even as King was emerging as a national black hero the nationalistic message preached so eloquently by Malcolm X resonated in the consciousness of hundreds of impatient, angry black people who saw no chance of entering white middle-class society. As far back as the middle of the nineteenth century Black Nationalism had been a strong ideological undercurrent in the United States, surfacing, as William J. Wilson has argued, when intense frustration and disillusionment follow a span of heightened expectations (1973:50).

As limited as its human and financial resources may have been, the Black Power Movement was, with the aid of a titillated white press, able to drown out the voices of the leaders of the Civil Rights Movement. "Power," not "love"; "defensive violence" and "any means necessary," not nonviolence; and "soul" or "blood," not "black and white together," were the cries resounding in the ghettos and repeated on the nation's television screens.

Even more so than do most social movements, the Black Power Movement failed to achieve its stated objectives. Blacks did not win even veto power in the politics of the nation, the states, or the cities. The sort of power they gained in predominantly black cities and congressional districts resulted from demographic changes, not from concessions to the demands of the movement. Neither the extravagant dream of a black republic in the South nor the moderate one of viable all-black municipalities, such as Soul City, North Carolina, was realized. Real advances in self-chosen separatism going beyond the historically black churches and fraternal organizations, primarily took the form of black studies departments, black cultural centers, and a few all-black dormitories in predominantly white universities.

Despite its near failure, the significance of the short-lived black power movement has been greatly underestimated. First of all, its very demise dramatized the lengths that the white power structure, at all levels, would go to suppress blacks who did not remain meek and mild. Of even greater importance was the change in the terms of the ongoing debate between whites and blacks and within each community about the future of blacks in U.S.

society. King's shining grail of integration had lost its luster, at least for the time being. Assimilation had long been the dominant theme among both black Americans and white liberals, but now both its feasibility and desirability were being questioned. Various forms of pluralism gained legitimacy. At best, assimilation was a dream to be deferred until after a period of benign race consciousness.

The theme of black consciousness underscored the pervasive persistence of ethnic diversity in the society. It was accompanied by a novel concept, that of ethnic group rights. The idea of civil rights, individual rights based on citizenship, was now supplemented by the idea of rights based on membership in an ethnic group with a collective claim to being or having been an oppressed minority.

This seed fell on fertile soil, for other ethnic groups, not only Latinos and Native Americans, but also what Michael Novak called the "unmeltable white ethnics," began to advance their claims (1972). A system of competitive pluralism coupled with what Barbara Lal has called "compulsory ethnicity" arose along with "the institutionalization of ethnic identification as a basis for the assertion of collective claims concerning the distribution of scarce resources" (1983:167). In this connection we should note that since 1980 citizens filling out the schedule of the decennial census have been called on to specify the ancestral group with which they identify—application of the rule of descent has received bureaucratic sanction at the federal level. Yet those are probably the most inaccurate data to be found in the census volumes. Careful research has shown about one-third of respondents are likely to change their ethnic responses from year to year. And, ironically, Stanley Lieberson suggests that a new ethnic group is now growing in the United States—unhyphenated whites. He identifies them for statistical purposes as that one sixth of the population who, in 1980, identified themselves simply as "American" or refused to report any ancestry (1982).

One of the last demands addressed to United States society in the spirit of black power was the call for reparations. The Black Manifesto read by James Forman on the steps of New York's Riverside Church on May 4, 1969, was not an angry, quixotic whim of Forman and the few associates who accompanied him. It was a document drawn up by the National Black Economic Development Conference at a meeting set up by the Interreligious Foundation for Community Organization. The latter was created by most of the mainline Protestant denominations in the nation.

In the Manifesto Forman and others charged that the white Christian churches and the Jewish synagogues were part and parcel of the capitalistic system which had exploited the resources, the minds, the bodies, and the labor of blacks for centuries. The NBEDC was demanding $500 million in reparations. The melodramatic rhetoric of the Manifesto proclaimed that this came to "$15 per nigger," but the demand was not for the distribution of such a pittance to 30 million black individuals. Instead it called for the establishment of a southern land bank to enable displaced black farmers to establish farm cooperatives, black-controlled publishing houses and audio-visual networks; skills training centers; and other such collective enterprises. Whether such projects would have succeeded is beside the point. What is important is that the demand for reparations called for compensation to a group in the name of ethnic group rights; it was not a plea for the funding of "black capitalism."

The Dreams Fade

The principal outcome of the Manifesto was an outpouring of resolutions by churches. As Arnold Schucter observed, the "great orgy of American guilt" seemed to have subsided by that time, as had the urban insurrections (1970:28). CointelPro was decimating the ranks of the Black Power Movement, and agents provocateurs were giving it a terrorist image. Even whites who had finally began sympathizing with the goals of the Civil Rights Movement were asking, "Haven't we done enough for the blacks?"

Already the trend toward white acceptance of the principle of racial equality, particularly as applied to education and equal job opportunity, was discernible in public opinion polls. It was widely agreed that "white racism" was a terrible evil—but what did this mean?

The term "racism," usually meaning "white racism," became a catchword after the Kerner Commission declared in the summary of its Report to the President on the causes of civil disorders, "White racism is essentially responsible for the explosive mixture which has been accumulating in our cities since the end of World War II" (1968:203). But who are the white racists—particularly in the eyes of the majority of whites who now claim to accept the principle of racial equality? It is not they themselves but those Klansmen and American Nazis and Skinheads. They themselves are innocent, for they have accepted the victories of the Civil Rights Movement. They don't object to sharing public accommodations with blacks and they will let their children go to school with them as long as there aren't too many. They believe that blacks should have equal job opportunities and if a lot of them remain poor it must be because they don't take advantage of the changes open to them. Schuchter was all too accurate when he wrote in 1970, "We are faced with a society in which racism has become institutionalized even though the majority of Americans vehemently protest their innocence" (1970:28).

Fruits of the Dreams

By the beginning of the 1970s both the Civil Rights Movement and the Black Power Movement were comparatively dormant. As pointed out earlier the Black Power Movement had consequences of greater significance than is generally recognized. These consequences are seen primarily in the world view of blacks in the U.S., symbolized by the fact that the vast majority now call themselves "Black," not "Negro," and some even prefer "African American." Concretely, black power is seen only in the political realm and then only dimly. There is an important but still very small black congressional caucus, but there has been no black senator since the defeat of Edward Brook in 1972. Numerous blacks have been elected to city, county, and state offices, but not until 25 years after the passage of the Voting Rights Act did a state elect a black governor. Black political power remains dependent upon a high degree of black residential concentration and the drawing of electoral boundaries to reflect that concentration.

The Civil Rights Movement, despite its apparent triumph with the passage of the Civil Rights Act and the Voting Rights Act, still won only intermediate objectives. *De jure* segregation was struck down. De facto segregation in public places was greatly reduced, but the illusion of equality created in the forum was not reflected at the hearth; American homes, neighborhoods, and private clubs remained highly segregated. King's dream of a society where people would not be judged on the basis of their color remained woefully un-fulfilled. Even Latinos, a newer minority in many areas, find it easier to escape from the barrio than do blacks from the ghetto.

But what were the objectives unattained by either movement? Let us look again for a moment at the response of the white churches to the Black Manifesto. They placed new emphasis on preaching and teaching against "racism and on welcoming blacks into the pews of white churches; they raised money—not a great deal—to put into the ghettos to aid the poor, the disenfranchised, and the uneducated. But the lesson of the failed dreams of the 1960s is that it is not sensitivity training, nor token integration, nor welfare that is needed to eradicate the destructive consequences of ethnic discrimination. It is drastic economic reform and that revolution of values that Martin Luther King said would "look uneasily on the glaring contrast of poverty and wealth." What the dreams did not produce was a society where black and white children would not only sit beside each other in school but also achieve equal gains in leaning; a society where blacks would not only have equal rights to jobs but also have jobs; a society where poverty not only would ignore ethnic boundaries but also would actually diminish. How much closer are we to that sort of society than we were in 1970?

A Glass Half Empty

Many times after the publication of *The Impossible Revolution?* I heard myself character-ized as a chronic pessimist who would always see a glass as half empty, never as half full (Killian 1968). The analogy itself is flawed, f course—in life good or bad is never stable but is always rising or falling.

Today when I look about me, particularly in the South, and see whites and blacks eat-ing, shopping, studying, working, and playing in each other's presence in places where once they were cruelly segregated, I think, "How great and wonderful the progress since 1954!" But when I look at the little clumps of black people sitting, talking, huddling together even in supposedly integrated settings, I wonder if we have not progressed only to that con-dition which Cayton and Drake called "the equality of anonymity" (1945:102). When I drive through a still segregated and often very poor black residential area, and when I look at the economic indicators, I am even more pessimistic. Indeed, I am convinced that the glass is surely half empty, for the level of black well-being is falling.

Reports and Reports

Testifying before the Kerner Commission in 1968 Kenneth B. Clark said, "I read that report . . . of the 1919 riot in Chicago, and it is as if I were reading the report of the inves-tigating committee on the Harlem riot of '35, the report of the investigating committee on the Harlem riot of '43, the report of the McCone Commission on the Watts riot. I must again in candor say to you members of this committee it is a kind of Alice in Wonderland—with the same moving picture shown over and over again, the same analysis, the same recommendations, and the same inaction" (1977:ix).

Now we have the latest of the massive, comprehensive studies of how blacks are faring, *Blacks in American Society,* put together by a team of distinguished social scientists (Jaynes et al. 1989). It comes 70 years after the Chicago research, 45 years after *An American Dilemma,* and 20 years after the Kerner report. This volume starts out with refreshing honesty. While acknowledging many improvements, the authors declare, "We also describe the continuance of conditions of poverty, segregation, discrimination, and social fragmentation of the most serious proportions" (1989:ix).

The analysis of trends since the great migration of blacks out of southern agriculture beginning in 1939 leads to the conclusion that the place of blacks in the American economy has been, and remains, that of a reserve army of labor. They have enjoyed some progress during periods of prosperity and high employment, usually war-induced. "But," says the study, "after initial reports of rising relative black economic status, black gains have stagnated on many measures of economic position since the early 1970s" (1989:274). Two examples of this stagnation are given. Poverty rates for blacks increased from 29.7% in 1974 to 31% in 1985. Blacks' real per capita income in 1984 was one-third higher than in 1968 but still stood in the same relationship to white income as in 1971—57%. Yet it is important to note that poverty had increased among whites also, from 7.3% in 1974 to 11% in 1985.

There is no need to repeat the much cited evidence of the accentuated differences in status among blacks, with some segments gaining drastically relative to whites and others losing ground. The major source of inequality within the black community, the authors note, is the increased fraction of black men with no earnings at all. The major reasons for black economic inequality are (1) the concentration of black workers, particularly men, in low-paying jobs and (2) the relatively high proportion of unemployed blacks, many of them not even in the labor force. In fact, while between 1973 and 1986 black men with jobs continued to approach whites in position on the occupational ladder and in hourly wage rates, the gains were offset by employment losses. The optimistic reports about employment rates released almost every month from Washington rarely note that black unemployment still continues at a rate twice that of whites and that the rates are based on persons in the labor force, not including the bitter, discouraged dropouts.

Jaynes and his coauthors reject the explanation that it is transfer payments—the much-maligned "welfare"—causing people to drop out of the labor force. They offer instead a structural explanation: "The shifting industrial base of the U.S. economy from blue-collar manufacturing to service industries, the slowdown in economic growth, and the consequent decline in real wages could be expected to produce a period of economic and social distress. For displaced and educationally or spatially misplaced workers, the rise in unemployment and increased competition for moderate-to-high-paying jobs might well lead to a rise in the number of discouraged workers" (1989:310).

The most ominous of the statistics drawn together by this committee pertain to poverty rates. We have seen a dramatic decline from the unbelievably high rates, in 1939, of 93% and 65% for black and white people, respectively. By 1974 the rates were 30% for blacks and 9% for whites, but by 1986 rates for both groups were higher, 31% and 11%. Even more alarming is the prevalence of poverty among black children—44% in 1985, compared with 16% among white children.

The pessimistic conclusion of the chapter "Blacks in the Economy" reads, "The economic fortunes of blacks are strongly tied (more so than those of whites) to a strong economy and vigorously enforced policies against discrimination. Without these conditions, the black midddle class may persist, but it is doubtful it can grow or thrive. And the position of lower status blacks cannot be expected to improve" (1989:324).

To add my own pessimistic coda, a "strong economy" must achieve more than merely providing low-paying jobs in the service sector to replace those lost in the industrial sector through automation or export. Yet this seems to be what many secure people accept as a measure of solving the problem of unemployment. Moreover, with the insecurity felt by many whites it cannot be expected that they will willingly share with blacks the risk of falling into poverty.

Hence the crescendo of rhetoric decrying growing white racism and calling for more affirmative action programs is simplistic, avoiding the main problems facing both blacks and the society. In addition to focusing on the economic nature of these problems, we must also consider the changes in the nature of what is now called "racism."

How Much and What Kind of "Racism"?

Although there is no doubt that "racism" subsumes a multitude of sins, the term itself is very imprecise. Scholars defining it usually list a number of varieties. Since the 1960s it seems to have replaced the older concepts "prejudice" and "discrimination" to denote those negative attitudes and behaviors that result in the subordination and oppression of some groups which are socially defined as "races."

Focusing on the attitudinal components of racism, Schuman, Steeh, and Bobo found a paradox in the attitudes of white Americans in public opinion surveys from 1942 through 1983 (1985). On the one hand, they found strong positive trends toward acceptance of the principle of racial equality and the rejection of absolute segregation. On the other hand, questions concerning governmental implementation of these abstract principles got relatively low levels of support, and there are few signs showing that such support has increased over time. In 1989 the authors of *Blacks in American Society,* who found no reason to disagree with this observation, added their own finding that measures of black alienation from white society suggest an increase from the late 1960s to the 1980s (1989:131).

Many theoretical explanations have been advanced for the paradox disclosed by Schuman and his associates. One theory focuses on the level of abstract principles, seeing agreement with them as evidence of a strong progressive trend. It underplays the contradictory aspect of the findings as well as the absence of proportional structural changes in society, such as the persistence of massive residential segregation.

A sharply contrasting explanation holds that underlying "racist" attitudes have not changed. Agreement with abstract principles of racial equality constitutes only lip service conforming to a new cultural norm rendering crude, overt expression of racial prejudice less than respectable. Racial prejudice is now expressed symbolically. Opposition to school busing, open housing laws, and affirmative action, as well as failure to vote for a black candidate for public office, is to be explained primarily in terms of symbolic, covert racism. The more complex explanation of competing values such as objections to governmental intrusion, individualism, and genuine concern about what happens to one's children is rejected out of hand.

In *Racial Formation in the United States* Michael Omi and Howard Winant similarly give little credence to attitudinal expressions of support for abstract principles unless they are paralleled by support for implementation (1986). Unlike other sociologists they offer a theory of how the persistence of covert racism has affected racial politics in what they define as still being a "racial state."

They concede that a great transformation in ideas about race took place in the United States during the 1950s and 1960s. This had two major consequences. One was new, self-conscious racial identities which persisted even after the movements through which they were forged disintegrated. The second they call the "rearticulation of racial ideology" in reaction to the partial victories of the Civil Rights Movement and, I would add, of the Women's Liberation Movement. The conservative, right-wing trend in U.S. politics rests on racism, they suggest. "As the right sees it," they say, "racial problems today center on the new forms of racial injustice which originated in the great transformation. This new injustice confers group rights on racial minority groups, thus granting a new form of privilege—that of preferential treatment" (1986:114). Further developing this theme Omi and Winant assert, "In this scenario, the victims of racial discrimination have dramatically shifted from racial minorities to whites, particularly white males" (1986:114). They make a persuasive case that even though they were alluded to by code words racial issues were central to support for President Reagan in his two elections and for President George Bush. Who can question that the Republican Party's "southern strategy" has included a strong component of this rearticulated racial ideology, one appealing not only to voters such as those who elected David Duke to the Louisiana legislature, but also to numerous white voters outside the South?

This pessimistic view of the United States as basically a racial state in which racism changes its face but does not disappear is frightening to anyone who hopes for movement toward greater equality in the 1990s. An even more ominous view of a majority of the electorate is offered by Edna Bonacich, who attaches more importance to class as a factor than do Omi and Winant. She asserts, "The United States is an immensely unequal society in terms of distribution of material wealth and consequently in the distribution of all the benefits and privileges that accrue to wealth. . . . This inequality is vast irrespective of race." Granting that people of color suffer disproportionately, she goes on to say, "I believe that racial inequality is inextricably tied to overall inequality and to an ideology that endorses vast inequality as justified and desirable." She concludes, "And even if some kind of racial parity at the level of averages could be achieved, the amount of suffering at the bottom would remain undiminished, hence unconscionable" (1989:80).

Bonacich cites dramatic statistics demonstrating the vastness of inequality and its frightening growth. In 1987, for example, 6.7 million American workers living on the minimum wage had incomes of $9,968 a year, while Lee Iacocca was paid over $20 million, or $9,615 an hour. In 1986 there were 26 billionaires in the country; in 1987, 49. "The Culture of Inequality" which Michael Lewis identified in 1978 is more entrenched than ever (1978).

In the 1960s James Baldwin asked, "Who wants to be integrated into a burning house?" The house is still burning, being slowly consumed by the heat of greed and fear. Speculators gamble with the nation's wealth but pass the bill to the government when the dice roll against them. The CEO's of corporations have learned to live comfortably with affirmative action at the middle levels of the occupational scale but are equally comfortable with reductions in the total size of their work force. Often unnoted in optimistic studies of affirmative action is that increases in minority shares of employment are usually accompanied by contraction in the number of all persons employed. The size of the piece of the pie is not as critical in these times as is the shrinking of the fraction of the pie left for the have-nots in a class-polarized society.

The ideology of inequality Bonacich addresses is sustained also by the insecurities of people who have left the work force and are living on fixed incomes, either from interest and dividends or from those transfer payments now known as "entitlements." They do not see as their enemies the 0.5% of the families who in 1983 held 35% of the net wealth of the nation. Instead they fear the faceless people at the bottom of the heap. Have they not been told in campaign after campaign that it is the demands of the poor for welfare, social services, and higher wages that might cause higher taxes and increased prices? Polarization does not start near the top of the income distribution but near the bottom. One of Jonathan Rieder's subjects in *Canarsie* put it exactly, "We never join the have-a-littles with the have-nots to fight the haves. We make sure the have-a-littles fight the have-nots" (1985:119).

Now, ironically, as the crisis of capitalism in America intensifies the attention of American voters is distracted by the failures of socialist polities and economies abroad, as if that made their own plight less perilous and their own future more secure. The prospects for a radical rejection of the culture of inequality, with its concomitant acceptance of racial inequality, seem dim. To me, some pessimistic warnings from the past seem more appropriate today than do optimistic predictions for the 1990s.

Voices from the Past

When I look at the retreat of the federal government from vigorous enforcement of civil rights laws, I am reminded of the warning of Frederick Douglass, issued as he witnessed a similar retreat. He wrote, "No man can be truly free whose liberty is dependent upon the thought, feeling, and actions of others, and who has himself no means in his own hands for guarding, protecting, defending, and maintaining that liberty" (1962:539).

During the Civil Rights and Black Power movements black Americans were catalysts in producing a national orgy of guilt, but they did not attain the sort of power Douglass described. After laws promising equal opportunity were passed, blacks lacked the political clout to get succeeding congresses to pass laws to implement these promises. They were forced to depend, instead, on sympathetic bureaucrats in the executive branch and a narrow majority in a relatively friendly Supreme Court to promote implementation in the absence of majority popular support. Now we see the administrative and judicial support fading because of the growing strength of a political party that does not depend on minority voters for victory and often appears downright hostile to their interests. As inadequate as were the responses of the liberal Kennedy, Johnson, and Carter administrations, they were magnificent when compared to those of elected officials who use "liberal" as a code word signifying softness on crime, welfare fraud, pauperism, reverse discrimination, and the spread of communism in the Third World.

Yet the black middle class still prospers relative to its past condition as the gap between the haves and have-nots grows in the black community, just as in the white. Here I am reminded of Stokely Carmichael's quip in the 1960s, "To most whites Black Power seems to mean that the Mau Mau are coming to the suburbs at night" (1966:5). Today we might say that, to most whites, actually accepting blacks as residents of their neighborhoods seems to mean that drug-ridden welfare recipients from the ghetto will be on their doorstep tomorrow. Julius Lester wrote at about the same time, "The black middle class is aware of its precarious position between the ghetto blacks and white society, and its members know that because they are black, they are dispensable" (1968:34). Even the qualified black person who seems to have achieved equality is regarded as the "exceptional" black and even then is often suspected of reaching that level because of affirmative action. Until the plight of the underclass is alleviated its shadow will continue to blight the lives and fortunes of those blacks who have partially escaped the bonds of past discrimination.

Lester said that the black middle class knew that it was dispensable. Sidney Willhelm asked, "Who needs the Negro?" (1970). Although asked in 1970, his question is still horrendously relevant today. Writing before the export of semiskilled jobs to Third World countries became another threat to workers in the United States, he warned about automation: "The Negro becomes a victim of neglect as he becomes useless to an emerging economy of automation. With the onset of automation the Negro moves out of his historical state of oppression into one of uselessness. Increasingly, he is not so much economically exploited as he is irrelevant" (1970:162).

Although he and Willhelm have been highly critical of each other's work, William J. Wilson pointed to the same problem in *The Declining Significance of Race.* He observed, "Representing the very center of the New American economy, corporate industries are characterized by vertically integrated production processes and technologically progressive systems of production and distribution. The growth of production depends more on technical progress and increases in physical capital per worker than on the growth of employment." He added, "In short, an increasing number of corporate sector workers have become redundant because the demand for labor is decreased in the short run by the gap between productivity and the demand for goods" (1978:96-97). Perhaps we must ask today, "Who needs people, except as consumers?" Willhelm characterized our situation as one in which "the new standard of living entails both production and distribution of goods without, however, involving either a producer or distributor through large-scale employment" (1978:203). Hence this oft-disparaged but frighteningly accurate prophet among sociologists advanced a truly radical proposition: "It will be incumbent for a society relying upon automation and dedicated to the well being of human beings to accept a new economic gauge, namely: *services are to be rendered and goods produced, distributed and consumed in keeping with a designated standard of living*" (1978:203). This is the sort of change in perspective of which Wilson said, in 1987, "It will require a radicalism that neither Democrat nor Republican parties have as yet been realistic enough to propose" (1987:139). Instead what we continue to see is platforms that imply that if profits are kept high and taxes low so that investment is encouraged, plenty of jobs will be created. Then, if blacks will get an education and develop the right attitudes toward work and the family, they can enjoy that portion of the prosperity that trickles down to them. This, unfortunately, is the dream of many white voters today. It is not, however, an accurate vision of things to come but a rose-tinted stereotype of an industrial era which is gone forever and was never good for minority workers.

Dream or Nightmares for the 1990s?

During those years after 1940 during which I studied, taught, and lived race relations in the South, I had my own dream. It was that my fellow white southerners, most of whom I knew as good, kind people, would have peeled from their eyes the veil which kept them from knowing what they were doing to black people. Someday they would see, I hoped, how segregation and discrimination, no matter how paternalistic, left cruel injuries which would handicap both current and future generations.

During the decade after 1954 I thought I was beginning to see that veil thinning under the assault of the Civil Rights Movement. I did witness heartening changes, but then I saw new complacency, with white America asking, "How much more are we supposed to do for them?" Now I see a new veil blinding people whom I still believe to be good-spirited. They are blind to institutional discrimination and to the poverty increasing in our nation even more rapidly than 20 years ago. Ironically, the behavior of most white people, particularly in the South has changed more than have their attitudes. Now they mix with their black fellow citizens, yet blacks still remain largely invisible to them. They admit selected, acceptable blacks to their company as individuals but ignore the tragedy of the masses who yearly become more separated and alienated from what appears to those on top as an affluent society. Poverty, black and white, is concealed in a way different from when the rich and the poor lived closer to each other. It is known to many Americans only by flitting images in the mass media. In the meantime defense of what security and prosperity one does enjoy, rather than concern for the social problems threatening the nation, anchors successful political appeals with the dominant theme, "no new taxes."

In 1961 James E. Conant wrote in *Slums and Suburbs,* "We are allowing social dynamite to accumulate in our large cities" (p. 2). In the 1960s there were explosions of that dynamite, but its potential for destruction was far from exhausted. Now, in 1990, more dynamite is accumulating and in more cities.

Yet at this very time there appears to be a new basis for optimism. Many Americans are celebrating the end of the Cold War and looking forward to a "peace dividend." The case for deferring spending on domestic programs because of the demands for military defense loses its cogency. Journalists and novelists ask, "Who will be the enemy now that the Soviet Union is no longer the evil empire?"

There has been another cold war, however—a war of heartless neglect of the burgeoning needs of the truly disadvantaged in our own affluent society. A bright new dream would feature the end of this cold war and the beginning of a new war on poverty. We can expect increasingly urgent demands for a concerted attack on underemployment, undereducation, crime which preys on the poor, and the hopelessness that causes young people to drop out not only from school but also from the labor force. But these problems cannot be adequately addressed with the meager surplus left after the requirements for deficit reduction and new foreign aid are met. New taxes and a more equitable distribution of wealth will be required. But what if the response of the "haves" and the "have-littles" to this summons for self-sacrifice is a new wave of blaming the victim? If this is the case, the new enemy will be our own underclass.

References

Bonacich, Edna. 1989. "Inequality in America: The Failure of the American System for People of Color." *Sociological Spectrum* 9:77–101.

Carmichael, Stokely. 1966. "What We Want." *New York Review of Books,* September 22.

Cayton, Horace W., and St. Clair Drake. 1945. *Black Metropolis.* Harcourt Brace.

Clark, Kenneth. 1977. P. ix In the Preface to *Commission Politics,* by Michael Lipsky and David J. Olson. Transaction.

Conant, James B. 1961. *Slums and Suburbs.* McGraw Hill.

Douglass, Frederick. 1962. *Life and Times of Frederick Douglass.* Collier.

Jaynes, Gerald, and Robin M. Williams. 1989. *Blacks and American Society.* National Academy Press.

Killian, Lewis M. 1968. *The Impossible Revolution? Black Power and the American Dream.* Random House.

King, Martin Luther, Jr. (1963). 1986. "I Have a Dream." In *A Testament of Hope. The Essential Writings of Martin Luther King, Jr.,* edited by James M. Washington. Harper & Row.

———. (1967). 1986. "A Time to Break Silence." Loc. cit.

———. (1968). 1986. "Where Do We Go From Here?" Loc. cit.

Lal, Barbara Lallis. 1983. "Perspectives on Ethnicity: Old Wines in New Bottles." *Ethnic and Racial Studies* 6:154–73.

Lewis, Michael. 1978. *The Culture of Inequality.* University of Massachusetts Press.

Lieberson, Stanley. 1982. "A New Ethnic Group in the United States." Pp. 259–67 in *Majority and Minority,* edited by Norman R. Yetman. 4th ed. Allyn & Bacon.

Myrdal, Gunnar. 1944. *An American Dilemma.* Harper.

Novak, Michael. 1972. *The Rise of the Unmeltable Ethnics.* Macmillan.

Omi, Michael, and Howard Winant. 1986. *Racial Formation in the United States from the 1960's to the 1980's.* Routledge & Kegan Paul.

Report of the National Advisory Commision on Civil Disorders. 1968. Bantam.

Rieder, Jonathan. 1985. *Canarsie: The Jews and Italians of Brooklyn Against Liberalism.* Harvard University Press.

Schucter, Arnold. 1970. *Reparations: The Black Manifesto and Its Challenge to White America.* J.B. Lippincott

Schuman, Howard, Charlotte Steeh, and Lawrence Bobo. 1985. *Racial Attitudes in America.* Harvard University Press.

Willhelm, Sydney. 1970. *Who Needs the Negro?* Schenkman.

Wilson, William J. 1973. *Power, Racism, and Privilege.* Macmillan.

———. 1980. *The Declining Significance of Race.* University of Chicago Press.

———. 1987. *The Truly Disadvantaged.* University of Chicago Press.

Discussion Questions

1. Killian argues that race relations and equality are in jeopardy because, although whites accept the principle of racial equality, they don't support policies that would make it possible. In your opinion, to what degree do people of your generation believe in racial equality? How much do they support the use of governmental policy to bring it about? Do you think any kind of governmental programs can further equality? If not, why not? If you believe there are programs that will work, which ones are they? Do you think the American people are willing to pay for them?

2. What do you think the future holds for ethnic relations and equality for Hispanic Americans? For Native Americans? For Asian Americans?

Chapter *10*

Inequalities of Gender and Age

What are the most crucial areas of gender inequality? Jobs? Income? Political power? These are all areas in which women suffer inequality. But equally important, women are much more frequently the victims of violence than men. As Toni Nelson points out, this pattern of violence is worldwide, and is often approved or even mandated by a nation's culture. Female genital mutilation (female circumcision) is a case in point. Can you imagine your family, community, and even your entire society requiring the mutilation of all the young women in your family?

It is possible to turn away with disgust from information about such a practice. After all, it isn't found in civilized nations like ours, is it? But Nelson points out that the lower status of women in societies throughout the world, including our own, encourages violence against them in almost every area of life. And it is costly. The personal impact on the victim is often enormous, but the author points to the cost to society as well, emphasizing health care costs and the effects on economic productivity.

Are there solutions? Nelson describes the recent trend in much of the world for women to speak out about violence against females. Of course, whether such movements and activities will make a significant long-term difference is open to question. Could it be possible that the victimization of women will disappear in your lifetime?

Violence Against Women

TONI NELSON

A Girl is Mutilated in Egypt

It is not a ritual that many people would expect—much less want—to witness. Yet in the fall of 1994, the television network CNN brought the practice of female genital mutilation (FGM) into living rooms around the world, by broadcasting the amputation of a young Egyptian girl's clitoris. Coinciding with the United Nations International Conference on Population and Development in Cairo, the broadcast was one of several recent events that have galvanized efforts to combat the various forms of violence that threaten women and girls throughout the world. The experience suffered by 10-year-old Nagla Hamza focused international attention on the plight of the more than 100 million women and girls in Africa victimized by FGM. In doing so, it helped spur conference delegates into formulating an official "Programme of Action" that condemned FGM and outlined measures to eliminate the practice.

Euphemistically referred to as female circumcision, FGM encompasses a variety of practices ranging from excision, the partial or total removal of the clitoris and labia minora, to infibulation, in which all the external genitals are cut away and the area is restitched, leaving only a small opening for the passage of urine and menstrual blood. Nagla's mutilation, performed by a local barber without anesthesia or sanitary precautions, was typical. Although the physical and psychological consequences of FGM are severe and often life-threatening, the practice persists due to beliefs that emerged from ancient tribal customs but which have now come to be associated with certain major religions. In Israel, for instance, FGM is practiced by Jewish migrants from the Ethiopian Falasha community; elsewhere in Africa, it is found among Christian and Islamic populations. But FGM has no inherent association with any of these religions. Although some Islamic scholars consider it an important part of that religion, FGM actually predates Islam, and neither the Qur'an, the

Nelson, Toni. The World's Violence against Women. *World Watch,* July/August 1996. Reprinted with permission of the Worldwatch Institute.

primary source for Islamic law, nor the Hadith, collections of the Prophet Mohammed's lessons, explicitly require the practice.

Justifications for FGM vary among the societies where it occurs (FGM is practiced in 28 African nations, as well as in scattered tribal communities in the Arabian Peninsula and various parts of South Asia). But most explanations relate in some way to male interest in controlling women's emotions and sexual behavior. One of the most common explanations is the need to lessen desire so women will preserve their virginity until marriage. The late Gad-Alhaq Ali Gad-Alhaq, Sheik of Cairo's al-Azhar Islamic University at the time of the CNN broadcast, explained it this way: the purpose of FGM is "to moderate sexual desire while saving womanly pleasures in order that women may enjoy their husbands." For Mimi Ramsey, an anti-FGM activist in the United States who was mutilated in her native Ethiopia at age six, FGM is meant to reinforce the power men have over women: "the reason for my mutilation is for a man to be able to control me, to make me a good wife." Today, migrants are bringing FGM out of its traditional societies and into Europe, North America, and Australia. Approximately 2 million girls are at risk each year.

As in other countries where the practice is commonplace, Egypt's official policy on FGM has been ambiguous. Although a Ministry of Health decree in 1959 prohibited health professionals and public hospitals from performing the procedure, and national law makes it a crime to permanently mutilate anyone, clitoridectomies and other forms of FGM are not explicitly prohibited. An estimated 80 percent of Egyptian women and girls, or more than 18 million people, have undergone some form of FGM, which is often carried out by barbers in street booths on the main squares of both small towns and large cities.

Before the CNN broadcast, Egyptian public opinion seemed to be turning against the practice. In early 1994, activists founded the Egyptian Task Force Against Female Genital Mutilation. Later that year, during the population conference, Population and Family Welfare Minister Maher Mahran vowed to delegates that "Egypt is going to work on the elimination of female genital mutilation." Plans were even laid for legislation that would outlaw FGM. But some members of Egypt's religious community saw the broadcast as a form of Western imperialism and used it to challenge both the secular government of Hosni Mubarak and the conference itself.

In October 1994, Sheik Gad-Alhaq ruled that FGM is a religious obligation for Muslims. The same month, Minister of Health Dr. Ali Abdel Fattah issued a decree permitting the practice in selected government hospitals. The Minister's directive came just 10 days after a committee of experts convened by him condemned FGM and denied that it had any religious justification. Fattah affirmed his personal opposition, but insisted that the decree was necessary to "save those victimized girls from being 'slaughtered' by unprofessionals."

In the wake of the Minister's decision, plans for the bill outlawing FGM were postponed. Contending that Fattah had effectively legalized the procedure, national and international nongovernmental organizations sought to reverse the decision through petition drives, public education initiatives, and lawsuits. And on October 17, 1995, Fattah reversed his decision, and the Ministry of Health once again banned FGM in public hospitals. The anti-FGM legislation, however, remains on hold.

Violence Is a Universal Threat

Egypt's confused and ambivalent response to FGM mirrors in many ways the intensifying international debate on all forms of violence against women. And even though FGM itself may seem just a grotesque anomaly to people brought up in cultures where it isn't practiced, FGM is grounded in attitudes and assumptions that are, unfortunately, all too common. Throughout the world, women's interior social status makes them vulnerable to abuse and denies them the financial and legal means necessary to improve their situations. Over the past decade, women's groups around the world have succeeded in showing how prevalent this problem is and how much violence it is causing—a major accomplishment, given the fact that the issue was not even mentioned during the first UN Women's Conference in 1975 or in the 1979 UN Convention on All Forms of Discrimination Against Women. But as the situation in Egypt demonstrates, effective policy responses remain elusive.

Violence stalks women throughout their lives, "from cradle to grave"—in the judgment of the *Human Development Report 1995,* the UN's annual assessment of social and economic progress around the world. Gender-specific violence is almost a cultural constant, both emerging from and reinforcing the social relationships that give men power over women. This is most obvious in the implicit acceptance, across cultures, of domestic violence—of a man's prerogative to beat his wife. Large-scale surveys in 10 countries, including Colombia, Canada, and the United States, estimate that as many as one-third of women have been physically assaulted by an intimate male partner. More limited studies report that rates of physical abuse among some groups in Latin America, Asia, and Africa may reach 60 percent or more.

Belying the oft-cited clichés about "family values," studies have shown that the biggest threat to women is domestic violence. In 1992, the *Journal of the American Medical Association* published a study that found that women in the United States are more likely to be assaulted, injured, raped, or murdered by a current or former male partner than by all other types of attackers combined. In Canada, a 1987 study showed that 62 percent of the women murdered in that year were killed by an intimate male partner. And in India, the husband or in-laws of a newly married woman may think it justified to murder her if they consider her dowry inadequate, so that a more lucrative match can be made. One popular method is to pour kerosene on the woman and set her on fire—hence the term "bride burning." One in four deaths among women aged 16 to 24 in the urban areas of Maharashtra state (including Bombay) is attributed to "accidental burns." About 5,000 "dowry deaths" occur in India every year, according to government estimates, and some observers think the number is actually much higher. Subhadra Chaturvedi, one of India's leading attorneys, puts the death toll at a minimum of 12,000 a year.

The preference for sons, common in many cultures, can lead to violence against female infants—and even against female fetuses. In India, for example, a 1990 study of amniocentesis in a large Bombay hospital found that 95.5 percent of fetuses identified as female were aborted, compared with only a small percentage of male fetuses. (Amniocentesis involves the removal of a sample of amniotic fluid from the womb; this can be used to determine the baby's sex and the presence of certain inherited diseases.) Female infanticide is still practiced in rural areas of India; a 1992 study by Cornell University demographer Sabu George found that 58 percent of female infant deaths (19 of 33) within a 12-village region of Tamil Nadu state were due to infanticide. The problem is especially pronounced in China, where the imposition of the one-child-per-family rule has led to a precipitous decline in the number of girls: studies in 1987 and 1994 found a half-million fewer female infants in each of those years than would be expected, given the typical biological ratio of male to female births.

Women are also the primary victims of sexual crimes, which include sexual abuse, rape, and forced prostitution. Girls are the overwhelming target of child sexual assaults; in the United States, 78 percent of substantiated child sexual abuse cases involve girls. According to a 1994 World Bank study, *Violence Against Women: The Hidden Health Burden,* national surveys suggest that up to one-third of women in Norway, the United States, Canada, New Zealand, Barbados, and the Netherlands are sexually abused during childhood. Often very young children are the victims: a national study in the United States and studies in several Latin American cities indicate that 13 to 32 percent of abused girls are age 10 and under.

Rape haunts women throughout their lives, exposing them to unwanted pregnancy, disease, social stigma, and psychological trauma. In the United States, which has some of the best data on the problem, a 1993 review of rape studies suggests that between 14 and 20 percent of women will be victims of completed rapes during their lifetimes. In some cultures, a woman who has been raped is perceived as having violated the family honor, and she may be forced to marry her attacker or even killed. One study of female homicide in Alexandria, Egypt, for example, found that 47 percent of women murdered were killed by a family member following a rape.

In war, rape is often used as both a physical and psychological weapon. An investigation of recent conflicts in the former Yugoslavia, Peru, Kashmir, and Somalia by the international human rights group, Human Rights Watch, found that "rape of women civilians has been deployed as a tactical weapon to terrorize civilian communities or to achieve 'ethnic cleansing'." Studies suggest that tens of thousands of Muslim and Serbian women in Bosnia have been raped during the conflict there.

A growing number of women and girls, particularly in developing countries, are being forced into prostitution. Typically, girls from poor, remote villages are purchased outright from their families or lured away with promises of jobs or false marriage proposals. They are then taken to brothels, often in other countries, and forced to work there until they pay off their "debts"—task that becomes almost impossible as the brother owner charges them for clothes, food, medicine, and often even their own purchase price. According to Human Rights Watch, an estimated 20,000 to 30,000 Burmese girls and women currently work in brothels in Thailand; their ranks are now expanding by as many as 10,000 new recruits each year. Some 20,000 to 50,000 Nepalese girls are working in Indian brothels. As the fear of AIDS intensifies, customers are demanding ever younger prostitutes, and the age at which girls are being forced into prostitution is dropping; the average age of the Nepalese recruits, for example, declined from 14–16 years in the 1980s, to 10–14 years by 1994.

The Hidden Costs of Violence

Whether it takes the form of enforced prostitution, tape, genital mutilation, or domestic abuse, gender-based violence is doing enormous damage—both to the women who experience it, and to societies as a whole. Yet activists, health officials, and development agencies have only recently begun to quantify the problem's full costs. Currently, they are focusing on two particularly burdensome aspects of the violence: the health care costs, and the effects on economic productivity.

The most visible effects of violence are those associated with physical injuries that require medical care. FGM, for example, often causes severe health problems. Typically performed in unsterile environments by untrained midwives or barbers working without anesthesia, the procedure causes intense pain and can result in infection or death. Long-term effects include chronic pain, urine retention, abscesses, lack of sexual sensitivity, and depression. For the approximately 15 percent of mutilated women who have been infibulated, the health-related consequences are even worse. Not only must these women be cut and stitched repeatedly, on their wedding night and again with each childbirth, but sexual dysfunction and pain during intercourse are common. Infibulated women are also much more likely to have difficulties giving birth. Their labor often results, for instance, in vesico-vaginal fistulas—holes in the vaginal and rectal areas that cause continuous leakage of urine and feces. An estimated 1.5 to 2 million African women have fistulas, with some 50,000 to 100,000 new cases occurring annually. Infibulation also greatly increases the danger to the child during labor. A study of 33 infibulated women in delivery at Somalia's Benadir Hospital found that five of their babies died and 21 suffered oxygen deprivation.

Other forms of violence are taking a heavy toll as well. A 1994 national survey in Canada, for example, found that broken bones occurred in 12 percent of spousal assaults, and internal injuries and miscarriages in 10 percent. Long-term effects may be less obvious but they are often just as serious. In the United States, battered women are four to five times more likely than non-battered women to require psychiatric treatment and five times more likely to attempt suicide. And even these effects are just one part of a much broader legacy of misery. A large body of psychological literature has documented the erosion of self esteem, of social abilities, and of mental health in general, that often follows in the wake of violence. And the problem is compounded because violence tends to be cyclical: people who are abused tend to become abusers themselves. Whether it's through such direct abuse or indirectly, through the destruction of family life, violence against women tends to spill over into the next generation as violence against children.

Only a few studies have attempted to assign an actual dollar value to gender-based violence, but their findings suggest that the problem constitutes a substantial health care burden. In the United States, a 1991 study at a major health maintenance organization (a type of group medical practice) found that women who had been raped or beaten at any point in their lifetimes had medical costs two-and-a-half times higher during that year than women who had not been victimized. In the state of Pennsylvania, a health insurer study estimated that violence against women cost the health care system approximately $326.6 million in 1992. And in Canada, a 1995 study of violence against women, which examined not only medical costs, but also the value of community support services and lost work, put the annual cost to the country at Cdn $1.5 billion (US $1.1 billion).

One important consequence of violence is its effect on women's productivity. In its *World Development Report 1993,* the World Bank estimated that in advanced market economies, 19 percent of the total disease burden of women aged 15 to 44—nearly one out of every five healthy days of life lost—can be linked to domestic violence or rape. (Violence against women is just as pervasive in developing countries, but because the incidence of disease is higher in those regions, it represents only 5 percent of their total disease burden.) Similarly, a 1993 study in the United States showed a correlation between violence and lower earnings. After controlling for other factors that affect income, the study found that women who have been abused earn 3 to 20 percent less each year than women who have not been abused, with the discrepancy depending on the type of sexual abuse experienced and the number of perpetrators.

Violence can also prevent women from participating in public life—a form of oppression that can cripple Third World development projects. Fear may keep women at home; for example, health workers in India have identified fear of rape as an impediment to their outreach efforts in rural sites. The general problem was acknowledged plainly in a UN report published in 1992, *Battered Dreams: Violence Against Women as an Obstacle to Development:* "Where violence keeps a woman from participating in a development project, force is used to deprive her of earnings, or fear of sexual assault prevents her from taking a job or attending a public function, development does not occur." Development efforts aimed at reducing fertility levels may also be affected, since gender-based violence, or the threat of it, may limit women's use of contraception. According to the 1994 World Bank study, a woman's contraceptive use often depends in large part on her partner's approval.

A recurrent motive in much of this violence is an interest in preventing women from gaining autonomy outside the home. Husbands may physically prevent their wives from attending development meetings, or they may intimidate them into not seeking employment or accepting promotions at work. The World Bank study relates a chilling example of the way in which violence can be used to control women's behavior: "In a particularly gruesome example of male backlash, a female leader of the highly successful government sponsored Women's Development Programme in Rajasthan, India, was recently gang raped [in her home in front of her husband] by male community members because they disapproved of her organizing efforts against child marriage." The men succeeded in disrupting the project by instilling fear in the local organizers.

Women Break the Silence

"These women are holding back a silent scream so strong it could shake the earth." That is how Dr. Nahid Toubia, Executive Director of the U.S.-based anti-FGM organization RAINBO, described FGM victims when she testified at the 1993 Global Tribunal on Violations of Women's Human Rights. Yet her statement would apply just as well to the millions of women all over the world who have been victims of other forms of violence. Until recently, the problem of gender-based violence has remained largely invisible.

Because the stigma attached to many forms of violence makes them difficult to discuss openly, and because violence typically occurs inside the home, accurate information on the magnitude of the problem has been extremely scarce. Governments, by claiming jurisdiction only over human rights abuses perpetrated in the public sphere by agents of the state, have reinforced this invisibility. Even human rights work has traditionally confined itself to the public sphere and largely ignored many of the abuses to which women are most vulnerable.

But today, the victims of violence are beginning to find their voices. Women's groups have won a place for "private sphere" violence on human rights agendas, and they are achieving important changes in both national laws and international conventions. The first major reform came in June 1993, at the UN Second World Conference on Human Rights in Vienna. In a drive leading up to the conference, activists collected almost half a million signatures from 124 countries on a petition insisting that the conference address gender violence. The result: for the first time, violence against women was recognized as an abuse of women's human rights, and nine paragraphs on "The equal status and human rights of women" were incorporated into the Vienna Declaration and Programme of Action.

More recently, 18 members of the Organization of American States have ratified the Inter-American Convention on the Prevention, Punishment and Eradication of Violence Against Women. Many activists consider this convention, which went into effect on March 5, 1995, the strongest existing piece of international legislation in the field. And the Pan American Health Organization (PAHO) has become the first development agency to make a significant financial commitment to the issue. PAHO has received $4 million from Sweden, Norway, and the Netherlands, with the possibility of an additional $2.5 million from the Inter-American Development Bank, to conduct research on violence and establish support services for women in Latin America.

National governments are also drawing up legislation to combat various forms of gender violence. A growing number of countries, including South Africa, Israel, Argentina, the Bahamas, Australia, and the United States have all passed special domestic violence laws. Typically, these clarify the definition of domestic violence and strengthen protections available to the victims. In September 1994, India passed its "Pre-natal Diagnostic Techniques (Regulation and Prevention of Misuse) Act," which outlaws the use of prenatal testing for sex-selection. India is also developing a program to eradicate female infanticide. FGM is being banned in a growing number of countries, too. At least nine European countries now prohibit the practice, as does Australia. In the United States, a bill criminalizing FGM was passed by the Senate in May, but had yet to become law. More significant, perhaps, is the African legislation: FGM is now illegal in both Ghana and Kenya.

It is true, of course, that laws don't necessarily translate into real-life changes. But it is possible that the movement to stop FGM will yield the first solid success in the struggle to make human rights a reality for women. Over the past decade, the Inter-African Committee on Traditional Practices Affecting the Health of Women and Children, an NGO dedicated to abolishing FGM, has set up committees in 25 African countries. And in March 1995, Ghana used its anti-FGM statute to arrest the parents and circumciser of an eight-year-old girl who was rushed to the hospital with excessive bleeding. In Burkina Faso, some circumcising midwives have been convicted under more general legislation. These are modest steps, perhaps, but legal precedent can be a powerful tool for reform.

In the United States, an important precedent is currently being set by a 19-year-old woman from the nation of Togo, in west Africa. Fleeing an arranged marriage and the ritual FGM that would accompany it, Fauziya Kasinga arrived in the United States seeking asylum in December 1994. She has spent much of the time since then in prison, and her request for asylum, denied by a lower court, is at the time of writing under appeal. People are eligible for asylum in the United States if they are judged to have a reasonable fear of persecution due to their race, religion, nationality, political opinions, or membership in a social group. However, U.S. asylum law makes no explicit provision for gender-based violence. In 1993, Canada became the world's first country to make the threat of FGM grounds for granting refugee status.

Whichever way the decision on Kasinga's case goes, it will be adopted as a binding general precedent in U.S. immigration cases (barring the passage of federal legislation that reverses it). But even while her fate remains in doubt, Kasinga has already won an important moral victory. Her insistence on her right *not* to be mutilated—and on the moral obligation of others to shield her from violence if they can—has made the threat she faces a matter of conscience, of politics, and of policy. Given the accumulating evidence of how deeply gender-based violence infects our societies, in both the developing and the industrialized countries, we have little choice but to recognize it as the fundamental moral and economic challenge that it is.

Discussion Questions

1. What are some types of gender violence you are familiar with? Which kinds are the most costly to the victim? Why? What are the hidden costs of such violence to society?

2. Nelson describes the recent willingness of women to speak out against gender violence as a start toward a solution, but obviously that isn't enough. Do you think gender violence can be eliminated from a society? Why or why not? What changes would have to take place in U.S. society for gender violence to be eliminated? How likely is each of these changes to occur?

Chapter *11*

Politics and Economics

In a capitalist economic system dedicated to competition in order to maximize profits, it would seem logical that jobs would be given to those who could perform best. But what happens when men and women enter career fields that are dominated by the opposite sex? In this article, Williams reports on her research on that question, focusing primarily on men who enter four traditionally female occupations.

Williams addresses several questions. Do men experience hiring discrimination in non-traditional occupations? Are they blocked from some career "tracks" after being hired? Do they face discrimination in promotion? What kind of relationship do they have with their supervisors? What is the main source of negative images and treatment? You may already suspect the answers to some of these questions. (No, they say they aren't aware of any hiring discrimination.) Other findings may be a surprise. (The main negative reaction comes from outside their occupations.) Keep all of these questions in mind as you read the article, and see if the answers give you a general picture of men in nursing or elementary school teaching.

The Glass Escalator
Hidden Advantages for Men in the "Female" Professions*

CHRISTINE L. WILLIAMS
University of Texas at Austin

The sex segregation of the U.S. labor force is one of the most perplexing and tenacious problems in our society. Even though the proportion of men and women in the labor force is approaching parity (particularly for younger cohorts of workers) (U.S. Department of Labor 1991:18), men and women are still generally confined to predominantly single sex occupations. Forty percent of men or women would have to change major occupational categories to achieve equal representation of men and women in all jobs (Reskin and Roos 1990:6), but even this figure underestimates the true degree of sex segregation. It is extremely rare to find specific jobs where equal numbers of men and women are engaged in the same activities in the same industries (Bielby and Baron 1984).

Most studies of sex segregation in the work force have focused on women's experiences in male-dominated occupations. Both researchers and advocates for social change have focused on the barriers faced by women who try to integrate predominantly male fields. Few have looked at the "flip-side" of occupational sex segregation: the exclusion of men from predominantly female occupations (exceptions include Schreiber 1979; Williams 1989; Zimmer 1988). But the fact is that men are less likely to enter female sex-typed occupations than women are to enter male-dominated jobs (Jacobs 1989). Reskin and Roos, for example, were able to identify 33 occupations in which female representation increased by more than nine percentage points between 1970 and 1980, but only three occupations in which the proportion of men increased as radically (1990:20–21).

In this paper, I examine men's underrepresentation in four predominantly female occupations—nursing, librarianship, elementary school teaching, and social work. Throughout the twentieth century, these occupations have been identified with "women's work"—

Williams, Christine L. The Glass Escalator: Hidden Advantages for Men in the "Female" Professions. *Social Problems, 39,* 3, August 1992, 253–267. By permission of the University of California Press.

even though prior to the Civil War, men were more likely to be employed in these areas. These four occupations, often called the female "semi-professions" (Hodson and Sullivan 1990). today range from 5.5 percent male (in nursing) to 32 percent male (in social work). (See Table 11.1.) These percentages have not changed substantially in decades. In fact, as Table 11.1 indicates, two of these professions—librarianship and social work—have experiences declines in the proportions of men since 1975. Nursing is the only one of the four experiencing noticeable changes in sex composition, with the proportion of men increasing 80 percent between 1975 and 1990. Even so, men continue to be a tiny minority of all nurses.

Although there are many possible reasons for the continuing preponderance of women in these fields, the focus of this paper is discrimination. Researchers examining the integration of women into "male fields" have identified discrimination as a major barrier to women (Jacobs 1989; Reskin 1988; Reskin and Hartmann 1996). This discrimination has taken the form of laws or institutionalized rules prohibiting the hiring or promotion of women into certain job specialties. Discrimination can also be "informal," as when women encounter sexual harassment, sabotage, or other forms of hostility from their male co-workers resulting in a poisoned work environment (Reskin and Hartmann 1986). Women in nontraditional occupations also report feeling stigmatized by clients when their work puts them in contact with the public. In particular, women in engineering and blue-collar occupations encounter gender-based stereotypes about their competence which undermine their work performance (Epstein 1988; Martin 1980). Each of these forms of discrimination— legal, informal, and cultural—contributes to women's underrepresentation in predominantly male occupations.

The assumption in much of this literature is that any member of a token group in a work setting will probably experience similar discriminatory treatment. Kanter (1977), who is best known for articulating this perspective in her theory of tokenism, argues that when any group represents less than 15 percent of an organization, its members will be subject to predictable forms of discrimination. Likewise, Jacobs argues that "in some ways, men in female-dominated occupations experience the same difficulties that women in male-dominated occupations face" (1989:167), and Reskin contends that any dominant group in an occupation will use their power to maintain a privileged position (1988:62).

TABLE 11.1   Percent Male in Selected Occupations, Selected Years

Profession	1990	1980	1975
Nurses	5.5	3.5	3.0
Elementary teachers	14.8	16.3	14.6
Librarians	16.7	14.8	18.9
Social workers	31.8	35.0	39.2

Source: U.S. Department of Labor. Bureau of Labor Statistics. *Employment and Earnings* 38:1 (January 1991), Table 22 (Employed civilians by detailed occupation), 185; 28:1 (January 1981), Table 23 (Employed persons by detailed occupation), 180; 22:7 (January 1976), Table 2 (Employed persons by detailed occupation), 11.

However, the few studies that have considered men's experience in gender atypical occupations suggest that men may not face discrimination or prejudice when they integrate predominantly female occupations. Zimmer (1988) and Martin (1988) both contend that the effects of sexism can outweigh the effects of tokenism when men enter nontraditional occupations. This study is the first to systematically explore this question using data from four occupations. I examine the barriers to men's entry into these professions; the support men receive from their supervisors, colleagues and clients; and the reactions they encounter from the public (those outside their professions).

Methods

I conducted in-depth interviews with 76 men and 23 women in four occupations from 1985–1991. Interviews were conducted in four metropolitan areas: San Francisco/Oakland, California; Austin, Texas; Boston, Massachusetts; and Phoenix, Arizona. These four areas were selected because they show considerable variation in the proportions of men in the four professions. For example, Austin has one of the highest percentages of men in nursing (7.7 percent), whereas Phoenix's percentage is one of the lowest (2.7 percent) (U.S. Bureau of the Census 1980). The sample was generated using "snowballing" techniques. Women were included in the sample to gauge their feelings and responses to men who enter "their" professions.

Like the people employed in these professions generally, those in my sample were predominantly white (90 percent).[1] Their ages ranged from 20 to 66 and the average age was 38. The interview questionnaire consisted of several open-ended questions on four broad topics: motivation to enter the profession; experiences in training; career progression; and general views about men's status and prospects within these occupations. I conducted all the interviews, which generally lasted between one and two hours. Interviews took place in restaurants, my home or office, or the respondent's home or office. Interviews were tape-recorded and transcribed for the analysis.

Data analysis followed the coding techniques described by Strauss (1987). Each transcript was read several times and analyzed into emergent conceptual categories. Likewise, Strauss' principle of theoretical sampling was used. Individual respondents were purposively selected to capture the array of men's experiences in these occupations. Thus, I interviewed practitioners in every specialty, oversampling those employed in the most gender atypical areas (e.g., male kindergarten teachers). I also selected respondents from throughout their occupational hierarchies—from students to administrators to retirees. Although the data do not permit within group comparisons, I am reasonably certain that the sample does capture a wide range of experiences common to men in these female-dominated professions. However, like all findings based on qualitative data, it is

[1]According to the U.S. Census, black men and women comprise 7 percent of all nurses and librarians, 11 percent of all elementary school teachers, and 19 percent of all social workers (calculated from U.S. Census 1980: Table 278, 1-197). The proportion of blacks in social work may be exaggerated by these statistics. The occupational definition of "social worker" used by the Census Bureau includes welfare workers and pardon and parole officers, who are not considered "professional" social workers by the National Association of Social Workers. A study of degreed professionals found that 89 percent of practitioners were white (Hardcastle 1997).

uncertain whether the findings generalize to the larger population of men in nontraditional occupations.

In this paper, I review individuals' responses to questions about discrimination in hiring practices, on-the-job rapport with supervisors and co-workers, and prejudice from clients and others outside their profession.

Discrimination in Hiring

Contrary to the experience of many women in the male-dominated professions, many of the men and women I spoke to indicated that there is a preference for hiring men in these four occupations. A Texas librarian at a junior high school said that his school district "would hire a male over a female."

> *I: Why do you think that is?*
> *R: Because there are so few, and the . . . ones that they do have, the library directors seem to really . . . think they're doing great jobs. I don't know, maybe they just feel they're being progressive or something, [but] I have had a real sense that they really appreciate having a male, particularly at the junior high. . . . As I said, when seven of us lost our jobs from the high schools and were redistributed, there were only four positions at junior high, and I got one of them. Three of the librarians, some who had been here longer than I had with the school district, were put down in elementary school as librarians. And I definitely think that be-ing male made a difference in my being moved to the junior high rather than an elementary school.*

Many of the men perceived their token status as males in predominantly female occupations as an *advantage* in hiring and promotions. I asked an Arizona teacher whether his specialty (elementary special education) was an unusual area for men compared to other areas within education. He said,

> *Much more so. I am extremely marketable in special education. That's not why I got into the field. But I am extremely marketable because I am a man.*

In several cases, the more female-dominated the specialty, the greater the apparent prefer-ence for men. For example, when asked if he encountered any problem getting a job in pediatrics, a Massachusetts nurse said,

> *No, no, none. . . . I've heard this from managers and supervisory-type people with men in pediatrics: "It's nice to have a man because it's such a female-dominated profession."*

However, there were some exceptions to this preference for men in the most female-dominated specialties. In some cases, formal policies actually barred men from certain jobs. This was the case in some rural Texas school districts, which refused to hire men in the youngest grades (K–3). Some nurses also reported being excluded from positions in obstetrics and gynecology wards, a policy encountered more frequently in private Catholic hospitals.

But often the pressures keeping men out of certain specialties were more subtle than this. Some men described being "tracked" into practice areas within their professions which were considered more legitimate for men. For example, one Texas man described how he was pushed into administration and planning in social work, even though "I'm not interested in writing policy; I'm much more interested in research and clinical stuff." A nurse who is interested in pursuing graduate study in family and child health in Boston said he was dissuaded from entering the program specialty in favor of a concentration in "adult nursing." A kindergarten teacher described the difficulty of finding a job in his specialty after graduation: "I was recruited immediately to start getting into a track to become an administrator. And it was men who recruited me. It was men that ran the system at that time, especially in Los Angeles."

This tracking may bar men from the most female-identified specialties within these professions. But men are effectively being "kicked upstairs' in the process. Those specialties considered more legitimate practice areas for men also tend to be the most prestigious, better paying ones. A distinguished kindergarten teacher, who had been voted city-wide "Teacher of the Year," told me that even though people were pleased to see him in the classroom, "there's been some encouragement to think about administration, and there's been some encouragement to think about teaching at the University level or something like that, or supervisory-type position." That is, despite his aptitude and interest in staying in the classroom, he felt pushed in the direction of administration.

The effect of this "tracking" is the opposite of that experienced by women in male-dominated occupations. Researchers have reported that many women encounter a "glass ceiling" in their efforts to scale organizational and professional hierarchies. That is, they are constrained by invisible barriers to promotion in their careers, caused mainly by the sexist attitudes of men in the highest positions (Freeman 1990).[2] In contrast to the "glass ceiling," many of the men I interviewed seem to encounter a "glass escalator." Often, despite their intentions, they face invisible pressures to move up in their professions. As if on a moving escalator, they must work to stay in place.

A public librarian specializing in children's collections (a heavily female-dominated concentration) described an encounter with this "escalator" in his very first job out of library school. In his first six-months evaluation, his supervisors commended him for his good work in storytelling and related activities, but they criticized him for "not shooting high enough."

> *Seriously. That's literally what they were telling me. They assumed that because I was a male—and they told me this—and that I was being hired right out of graduate school, that somehow I wasn't doing the kind of management-oriented work*

---

[2]In April 1991, the Labor Department created a "Glass Ceiling Commission" to "conduct a thorough study of the underrepresentation of women and minorities in executive, management, and senior decision-making positions in business" (U.S. House of Representatives 1991:20).

that they thought I should be doing. And as a result, really they had a lot of bad marks, as it were, against me on my evaluation. And I said I couldn't believe this!

Throughout his ten-year career, he has had to struggle to remain in children's collections.

The glass escalator does not operate at all levels. In particular, men in academia reported some gender-based discrimination in the highest positions due to their universities' commitment to affirmative action. Two nursing professors reported that they felt their own chances of promotion to deanships were nil because their universities viewed the position of nursing dean as a guaranteed female appointment in an otherwise heavily male-dominated administration. One California social work professor reported his university canceled its search for a dean because no minority male or female candidates had been placed on their short list. It was rumored that other schools on campus were permitted to go forward with their searches—even though they also failed to put forward names of minority candidates—because the higher administration perceived it to be "easier" to fulfill affirmative action goals in the social work school. The interviews provide greater evidence of the "glass escalator" at work in the lower levels of these professions.

Of course, men's motivations also play a role in their advancement to higher professional positions. I do not mean to suggest that the men I talked to all resented the informal tracking they experienced. For many men, leaving the most female-identified areas of their professions helped them resolve internal conflicts involving their masculinity. One man left his job as a school social worker to work in a methadone drug treatment program not because he was encouraged to leave by his colleagues, but because "I think there was some macho shit there, to tell you the truth, because I remember feeling a little uncomfortable there . . . ; it didn't feel right to me." Another social worker, employed in the mental health services department of a large urban area in California, reflected on his move into administration:

The more I think about it, through our discussion, I'm sure that's a large part of why I wound up in administration. It's okay for a man to do the administration. In fact, I don't know if I fully answered a question that you asked a little while ago about how did being male contribute to my advancing in the field. I was saying it wasn't because I got any special favoritism as a man, but . . . I think . . . because I'm a man, I felt a need to get into this kind of position. I may have worked harder toward it, may have competed harder for it, than most women would do, even women who think about doing administrative work.

Elsewhere I have speculated on the origins of men's tendency to define masculinity through single-sex work environments (Williams 1989). Clearly, personal ambition does play a role in accounting for men's movement into more "male-defined" arenas within these professions. But these occupations also structure opportunities for males independent of their individual desires or motives.

The interviews suggest that men's underrepresentation in these professions cannot be attributed to discrimination in hiring or promotions. Many of the men indicated that they received preferential treatment because they were men. Although men mentioned gender discrimination in the hiring process, for the most part they were channelled into more "masculine" specialties within these professions, which ironically meant being "tracked" into better paying and more prestigious specialties.

Supervisors and Colleagues: The Working Environment

Researchers claim that subtle forms of work place discrimination push women out of male-dominated occupations (Jacobs 1989; Reskin and Hartmann 1986). In particular, women report feeling excluded from informal leadership and decision-making networks, and they sense hostility from their male co-workers, which makes them feel uncomfortable and unwanted (Carothers and Crull 1984). Respondents in this study were asked about their relationships with supervisors and female colleagues to ascertain whether men also experienced "poisoned" work environments when entering gender atypical occupations.

A major difference in the experience of men and women in nontraditional occupations is that men in these situations are far more likely to be supervised by a member of their own sex. In each of the four professions I studied, men are overrepresented in administrative and managerial capacities, or, as is the case of nursing, their positions in the organizational hierarchy are governed by men (Grimm and Stern 1974; Phenix 1987; Schmuck 1987; Williams 1989; York, Henley and Gamble 1987). Thus, unlike women who enter "male fields," the men in these professions often work under the direct supervision of other men.

Many of the men interviewed reported that they had good rapport with their male supervisors. Even in professional school, some men reported extremely close relationships with their male professors. For example, a Texas librarian described an unusually intimate association with two male professors in graduate school:

> *I can remember a lot of times in the classroom there would be discussions about a particular topic or issue, and the conversation would spill over into their office hours, after the class was over. And even though there were . . . a couple of the other women that had been in on the discussion, they weren't there. And I don't know if that was preferential or not . . . It certainly carried over into personal life as well. Not just at the school and that sort of thing. I mean, we would get together for dinner . . .*

These professors explicitly encouraged him because he was male:

> *I: Did they ever offer you explicit words of encouragement about being in the profession by virtue of the fact that you were male? . . .*
> *R: Definitely. On several occasions. Yeah. Both of these guys, for sure, including the Dean who was male also. And it's an interesting point that you bring up because it was, oftentimes, kind of in a sign, you know. It wasn't in the classroom, and it wasn't in front of the group, or if we were in the student lounge or something like that. It was . . . if it was just myself or maybe another one of the guys, you know, and just talking in the office. It's like . . . you know, kind of an opening-up and saying, "You know, you are really lucky that you're in the profession because you'll really go to the top real quick, and you'll be able to make real definite*

improvements and changes. And you'll have a real influence," and all this sort of thing. I mean, really, I can remember several times.

Other men reported similar closeness with their professors. A Texas psychotherapist recalled his relationships with his male professors in social work school:

I made it a point to make a golfing buddy with one of the guys that was in administration. He and I played golf a lot. He was the guy who kind of ran the research training, the research part of the master's program. Then there was a sociologist who ran the other part of the research program. He and I developed a good friendship.

This close mentoring by male professors contrasts with the reported experience of women in nontraditional occupations. Others have noted a lack of solidarity among women in non-traditional occupations. Writing about military academics, for example, Yoder describes the failure of token women to mentor succeeding generations of female cadets. She argues that women attempt to play down their gender difference from men because it is the source of scorn and derision.

Because women felt unaccepted by their male colleagues, one of the last things they wanted to do was to emphasize their gender. Some women thought that, if they kept company with other women, this would highlight their gender and would further isolate them from male cadets. These women desperately wanted to be accepted as cadets, not as women *cadets. Therefore, they did everything from not wearing skirts as an option with their uniforms to avoiding being a part of a group of women. (Yoder 1989:532)*

Men in nontraditional occupations face a different scenario—their gender is construed as a *positive* difference. Therefore, they have an incentive to bond together and emphasize their distinctiveness from the female majority.

Close, personal ties with male supervisors were also described by men once they were established in their professional careers. It was not uncommon in education, for example, for the male principal to informally socialize with the male staff, as a Texas special education teacher describes:

Occasionally I've had a principal who would regard me as "the other man on the campus" and "it's us against them," you know? I mean, nothing really that extreme, except that some male principals feel like there's nobody there to talk to except the other man. So I've been in that position.

These personal ties can have important consequences for men's careers. For example, one California nurse, whose performance was judged marginal by his nursing supervisors, was transferred to the emergency room staff (a prestigious promotion) due to his personal friendship with the physician in charge. A Massachusetts teacher acknowledged that his principal's personal interest in him landed him his current job.

I: You had mentioned that your principal had sort of spotted you at your previous job and had wanted to bring you here [to this school]. Do you think that has anything to do with the fact that you're a man, aside from your skills as a teacher?
R: Yes, I would say in that particular case, that was part of it. . . . We have certain things in common, certain interests that really lined up.
I: Vis-à-vis teaching?
R: Well, more extraneous things—running specifically, and music. And we just seemed to get along real well right off the bat. It is just kind of a guy thing; we just liked each other . . .

Interviewees did not report many instances of male supervisors discriminating against them, or refusing to accept them because they were male. Indeed, these men were much more likely to report that their male bosses discriminated against the *females* in their professions. When asked if he thought physicians treated male and female nurses differently, a Texas nurse said:

I think yeah, some of them do. I think the women seem like they have a lot more trouble with the physicians treating them in a derogatory manner. Or, if not derogatory, then in a very paternalistic way than the men [are treated]. Usually if a physician is mad at a male nurse, he just kind of yells at him. Kind of like an employee. And if they're mad at a female nurse, rather than treat them on an equal basis, in terms of just letting their anger out at them as an employee, they're more paternalistic or there's some sexual harassment component to it.

A Texas teacher perceived a similar situation where he worked:

I've never felt unjustly treated by a principal because I'm a male. The principals that I've seen that I felt are doing things that are kind of arbitrary or not well thought out are doing it to everybody. In fact, they're probably doing it to the females worse than they are to me.

Openly gay men may encounter less favorable treatment at the hands of their supervisors. For example, a nurse in Texas stated that one of the physicians he worked with preferred to staff the operating room with male nurses exclusively—as long as they weren't gay. Stigma associated with homosexuality leads some men to enhance, or even exaggerate their "masculine" qualities, and may be another factor pushing men into more "acceptable" specialties for men.

Not all the men who work in these occupations are supervised by men. Many of the men interviewed who had female bosses also reported high levels of acceptance—although levels of intimacy with women seemed lower than with other men. In some cases, however, men reported feeling shut-out from decision making when the higher administration was constituted entirely by women. I asked an Arizona librarian whether men in the library profession were discriminated against in hiring because of their sex:

Professionally speaking, people go to considerable lengths to keep that kind of thing out of their [hiring] deliberations. Personally, is another matter. It's pretty common around here to talk about the "old girl network." This is one of the few libraries that I've had any intimate knowledge of which is actually controlled by women. . . . Most of the department heads and upper level administrators are women. And there's an "old girl network" that works just like the "old boy network," except that the important conferences take place in the women's room rather than on the golf course. But the political mechanism is the same, the exclusion of the other sex from decision making is the same. The reasons are the same. It's somewhat discouraging . . .

Although I did not interview many supervisors, I did include 23 women in my sample to ascertain their perspectives about the presence of men in their professions. All of the women I interviewed claimed to be supportive of their male colleagues, but some conveyed ambivalence. For example, a social work professor said she would like to see more men enter the social work profession, particularly in the clinical specialty (where they are underrepresented). Indeed, she favored affirmative action hiring guidelines for men in the profession. Yet, she resented the fact that her department hired "another white male" during a recent search. I questioned her about this ambivalence:

I: I find it very interesting that, on the one hand you sort of perceive this preference and perhaps even sexism with regard to how men are evaluated and how they achieve higher positions within the profession, yet, on the other hand, you would be encouraging of more men to enter the field. Is that contradictory to you, or . . . ?
R: Yeah, it's contradictory.

It appears that women are generally eager to see men enter "their" occupations. Indeed, several men noted that their female colleagues had facilitated their careers in various ways (including mentorship in college). However, at the same time, women often resent the apparent ease with which men advance within these professions, sensing that men at the higher levels receive preferential treatment which closes off advancement opportunities for women.

But this ambivalence does not seem to translate into the "poisoned" work environment described by many women who work in male-dominated occupations. Among the male interviewees, there were no accounts of sexual harassment. However, women do treat their male colleagues differently on occasion. It is not uncommon in nursing, for example, for men to be called upon to help catheterize male patients, or to lift especially heavy patients. Some librarians also said that women asked them to lift and move heavy boxes of books because they were men. Teachers sometimes confront differential treatment as well, as described by this Texas teacher:

As a man, you're teaching with all women, and that can be hard sometimes. Just because of the stereotypes, you know. I'm real into computers . . . , and all the time people are calling me to fix their computer. Or if somebody gets a flat tire, they come and get me. I mean, there are just a lot of stereotypes. Not that I mind doing any of those things, but it's . . . you know, it just kind of bugs me that it is a stereotype, "A man should do that." Or if their kids have a lot of discipline problems, that kiddo's in your room. Or if there are kids that don't have a father in their home, that kid's in your room. Hell, nowadays that'd be half the school in my room (laughs). But you know, all the time I hear from the principal or from other teachers, Well, this child really needs a man . . . a male role model" (laughs). So there are a lot of stereotypes that . . . men kind of get stuck with.

This special treatment bothered some respondents. Getting assigned all the "discipline problems" can make for difficult working conditions, for example. But many men claimed this differential treatment did not cause distress. In fact, several said they liked being appreciated for the special traits and abilities (such as strength) they could contribute to their professions.

Furthermore, women's special treatment sometimes enhanced—rather than poisoned—the men's work environments. One Texas librarian said he felt "more comfortable working with women than men" because "I think it has something to do with control. Maybe it's that women will let me take control more than men will." Several men reported that their female colleagues often cast them into leadership roles. Although not all savored this distinction, it did enhance their authority and control in the work place. In subtle (and not-too-subtle) ways, then, differential treatment contributes to the "glass escalator" men experience in nontraditional professions.

Even outside work, most of the men interviewed said they felt fully accepted by their female colleagues. They were usually included in informal socializing occasions with the women—even though this frequently meant attending baby showers or Tupperware parties. Many said that they declined offers to attend these events because they were not interested in "women's things," although several others claimed to attend everything. The minority men I interviewed seemed to feel the least comfortable in these informal contexts. One social worker in Arizona was asked about socializing with his female colleagues:

I: So in general, for example, if all the employees were going to get together to have a party, or celebrate a bridal shower or whatever, would you be invited along with the rest of the group?
R: They would invite me. I would say, somewhat reluctantly. Being a black male, working with all white females, it did cause some outside problems. So I didn't go to a lot of functions with them . . .
I: You felt that there was some tension there on the level of your acceptance . . . ?
R: Yeah. It was OK working, but on the outside, personally, there was some tension there. It never came out, that they said, "Because of who you are we can't invite you" (laughs), and I wouldn't have done anything anyway. I would have probably respected them more for saying what was on their minds. But I never felt completely in with the group.

Some single men also said they felt uncomfortable socializing with married female colleagues because it gave the "wrong impression." But in general, the men said that they felt very comfortable around their colleagues and described their work places as very congenial for men. It appears unlikely, therefore, that men's underrepresentation in these professions is due to hostility towards men on the part of supervisors or women workers.

Discrimination from "Outsiders"

The most compelling evidence of discrimination against men in these professions is related to their dealings with the public. Men often encounter negative stereotypes when they come into contact with clients or "outsiders"—people they meet outside of work. For instance, it is popularly assumed that male nurses are gay. Librarians encounter images of themselves as "wimpy" and asexual. Male social workers describe being typecast as "feminine" and "passive." Elementary school teachers are often confronted by suspicions that they are pedophiles. One kindergarten teacher described an experience that occurred early in his career which was related to him years afterwards by his principal:

> *He indicated to me that parents had come to him and indicated to him that they had a problem with the fact that I was a male. . . . I recall almost exactly what he said. There were three specific concerns that the parents had: One parent said, "How can he love my child; he's a man." The second thing that I recall, he said the parent said, "He has a beard," And the third thing was, "Aren't you concerned about homosexuality?"*

Such suspicions often cause men in all four professions to alter their work behavior to guard against sexual abuse charges, particularly in those specialties requiring intimate contact with women and children.

Men are very distressed by these negative stereotypes, which tend to undermine their self-esteem and to cause them to second-guess their motivations for entering these fields. A California teacher said,

> *If I tell men that I don't know, that I'm meeting for the first time, that that's what I do. . . . sometimes there's a look on their faces that, you know, "Oh, couldn't get a real job?"*

When asked if his wife, who is also an elementary school teacher, encounters the same kind of prejudice, he said,

> *No, it's accepted because she's a woman. . . .I think people would see that as a . . . step up, you know. "Oh, you're not a housewife, you've got a career. That's great . . . that you're out there working. And you have a daughter, but you're still out there working. You decided not to stay home, and you went out there and got a job." Whereas for me, it's more like I'm supposed to be out working anyway, even though I'd rather be home with [my daughter].*

Unlike women who enter traditionally male professions, men's movement into these jobs is perceived by the "outside world" as a step down in status. This particular form of discrimination may be most significant in explaining why men are underrepresented in these professions. Men who otherwise might show interest in and aptitude for such careers are probably discouraged from pursuing them because of the negative popular stereotypes associated with the men who work in them. This is a crucial difference from the experience of women in nontraditional professions: "My daughter, the physician," resonates far more favorably in most peoples' ears than "My son, the nurse."

Many of the men in my sample identified the stigma of working in a female-identified occupation as the major barrier to more men entering their professions. However, for the most part, they claimed that these negative stereotypes were not a factor in their own decisions to join these occupations. Most respondents didn't consider entering these fields until well into adulthood, after working in some related occupation. Several social workers and librarians even claimed they were not aware that men were a minority in their chosen professions. Either they had no well-defined image or stereotype, or their contacts and mentors were predominantly men. For example, prior to entering library school, many librarians held part-time jobs in university libraries, where there are proportionally more men than in the profession generally. Nurses and elementary school teachers were more aware that mostly women worked in these jobs, and this was often a matter of some concern to them. However, their choices were ultimately legitimized by mentors, or by encouraging friends or family members who implicitly reassured them that entering these occupations would not typecast them as feminine. In some cases, men were told by recruiters there were special advancement opportunities for men in these fields, and they entered them expecting rapid promotion to administrative positions.

> *I: Did it ever concern you when you were making the decision to enter nursing school, the fact that it is a female-dominated profession?*
> *R: Not really. I never saw myself working on the floor. I saw myself pretty much going into administration, just getting the background and then getting a job someplace as a supervisor, and then working, getting up into administration.*

Because of the unique circumstances of their recruitment, many of the respondents did not view their occupational choices as inconsistent with a male gender role, and they generally avoided the negative stereotypes directed against men in these fields.

Indeed, many of the men I interviewed claimed that they did not encounter negative professional stereotypes until they had worked in these fields for several years. Popular prejudices can be damaging to self-esteem and probably push some men out of these professions altogether. Yet, ironically, they sometimes contribute to the "glass escalator" effect I have been describing. Men seem to encounter the most vituperative criticism from the public when they are in the most female-identified specialties. Public concerns sometimes result in their being shunted into more "legitimate" positions for men. A librarian formerly in charge of a branch library's children's collection, who now works in the reference department of the city's main library, describes his experience:

> *R: Some of the people (who frequented the branch library] complained that they didn't want to have a man doing the storytelling scenario. And I got transferred*

> *here to the central library in an equivalent job . . . I thought that I did a good job.*
> *And I had been told by my supervisor that I was doing a good job.*
> *I: Have you ever considered filing some sort of lawsuit to get that other job back?*
> *R: Well, actually, the job I've gotten now . . . well, it's a reference librarian; it's*
> *what I wanted in the first place. I've got a whole lot more authority here. I'm also*
> *in charge of the circulation desk. And I've recently been promoted because of my*
> *new stature, so . . . no, I'm not considering trying to get that other job back.*

The negative stereotypes about men who do "women's work" can push men out of specific jobs. However, to the extent that they channel men into more "legitimate" practice areas, their effects can actually be positive. Instead of being a source of discrimination, these prejudices can add to the "glass escalator effect" by pressuring men to move *out* of the most female-identified areas, and *up* to those regarded more legitimate and prestigious for men.

Conclusion: Discrimination against Men

Both men and women who work in nontraditional occupations encounter discrimination, but the forms and consequences of this discrimination are very different. The interviews suggest that unlike "nontraditional" women workers, most of the discrimination and prejudice facing men in the "female professions" emanates from outside those professions. The men and women interviewed for the most part believed that men are given fair—if not preferential—treatment in hiring and promotion decisions, are accepted by supervisors and colleagues, and are well-integrated into the work place subculture. Indeed, subtle mechanisms seem to enhance men's position in these professions—a phenomenon I refer to as the "glass escalator effect."

The data lend strong support for Zimmer's (1988) critique of "gender neutral theory" (such as Kanter's [1977] theory of tokenism) in the study of occupational segregation. Zimmer argues that women's occupational inequality is more a consequence of sexist beliefs and practices embedded in the labor force than the effect of numerical underrepresentation per se. This study suggests that token status itself does not diminish men's occupational success. Men take their gender privilege with them when they enter predominantly female occupations; this translates into an advantage in spite of their numerical rarity.

This study indicates that the experience of tokenism is very different for men and women. Future research should examine how the experience of tokenism varies for members of different races and classes as well. For example, it is likely that informal work place mechanisms similar to the ones identified here promote the careers of token whites in predominantly black occupations. The crucial factor is the social status of the token's group—not their numerical rarity—that determines whether the token encounters a "glass ceiling" or a "glass escalator."

However, this study also found that many men encounter negative stereotypes from persons not directly involved in their professions. Men who enter these professions are often considered "failures," or sexual deviants. These stereotypes may be a major impediment to men who otherwise might consider careers in these occupations. Indeed, they are likely to be important factors whenever a member of a relatively high status group crosses over into a lower status occupation. However, to the extent that these stereotypes contribute to the "glass escalator effect" by channeling men into more "legitimate" (and higher paying) occupations, they are not discriminatory.

Women entering traditionally "male" professions also face negative stereotypes suggesting they are not "real women" (Epstein 1981; Lorber 1984; Spencer and Podmore 1987). However, these stereotypes do not seem to deter women to the same degree that they deter men from pursuing nontraditional professions. There is ample historical evidence that women flock to male-identified occupations once opportunities are available (Cohn 1985; Epstein 1988). Not so with men. Examples of occupations changing from predominantly female to predominantly male are very rare in our history. The few existing cases—such as medicine—suggest that redefinition of the occupations as appropriately "masculine" is necessary before men will consider joining them (Ehrenreich and English 1978).

Because different mechanisms maintain segregation in male- and female-dominated occupations, different approaches are needed to promote their integration. Policies intended to alter the sex composition of male-dominated occupations—such as affirmative action— make little sense when applied to the "female professions." For men, the major barriers to integration have little to do with their treatment once they decide to enter these fields. Rather, we need to address the social and cultural sanctions applied to men who do "women's work" which keep men from even considering these occupations.

One area where these cultural barriers are clearly evident is in the media's representation of men's occupations. Women working in traditionally male professions have achieved an unprecedented acceptance on popular television shows. Women are portrayed as doctors ("St. Elsewhere"), lawyers ("The Cosby Show," "L.A. Law"), architects ("Family Ties"), and police officers ("Cagney and Lacey"). But where are the male nurses, teachers and secretaries? Television rarely portrays men in nontraditional work roles, and when it does, that anomaly is made the central focus—and joke—of the program. A comedy series (1991–92) about a male elementary school teacher ("Drexell's Class") stars a lead character who *hates children!* Yet even this negative portrayal is exceptional. When a prime time hospital drama series ("St. Elsewhere") depicted a male orderly striving for upward mobility, the show's writers made him a "physician's assistant," not a nurse or nurse practitioner—the much more likely "real life" possibilities.

Presenting positive images of men in nontraditional careers can produce limited effects. A few social workers, for example, were first inspired to pursue their careers by George C. Scott, who played a social worker in the television drama series, "Eastside/Westside." But as a policy strategy to break down occupational segregation, changing media images of men is no panacea. The stereotypes that differentiate masculinity and femininity, and degrade that which is defined as feminine, are deeply entrenched in culture, social structure, and personality (Williams 1989). Nothing short of a revolution in cultural definitions of masculinity will effect the broad scale social transformation needed to achieve the complete occupational integration of men and women.

Of course, there are additional factors besides societal prejudice contributing to men's underrepresentation in female-dominated professions. Most notably, those men I interviewed mentioned as a deterrent the fact that these professions are all underpaid relative to comparable "male" occupations, and several suggested that instituting a "comparable worth" policy might attract more men. However, I am not convinced that improved salaries will substantially alter the sex composition of these professions unless the cultural stigma faced by men in these occupations diminishes. Occupational sex segregation is remarkably resilient, even in the face of devastating economic hardship. During the Great Depression of the 1930s, for example, "women's jobs" failed to attract sizable numbers of men (Blum 1991:154). In her study of American Telephone and Telegraph (AT&T) workers, Epstein (1989) found that some men would rather suffer unemployment than accept relatively high paying "women's jobs" because of the damage to their identities this would cause. She quotes one unemployed man who refused to apply for a female-identified telephone operator job:

> *I think if they offered me $1000 a week tax free. I wouldn't take that job. When I . . . see those guys sitting in there [in the telephone operating room], I wonder what's wrong with them. Are they pansies or what? (Epstein 1989: 577)*

This is not to say that raising salaries would not affect the sex composition of these jobs. Rather, I am suggesting that wages are not the only—or perhaps even the major—impediment to men's entry into these jobs. Further research is needed to explore the ideological significance of the "woman's wage" for maintaining occupational stratification.[3]

At any rate, integrating men and women in the labor force requires more than dismantling barriers to women in male-dominated fields. Sex segregation is a two-way street. We must also confront and dismantle the barriers men face in predominantly female occupations. Men's experiences in these nontraditional occupations reveal just how culturally embedded the barriers are, and how far we have to travel before men and women attain true occupational and economic equality.

References

Bielby, William T., and James N. Baron. 1984. "A women's place is with other women: Sex segregation within organizations." In Sex Segregation in the Workplace: Trends, explanations, remedies, ed. Barbara Reskin, 27–55. Washington, D.C.: National Academy Press.

Blum, Linda M. 1991. Between Feminism and Labor: The Significance of the Comparable Worth Movement. Berkeley and Los Angeles: University of California Press.

Carothers, Suzanne C., and Peggy Crull. 1984. "Contrasting sexual harassment in female-dominated and male-dominated occupations." In My Troubles are Going to have Trouble with Me: Everyday Trials and Triumphs of Women Workers, ed. Karen B. Sacks and Dorothy Remy,

[3]Alice Kessler-Harris argues that the lower pay of traditionally female occupations is symbolic of a patriarchal order that assumes female dependence on a male breadwinner. She writes that pay equity is fundamentally threatening to the "male worker's sense of self, pride, and masculinity" because it upsets his individual standing in the hierarchical ordering of the sexes (1990:125). Thus, men's reluctance to enter these occupations may have less to do with the actual dollar amount recorded in their paychecks, and more to do with the damage that earning "a woman's wage" would wreak on their self-esteem in a society that privileges men. This conclusion is supported by the interview data.

220–227. New Brunswick, N.J.: Rutgers University Press.

Cohn, Samuel. 1985. The Process of Occupational Sex-Typing. Philadelphia: Temple University Press.

Ehrenreich, Barbara, and Deirdre English. 1978. For Her Own Good: 100 Years of Expert Advice to Women. Garden City, N.Y.: Anchor Press.

Epstein, Cynthia Fuchs. 1981. Women in Law. New York: Basic Books.

———. 1988. Deceptive Distinctions: Sex, Gender and the Social Order. New Haven, Conn.: Yale University Press.

———. 1989. "Workplace boundaries: Conceptions and creations." Social Research 56:571–590.

Freeman, Sue J.M. 1990. Managing Lives: Corporate Women and Social Change. Amherst, Mass.: University of Massachusetts Press.

Grimm, James W., and Robert N. Stern. 1974. "Sex roles and internal labor market structures: The female semi-professions." Social 21:690–705.

Hardcastle, D.A. 1987. "The social work labor force." Austin, Tex.: School of Social Work, University of Texas.

Hodson, Randy, and Teresa Sullivan. 1990. The Social Organization of Work. Belmont, Calif.: Wadsworth Publishing Co.

Jacobs, Jerry. 1989. Revolving Doors: Sex Segregation and Women's Careers. Stanford, Calif.: Stanford University Press.

Kanter, Rosabeth Moss. 1977. Men and Women of the Corporation. New York: Basic Books.

Kessler-Harris, Alice. 1990. A Woman's Wage: Historical Meanings and Social Consequences. Lexington, Ky.: Kentucky University Press.

Lorber, Judith. 1984. Women Physicians: Careers, Status, and Power. New York: Tavistock.

Martin, Susan E. 1980. Breaking and Entering: Police Women on Patrol. Berkeley, Calif.: University of California Press.

———. 1988. "Think like a man, work like a dog, and act like a lady: Occupational dilemmas of policewomen." In The Worth of Women's Work: A Qualitative Synthesis, ed. Anne Statham, Eleanor M. Miller, and Hans O. Mauksch, 205–223. Albany, N.Y.: State University of New York Press.

Phenix, Katharine. 1987. "The status of women librarians." Frontiers 9:36–40.

Reskin, Barbara. 1990. "Bringing the men back in: Sex differentiation and the devaluation of women's work." Gender & Society 2:58–81.

Reskin, Barbara, and Heidi Hartmann. 1986. Women's Work, Men's Work: Sex Segregation on the Job, Washington, D.C.: National Academy Press.

Reskin, Barbara, and Patricia Roos. 1990. Job Queues Gender Queues: Explaining Women's Inroads into Male Occupations. Temple University Press.

Schmuck, Patricia A. 1987. "Women school employees in the United States." In Women Educators: Employees of Schools in Western Countries, ed. Patricia A. Schmuck, 75–97. Albany, N.Y.: State University of New York Press.

Schreiber, Carol. 1979. Men and Women in Transitional Occupations. Cambridge, Mass.: MIT Press.

Spencer, Anne, and David Podmore. 1987. In A Man's World: Essays on Women in Male-dominated Professions. London: Tavistock.

Strauss, Anselm L. 1987. Qulitative Analysis for Social Scientists. Cambridge, England: Cambridge University Press.

U.S. Bureau of the Census. 1980. Detailed Population Characteristics, Vol. 1, Ch. D. Washington, D.C.: Government Printing Office.

U.S. Department of Labor. Bureau of Labor Statistics. 1991. Employment and Earnings. January. Washington, D.C.: Government Printing Office.

U.S. Congress. House. 1991. Civil Rights and Women's Equity in Employment Act of 1991. Report. (Report 102–40, Part I.) Washington, D.C.: Government Printing Office.

Williams, Christine L. 1989. Gender Differences at Work: Women and Men in Nontraditional Occupations. Berkeley, Calif.: University of California Press.

Yoder, Janice D. 1989. "Women at West Point: Lessons for token women in in male-domiated occupations." In Women: A Feminist Perspective, ed. Jo Freeman, 523–537. Mountain View, Calif.: Mayfield Publishing Company.

York, Reginald O., H. Carl Henley, and Dorothy N. Gamble. 1987. "Sexual discrimination in social work: Is it salary or advancement?" Social Work 32:336–340.

Zimmer, Lynn. 1988. "Tokenism and women in the workplace." Social Problems 35:64–77.

Discussion Questions

1. Which majors offered at your school would you classify as leading to women's careers and which to men's careers? How likely do you think it is that any one of these majors has almost no students of the opposite sex? Are there any majors changing from their traditional gender designations to more neutral ones? If so, why?

2. What is you major (or interest, if you haven't decided)? Is it traditionally male, female, or neither? What influences before college led you to your major? Was your major's tradition as either a female or male occupation a factor in choosing it? If you are male, would you consider a major in nursing? If you are female, would you consider on in engineering? Why or why not?

Chapter *12*

Marriage and Family

Obviously, something all families do is to divide up the necessary family tasks among their members. When there are no children, this means the husband and wife must decide between themselves on who does what. It is probably no surprise that the woman usually does most of the inside, "domestic" chores, while her husband is more likely to do the outside jobs. But what happens when that first baby arrives? Susan Walzer's article reports on research exploring a special aspect of that topic, focusing on what she calls "mental work." Rather than looking at physical tasks involved with child care, Walzer studied the "invisible" work of infant care involving worrying, processing information, and managing the division of labor.

Are there really differences between parents in these mental tasks? Walzer's data indicate that there are. As you read her article, notice who worries the most, who is most involved in getting information on what needs to be done for the infant, and who does most of the negotiating on which parent will do which task.

Walzer argues that the distribution of mental work has a marked result: a decline in marital satisfaction. Here again is an example of sociological research uncovering a hidden dimension of social life that answers some very practical questions.

Thinking About the Baby
Gender and Divisions of Infant Care*

SUSAN WALZER
University at Albany, State University of New York

The tendency for women and men to become more differentiated from each other in work and family roles upon becoming parents has been documented in longitudinal studies of transitions into parenthood (see summaries in Belsky and Kelly 1994; Cowan and Cowan 1992). New mothers are more apt than new fathers to leave or curtail their employment (Belsky and Kelly 1994). And despite couples' previous intentions (Cowan and Cowan 1992), mothers provide more direct care to babies than fathers do (Belsky and Volling 1987; Berman and Pedersen 1987; Dickie 1987; Thompson and Walker 1989). Fathers tend to act as "helpers" to mothers, who not only spend more time interacting with babies, but planning for them as well (LaRossa 1986).

This pattern of increased gender differentiation following the birth of a baby has been associated with decreases in marital satisfaction, particularly for wives (Belsky, Lang, and Huston 1986; Cowan and Cowan 1988; Harriman 1985; Ruble et al. 1988). A number of researchers have interpreted new mothers' marital dissatisfaction as connected with "violated expectations" of more shared parenting (Belsky 1985; Belsky, Lang, and Huston 1986; Ruble et al. 1988), although some researchers express surprise that wives expect so much in the first place (Ruble et al. 1988). Nevertheless, traditional divisions of household labor have been implicated in marital stress following the birth of a first baby (Belsky. Lang, and Huston 1986; Schuchts and Witkin 1989).

In this paper I focus on the more invisible, mental labor that is involved in taking care of a baby and suggest that gender imbalances in this form of baby care play a particular role in reproducing differentiation between mothers and fathers and stimulating marital tension. My use of the term "mental" labor is meant to distinguish the thinking, feeling, and interpersonal work that accompanies the care of babies from physical tasks, as has been done in recent studies of household labor (see, e.g., Hochschild 1989; DeVault 1991; Mederer

Walzer, Susan. Thinking about Baby: Gender and Divisions of Infant Care. *Social Problems, 43,* 2, May 1996, 219–233. By permission of the University of California Press.

1993).[1] I include in the general category of mental labor what has been referred to as "emotion" work, "thought" work, and "invisible" work (Hochschild 1983; DeVault 1991); that is, I focus on aspects of baby care that involve thinking or feeling, managing thoughts or feelings, and that are not necessarily perceived as work by the person performing it (DeVault 1991).

Using qualitative data from interviews with 50 new mothers and fathers (25 couples), this paper describes three categories of mental baby care and suggests that the tendency for mothers to take responsibility for this kind of work is an underrecognized stress on marriages as well as a primary way in which mothering and fathering are reproduced as gendered experiences. While the tendency for mothers to feel ultimately responsible for babies has been identified in other studies (see, e.g., McMahon 1995), this paper describes some of the interactional and institutional contexts within which differences between maternal and paternal responsibilities are reproduced. I suggest that the way that new parents divide the work of thinking about their babies reflects an accountability to socially constructed and institutionalized differentiation between women and men.

Data and Method

The data grounding this discussion are from a qualitative interview study of 50 mothers and fathers who had become new parents approximately one year before the time of the data collection. The sample was located through birth announcements published in the local newspaper of a small city in upstate New York. This method for locating new parents was an attempt to improve upon the self-selection bias present in many studies of transitions to parenthood in which voluntary samples are generated through obstetrics practices, childbirth classes, or community announcements.

Preliminary letters were sent in stages telling potential respondents about the study and inviting them to be interviewed. These letters were then followed with a phone call to answer any questions and schedule interviews. The response rate for those couples who received letters, were reached by telephone, and fit the sample parameters was 68 percent.

The parents in the sample ranged in age from 21 to 44 years old and the age of the babies ranged from 11 to 18 months. Fourteen of the babies were boys and 11 were girls. Fifteen of the pregnancies were planned while 10 were not. Twenty-three of the couples in the sample were married while two were not. Four of the fathers and three of the mothers had had a previous marriage.

All of the parents in the sample had finished high school or a GED, 23 had a college degree, 4 had masters degrees, and 2 had professional degrees. The median family income range was $40,000–$49,999 with 6 families under $30,000 and five over $75,000. Two couples reported having received some public assistance. About 40 percent of the sample described growing up in households that could be characterized as poor to working class while 60 percent grew up in middle- to upper middle-class households.

[1]DeVault's (1991) examination of feeding work, for example, elaborates the notion that feeding involves mental labor preceding and beyond the physical act of meal preparation. Feeding the family includes planning, strategizing, juggling various individuals' needs as well as facilitating group interaction.

Ten of the mothers were employed full time, 7 were employed part time, and 2 were students. Six of the mothers described themselves as stay-at-home mothers, although two of them provided regular baby-sitting for pay. All except one of the fathers were employed at the time of the interview.

In most cases, wives and husbands were interviewed on the same occasion, first separately and with as much privacy as possible, and then more briefly together upon the completion of their separate interviews. Interview sessions ranged from two to four hours long. In three cases, wives and husbands were interviewed on separate occasions. All of the interviews took place in the couples' homes except for one father who requested an interview in his workplace.

The data used in this paper are part of a larger data set about new parents' transitions into parenthood. The interview protocol was semi-structured and designed to elicit parents' experiences of having become mothers or fathers as well as to discuss possible influences on the nature of their transitions into parenthood. All of the interviews were taped and then transcribed, coded, and analyzed using a constant comparative method (see Glaser and Strauss 1967). This paper represents data and analysis that emerged during the course of this grounded theoretical study.

Thinking About the Baby as "Women's Work"

Three categories of mental labor associated with taking care of a baby surfaced in my respondents' reports: worrying, processing information, and managing the division of labor (see also Ehrensaft 1987; LaRossa and LaRossa 1989).

Worrying

In this section I contextualize the disproportionate amount of worrying that new mothers do in interactional dynamics between mothers and fathers; that is, I suggest that mothers worry about babies, in part, because fathers do not. In this sense my analysis emphasizes other dynamics surrounding worrying besides the internalization of gendered personality differences (as in Ehrensaft's 1987 account).[2] I also suggest that gender differences in whether and how new parents worry are linked to socially constructed expectations for mothers and fathers to which new parents feel accountable (see West and Fenstermaker 1993 on the role of accountability in reproducing gender).

The "mental" experience of being a new mother—thinking about the baby, worrying "about everything"—is one that many of the women in my sample shared (see also Ehrensaft 1987; Hays 1993):

> *I don't walk around like a time bomb ready to explode. I don't want you to think that. It's just that I've got this stuff in the back of my head all the time.*

---

[2]See Risman and Schwartz (1989) for a discussion of individualist versus microstructural approaches to gender; see also Ferree (1991).

I worry about her getting cavities in teeth that are not even gonna be there for her whole life. Everything is so important to me now. I worry about everything.

It's like now you have this person and you're always responsible for them, the baby. You can have a sitter and go out and have a break, but in the back of your mind, you're still responsible for that person. You're always thinking about that person.

These new mothers described thinking about their babies as something that mothers do: "Mothers worry a lot." Worrying was such an expected part of mothering that the absence of it might challenge one's definition as a good mother. One of my respondents described returning to her job and feeling on her first day back that she should be worrying about her baby. She said that she had to "remind" herself to check on how her baby was doing at the baby-sitter's "or I'd be a bad mother."

Fathers do not necessarily think about their children while they are at work or worry that this reflects on them as parents (Ehrensaft 1987). My respondents did not report feeling like "bad" fathers if they took their minds off of their babies; some even expressed stress when their babies had to have their attention:

Sitting two hours playing with him, when I first did it was like, this is a waste of my time. I said, "I have more important things to do." And I'm still thinking, "Look at the time I've spent with him. What would I have done otherwise?"

This father's concern with his perceived lack of productivity while spending time with his baby might be a response to the social construction of fathers' roles as primarily economic (see Benson 1968; Thompson and Walker 1989). Another new father in my sample described a sense of loss about time he missed with his baby when he had to travel for work, "but," he said, "it goes back to the idea of being a father . . . I do think in a traditional sense where I'm the father, I'm the husband, it's my job to support the family."

A couple I will call Brendan and Eileen illustrate the relationship between parental worry and social constructions of motherhood and fatherhood. Brendan and Eileen both have professional/managerial careers, each reporting salaries of more than $75,000. When Eileen had to travel for work, Brendan would function as Jimmy's primary caregiver. But when she was home, Eileen wanted to do "the baby stuff." She referred to her caregiving of Jimmy as her "stake" in his life:

This is going to be hard to say. It's really important to me that Jimmy understands I'm his mother, whatever that means, because I'm probably not a traditional mother by any stretch.

When I asked what it means to her for Jimmy to know that she's his mother, Eileen responded:

It means that if I come home some night and he's with [his] day care [provider] and he doesn't want to leave her, it'll kill me, is what it means. So I don't know if the rest of this is trying to ensure that doesn't happen. I don't know if the rest is trying to ensure that I have that very special role with him.

For Eileen, anything that she was *not* doing for Jimmy had the potential to damage her "special role" with him. If she was not the most special person to him, she was inadequate as a mother—something she noted that Brendan did not feel. She connected these concerns with what she referred to as "the good mother image": "She's somehow all nurturing and all present and always there." And she added: "Now, I'm not even going to be able to have a shot at it because I'm not a lot of those things."

Brendan said that his behavior with Jimmy was not driven by guilt and anxiety as he perceived Eileen's to be:

I think she feels that need. She wants to be a good mother . . . Being a father, it's not a guilt thing. It's not like I'm going to do this because I don't want to be a bad daddy.

Brendan noted that his relationship with Jimmy was based on fun while he perceived Eileen's actions to be driven by insecurity. Eileen recognized that her concerns made her less of a good mother in Brendan's eyes. "I think his issue with me as a mother is that I worry a lot. The fact is that I do, but I also think mothers worry a lot." Although Eileen worried that she couldn't match the good mother image she described herself as "absolutely" buying into, worrying itself made her feel like a good mother.

Why is worrying associated with being a mother? I suggest two general reasons, which generate two kinds of worry. The first reason is that worrying is an integral part of taking care of a baby; it evokes, for example, the scheduling of medical appointments, babyproofing, a change in the baby's diet. There appears to be a connection between taking responsibility for physical care and carrying thoughts that reinforce the care (see Coltrane 1989; Ruddick 1983). This kind of worry, which I refer to as *"baby worry,"* is generated by the question: What does the baby need? And babies need a lot. As Luxton (1980:101) points out, women are often anxious because babies are "so totally dependent" and perceived as highly vulnerable to illness and injury.[3]

A second reason that new mothers worry is, as I suggest above, because they are expected to, and because social norms make it difficult for mothers to know whether they are doing the right thing for their babies. I call this *"mother worry,"* and it is generated by the question: Am I being a good mother? While it has been suggested that mothers are more identified with their children than fathers are (Ehrensaft 1987), I suggest that mothers' worrying is induced by external as well as by internal mechanisms. That is, perhaps mothers experience their children as extensions of themselves as Ehrensaft (1987) argues, but mothers are also aware that their children are perceived by others as reflecting on them. Mothers worry, in part, because they are concerned with how others evaluate them as mothers:

[3]See Lamb (1978) and LaRossa and LaRossa (1989) for discussions of how babies' dependency contributes to traditionalization in parental roles.

I think that people don't look at you and say, "oh there's a good mother," but they will look at people and say, "oh there's a bad mother."

Being a mother I worry about what everyone else is going to think.

The mother just quoted perceived mothers as uniquely responsible for their children's behavior, and even street violence:

The behavior of the child reflects the mother's parenting . . . I mean kids, you have all these things with kids shooting people, and I blame it on . . . mothers not being around.

The association of mothers with worrying provides a source of differentiation between mothers and fathers and presents women with a paradox, often played out in interactions with their male partners. Worrying is associated with irrationality and unnecessary anxiety, and some fathers suggested that their partners worried too much about their babies:

Sometimes I say, "He's fine, he's fine," but he's not fine enough for her.

However, worrying is perceived as something that "good" mothers do. A number of fathers made an explicit connection between good mothering and their wives' mental vigilance:

She's a very good mother. She worries a lot.

She's always concerned about how she's doing or she's always worried about if [child's] feelings are hurt or did she say something wrong to her.

This paradoxical message—good mothers worry; worrying too much isn't good— underlies the tendency for mothers to worry and for fathers to express ambivalence about their worrying. One mother described a division of labor in which she was stressed and got things done while her husband's job was to tell her to lighten up:

I'm the one who stresses out more. He is very laid back. He doesn't worry about things. In fact he procrastinates. And I'm the one, run run run run run. . . . But one of us has to get things done on time and the other one has to keep the other one from totally losing it and make them be more relaxed. So it kind of balances us out.

A father described the care that his wife's worrying ensures for their baby while also suggesting that some of it might be unnecessary:

She worries a lot. I'm probably too easygoing, but she makes sure he goes to the doctor, makes sure he has fluoride, makes sure he has all of his immunizations. She's hypervigilant to any time he might be acting sick. She's kind of that way her-

self. I kid her about being a hypochondriac. She makes sure he gets to bed on time, makes sure he's eating enough, whereas I'm a little more lackadaisical on that.

In both of these cases, as with Brendan and Eileen, the respondents described a kind of balance between the mother and father: The mother worries, the father doesn't; his job, in fact, might be to tell her not to worry. This dynamic reinforces a gendered division of mental labor. Although there is a subtext that the mother's worrying is unnecessary and/or neurotic, she does not stop. In fact, the suggestion that the mother "relax" serves to reinforce her worrying because although she does not recognize it as work, she does recognize that worrying gets things done for the baby. If the father offered to share the worrying rather than telling the mother to stop, the outcome might be quite different.

While I would not argue that it is possible for a baby to be cared for without having some assortment of adults performing "baby worry," the "mother worry" I have described here is heightened in our society by assumptions that good parenting is done exclusively and privately by a mother (with perhaps some "help" from a father) and that veering from this model may have severe consequences for children (see Coontz 1992 for a critique of "American standards of childrearing"). Examining another area of mental labor—the work of processing "expert" information about baby care—further reveals the norms attached to the work of thinking about babies.

Processing Information: "What to Expect"

LaRossa and LaRossa (1989) make a direct connection between the fact that wives tend to buy and read how-to books on parenting and their being "in charge" of the baby. Because mothers read the books more thoroughly, they are more informed, and both parents assume that the mother will orchestrate and implement the care: "Her purchase of the books reflects what is generally accepted: Babies are 'women's work' " (LaRossa and LaRossa 1989: 144). In this section, I suggest that processing information about baby care is itself part of the work of taking care of a baby. I also argue that the assumption that mothers will do this work is embedded and reinforced in the "information" that mothers get from expert advice (see also Hays 1993).

There are a number of steps that may be involved in the mental labor of processing information about babies:

1. Deciding on the need for advice
2. Locating the advice (often from more than one source)
3. Reading/listening to the advice
4. Involving/instructing one's partner
5. Contemplating and assessing the advice
6. Planning for the implementation of the advice

What I label here as steps 1–3 are carried out by mothers usually (LaRossa and LaRossa 1989; Hays 1993). In my sample, 23 out of 25 of the mothers reported reading parenting literature while 5 of the 25 fathers did.

Step 4 occurs in a number of variations: Mothers tell fathers what to read; mothers tell fathers specifically what they have read; mothers tell fathers what to do based on their own reading. These approaches to disseminating information were apparent in my sample:

He would say, "Well you're the mother, so what's the answer here?" And I said, "What do you think I have that I would know just because I'm the mother?" But I would do a lot more reading.

Sarah [wife] has read quite a few and I just pretty much go with her. She hasn't really told me I'm doing anything wrong.

Every once in a while she might pull something out and show me if she found something she thinks I should read, but I usually don't have time.

Step 5—contemplation and assessment of the advice—is often complicated, since what women find in advice books is ideology as well as information. According to a content analysis performed by Hays (1993; see also Marshall 1991), underlying the advice provided by child care experts is an "ideology of intensive mothering" that, among other things, holds individual mothers primarily responsible for child-rearing and treats mothering as expert-guided, emotionally absorbing, and labor-intensive. Mothers therefore take responsibility for gathering information from sources that reinforce their primary responsibility for the care of babies. As described by one respondent below, mothers have to confront the ideology underlying the advice in order to assess whether they can or want to implement it (Step 6).

The book relied on by a majority of the mothers in my sample was *What to Expect the First Year* (Eisenberg, Murkoff, and Hathaway 1989), a book that one of the authors writes was conceived to address new mothers' "numerous worries." Several of the women in my sample referred to it as their "bible," and, because it is not included in content analyses of expert advice books (see, e.g., Hays 1993; Marshall 1991), I include some excerpts in this paper. These excerpts illustrate how gendered divisions of mental labor are reinforced on an institutional level through "expert" advice for new parents.

The book is divided into two main parts—"The First Year" and "Of Special Concern"—and has a third "Ready Reference" section at the end. "Becoming a Father" is the 25th of 26 chapters in the book and is included in the issues "of special concern." Much of the information given throughout the book is in the form of answers to specific questions that are presented with quotation marks, as if particular mothers had asked them.

One of the mothers in my sample who preferred *What to Expect* over other books nevertheless had questions about its "accuracy." Her statements were sarcastic in response to the book's advice about the effort that mothers should exert to see that their babies eat healthy foods:

I like to read What to Expect. *Although I don't think they're too accurate . . . So your baby should be doing this and the other thing. And never give him any white sugar. Don't give him any cookies. Make sure they're muffins made from fruit juice. Yeah, okay. I'll just pop off in the kitchen and make some muffins.*

Following are the comments that open a consideration of when to introduce solid foods to a baby—something that a father can do whether or not the baby is being breast-fed:

> *The messages that today's new mother receives about when to start feeding solids are many and confusing. . . . Whom do you listen to? Does mother know best? Or doctor? Or friends? (Eisenberg, Murkoff, and Hathaway 1989:202)*

This passage illustrates the mental labor that is expected to accompany the introduction of solid foods: choosing when to do it, consulting with others about the issue, making a decision about whose advice to take. It also presumes that it is the mother who is making the decision in consultation with her mother, doctor, friends, yet her male partner is not mentioned.

The one chapter addressed to fathers begins with the following question from a presumably typical father:

> *"I gave up a lot of my favorite foods when my wife was pregnant so I could support her efforts to eat right for our baby. But enough's enough. Now that our son's here, shouldn't I be able to eat what I like?" (Eisenberg, Murkoff, and Hathaway 1989:591)*

The tone of the question suggests that the father is getting guff from someone about his diet. Implication: It may not be only babies whose diets new mothers need to worry about. Regardless of who is nagging this father, the question suggests that fathers will not be independently motivated to eat a healthy diet in the interest of their babies and themselves (although given the comments of the mother in my sample, this father may just want some cookies and white sugar in his diet).

As Hays (1993) points out, authors of advice books may not have created gender differentiation in parenting responsibility, but they certainly play a role in reproducing it. Mothers in my sample who already felt that they had the primary responsibility for their babies did not get any disagreement from the advice book they consulted most frequently about "what to expect":

> *If your husband, for whatever reason, fails to share the load with you, try to understand why this is so and to communicate clearly where you stand. Don't expect him to change overnight, and don't let your resentment when he doesn't trigger arguments and stress. Instead explain, educate, entice; in time, he'll meet you— partway, if not all the way (Eisenberg, Murkoff, and Hathaway 1989:545).*

This advice directs women to do "emotion work" (Hochschild 1983) to contain their responses to their husbands' lack of participation. Rather than experiencing stress or conflict, new mothers are directed to keep a lid on their feelings and focus on instructing and enticing their husbands into participation (and after all this, not to expect equity).

This kind of "advice" provides reinforcement for new parents' gendered divisions of mental labor, including the tendency for mothers to have the responsibility for getting the advice in the first place. The suggestion from these experts that new mothers should not argue with or expect equity from their husbands may also be a factor in the decreases in marital satisfaction that some experience.

Managing the Division of Labor

In this section I expand the concept of "managing" that has already been applied to infant care in past studies and suggest that it is not only the baby's appointments and supplies that mothers tend to manage (Belsky and Kelly 1994), but their babies' fathers as well (see also Ehrensaft 1987). To use the language from *What to Expect the First Year,* "enticing" fathers into helping out with their babies is another invisible, mental job performed by new mothers, as one respondent said of her husband:

> *Peter is very good at helping out if I say, "Peter, I'm tired, I'm sick, you've got to do this for me, you've got to do that," that's fine, he's been more than willing to do that.*

Even in situations in which fathers report that they and their partners split tasks equally, mothers often have the extra role of delegating the work, as the following fathers in my sample indicate (Coltrane 1989 and Ehrensaft 1987 also describe "manager-helper" dynamics in couples who "share" the care of children):

> *I don't change her [diaper] too often—as much as I can get out of it.*

> *Then at night either one of us will give him a bath. She'll always give him a bath, or if she can't, she'll tell me to do it because I won't do it unless she tells me, but if she asks me to do it I'll do it.*

These quotes from two fathers, who perceived that they split tasks equally with their partners, reflect a division of labor in which the mothers are the ultimate managers. Both of these fathers had described themselves as sharing tasks with their wives—when their wives told them to.

Diaper changes were a particular area in which enticing was evident:

> *I mean diapering, that's hard to say. He won't volunteer, but if I say, "Honey, she needs a diaper change, could you do it?" he does it.*

> *It took me a little while to get him to change the nasty diapers . . . but now he changes 'em all. He's a pro.*

Mothers also made decisions about when not to delegate:

> *I do diapers. Joel can't handle it well. You know, he does diapers too, but not if there's poop in them.*

> *I'm pretty much in charge of that, which is fine because it's really not that big of a deal. And she's more, it seems like she's easier for me than she is for him when it comes to diapering 'cause I just all the time do it, you know?*

The mother just quoted illustrates how habitual patterns become perceived as making sense—doing becomes a kind of knowing (Daniels 1987; DeVault 1991)—just as being the one to read the book makes the mother the expert. Another woman described how her husband sits and eats while she "knows" what is involved in feeding their baby (and him):

> *I know what has to be done. I know that like when we sit down for dinner, she [child] has to have everything cut up, and then you give it to her, you know, where he sits down and he eats his dinner. Then I have to get everything on the table, get her stuff all done. By the time I'm starting to eat, he's almost finished. Then I have to clean up and I also have to get her cleaned up and I know that like she'll always have to have a bath, and if she has to have a bath and if I need him to give it to her, "Can you do it?" I have to ask . . . because he just wouldn't do it if I didn't ask him. You know, it's just assumed that he doesn't have to do it.*

While on one level it appears that women are "in charge" of the division of labor, the assumption of female responsibility means that, on another level, men are in charge—because it is only with their permission and cooperation that mothers can relinquish their duties. One mother talked about feeling that she had to check with her husband before making plans that did not include their baby, while her husband did not check with her first. She described herself asking her husband, "Can I do this in 3 weeks?" Another young woman complained that her partner would leave the house while their child was taking a nap:

> *It's always the father that can just say, "Okay, I'm gonna go." Well I obviously can't leave, he's ready for a nap, you know? It's nap time. Mommy seems to always have to stay. I think that fathers have more freedom.*

These statements go against suggestions that mothers may not want to relinquish control to their male partners because motherhood is a source of power for women (see, e.g., Kranichfeld 1987). What is powerful, perhaps, is the desire of mothers to be perceived as good mothers, and this may be what they feel they are trading off if they are not taking responsibility for the care of their babies. While mothers may instruct their husbands to do things, the data here suggest that husbands' responses to and compliance with orders are not compulsory (see also DeVault 1991). Fathers who considered themselves equal participants in the division of labor would use the fact that they were "willing" to do diapers as an example:

> *We each will do whatever we have to do. It's not like I won't change diapers.*

Mothers did not necessarily see any baby task as optional for them:

> *It's kind of give and take. As far as diaper changing, I think I do more . . . it's not one of his favorite tasks.*

Women are the "bosses" in the sense that they carry the organizational plan and delegate tasks to their partners, but they manage without the privileges of paid managers. Their ultimate responsibility for baby care may, in fact, disempower them in relation to their husbands, since for many women it means a loss of economic power (see Blumberg and Coleman 1989) and greater dependence on their male partners (LaRossa and LaRossa 1989; Waldron and Routh 1981).

Mental Baby Care and Marital Changes

While having a baby may foster greater dependence by women on their husbands, Belsky and Kelly (1994) report that new mothers are often disappointed by the level of emotional support they get from their husbands. I suggest that women's disproportionate responsibility for mental baby care plays an important role in generating women's dissatisfaction. Mothers in my sample were not necessarily appreciated and were even criticized by their partners for worrying; the advice they were in charge of getting told them not to be open with their husbands about their experiences; and their sense of being ultimately responsible for their babies' care affected their access to other sources of validation and power, such as paid work and social networks.

One of the primary ways in which women's sense of responsibility for babies surfaced was in decisions they made about employment. In my sample, many women changed their paid work patterns, quitting jobs or cutting back their hours (see also Cowan and Cowan 1992). These changes had implications for the balance of power in their marriages:

> *It's funny now because he is the breadwinner so there have been opportunities where he has interviewed for positions, had opportunities to relocate and get a better position and the money was better. You're just put in a position where you have to just follow. Before when we were both working we would talk it out. I'd say, "No, I want to stay here." And now you really can't.*

On an institutional level, men's bigger pay checks and women's experiences of low-wage, low-prestige jobs structured some of my respondents' traditional parenting arrangements. But there were also women in my sample, such as Eileen, who made as much money as their husbands and were very satisfied with their jobs, yet felt that they had to answer for their work in ways that their husbands did not. Laura, for example, described her decision to let go of a part of her job that she enjoyed the most because she did not want to see her baby at the sitter for more hours:

> *I can't do that, I can't emotionally. I probably could, we'd have to pay more money for the sitter, but I don't want him at the sitter like for 10 hours a day. To me, that's, I'm doing something that I want to do, but in the long run I'm hurting him, you know? In my mind. I think that.*

Laura's husband, Stuart, had not cut back on any parts of his job and was struggling with maintaining his performance in extracurricular activities:

I either want to be involved and do it the right way or I almost don't want to be involved at all. Because I don't want to do a less than good job.

Laura did not mention how the hours required by Stuart's activities influenced the time spent by their child at the baby-sitter's, but she did acknowledge that her marriage was stressed by her resentment of her husband's "freedom." Even though both Laura and Stuart were employed and made similar wages, Laura felt more directly accountable for their baby's care. She could not allow herself to stay at work, she said, because it would hurt their baby: "In my mind, I think that." What Laura resented perhaps is that her husband was free from these kinds of thoughts.

Women's disappointment with their partners may stem from their loneliness in particular with the thinking they do about their babies. One woman in my sample, who did not question her primary responsibility for baby care, was upset by her perception that her husband did not recognize what goes on inside her head (emphases added):

It really hurts, because he doesn't know how high my intentions or whatever or goals for being a good mom are . . . (crying) He doesn't know what I think and when he's at work he doesn't know when she starts screaming and throwing fits, or pulling everything out of the dishwasher when I'm trying to load it, and I've got this in the back of my head that I have to do for school, and the house is a mess, and supper's not cooked and he'll be home in 30 minutes. He doesn't know that I have to keep telling myself. "Be calm. Love your child." You know? He doesn't know. So I just get upset when sometimes I really think he would say, "Well she could be a better mom."

Hochschild (1989) notes that when couples experience conflict about housework, it is generally not simply about who does what, but about who should be grateful to whom. This "economy of gratitude," Hochschild suggests, relates to how individuals define what should be expected of them as men and women. Applying this notion to divisions of baby care, if mental labor is defined as an idiosyncrasy of mothers rather than as work, there is nothing for a man to feel grateful for if his wife does it. If fathers are seen as doing mothers a favor when they participate in baby care, fathers will receive more appreciation from their partners than they give back, which may contribute to new mothers' disappointment in the lack of emotional support they receive from their husbands (Belsky and Kelly 1994).

Mothers' sense of responsibility may also keep them from other sources of support, which is another factor that puts stress on their marriages. Several of the mothers in my sample reported that their ability to keep up with social networks was affected by their sense of needing to get home to their babies. Women who lost contact with work or other social networks became more aware of what they did not get from their husbands:

I need him sometimes to be my girlfriend and he's not . . . I feel sorry for him because he wasn't ready for that . . . You don't realize how much you need those other people until you see them less frequently.

Decreases in new mothers' marital satisfaction, I am suggesting, are related both to the lack of recognition and sharing of mental labor by their husbands and to the loss of independence and support from other people that mothers' exclusive mental responsibility generates. If men and women who become parents together shared the mental labor associated with taking care of a baby, neither one would be "free," but perhaps neither one would be unhappy.[4]

Invisible Work and Doing Gender

One prominent explanation for gendered divisions of baby care in general is that the capacity to soothe or respond to a baby's hunger is more innate in mothers than fathers, yet it is not clear why a new mother would feel more worried and driven to read baby-care books if she has more "natural" ability. While the notion that mothers and fathers differ in caretaking competence has been refuted by some research (see, e.g., Parke and Sawin 1976), even those social scientists who argue for the salience of sex differences in caretaking capacity suggest that societies will ascribe more or less meaning to these differences. In Rossi's (1985) "biosocial" approach, biological and cultural factors interact in determining male and female parenting roles. In this discussion I focus on the cultural part of this equation and examine the role of gender in the reproduction of differentiation between new mothers and fathers.

As discussed, new parents experience distinct and different norms attached to motherhood and fatherhood. While fatherhood is equated foremost with economic provision, motherhood is socially constructed as a "constant and exclusive responsibility" (Thompson and Walker 1989:860). These norms have been linked in sociohistorical accounts with Western, dichotomized images of public and private, work and love, that became especially pronounced during nineteenth-century industrialization. As manufacturing took paid work out of households, the "public" sphere of the economy and state became perceived as a male sphere and economic provision the job of fathers, while women were left (at least ideologically if not in reality) to the "private" domain of the household and children (see Glenn 1994; Osmond and Thorne 1993).

This ideology continues to be reflected in pay inequity, occupational segregation, and other gendered workplace processes that both assume and reinforce divisions of labor in which women take primary responsibility for families (Reskin and Padavic 1994). The devaluation of "women's work," both paid and unpaid, has been a particular point of entry for the feminist argument that the ideological separation of public and private, production from reproduction, is a source of exploitation of women (see, e.g., Hartmann 1981).

One question that has puzzled social scientists, however, is why many women do not experience their disproportionate responsibility for household labor as oppressive (Berk 1985; Thompson 1991; Thompson and Walker 1989). The theoretical answers to this question are relevant for understanding divisions of mental baby care. DeVault (1991:11)

---

[4]Ross, Mirowsky, and Huber (1983), for example, find that wives are less depressed when their husbands help with housework; and the husbands are no more depressed as a result of their contributions. Marshall and Barnett (1995) find that when husbands share supervision of children, both husbands and wives report lower psychological distress.

suggests, for example, that women often do not recognize feeding their families as work because it is perceived as "embedded in family relations," "part of being a parent . . . or of being a wife." The notion that housework is considered to be an integral part of being a wife is reinforced by South and Spitze's (1994) finding in their analysis of housework patterns across marital statuses that married couples have the highest gender gaps in housework.

Studies of divisions of housework provide support for the theoretical notion that imbalances in household labor when men and women live together is a way in which they "do gender" (West and Zimmerman 1987); that is, they construct their social identities as "women" and "men" through their performance (or not) of "women's work" (Berk 1985; DeVault 1991). The fact that much of the mental work associated with household labor is invisible to the women who do it reinforces the notion that it is simply part of their identities and something for which they are perceived as having a "natural" propensity (Daniels 1987). For women to not do this work might challenge their social definition as women.

Taking responsibility for babies is socially constructed as "women's work," and men and women participate in reproducing this construction through their interactions with each other. One of the women in my sample said of what it means to be "the wife and mother":

> *If I hear him [baby] cry during the night, I'm more apt to get right up than Jake. Or if it's time to get up in the morning and I hear him, I'm more apt to get up and go get him. Jake is more apt to stay in bed and see what happens.*

According to this respondent, "wives and mothers" do not wait to see if their male partners will take care of the baby. Her husband agreed that although they share their baby's care, his wife does "a little more . . . because she is his mother."

In a hypothetical game of "chicken," in which the winner is the parent who can wait longer for the other parent to take responsibility for a baby's needs, it is difficult for mothers not to lose. There is a much greater threat to their social identities as mothers than there is for fathers if, in any particular moment, they are not taking responsibility for their baby (see also McMahon 1995). One explanation for why new parents reproduce differentiated images of mothering and fathering therefore is because they feel accountable to these already established images, "to normative conceptions regarding the essential womanly nature of child care" (West and Fenstermaker 1993:165).

Perhaps more than any other aspect of gender, Glenn (1994:3) suggests, mothering is perceived as "natural, universal, and unchanging," and in this sense, worrying and knowing about the baby may be constructed simply as part of being a mother in the way that feeding the family is. As with the invisible parts of feeding, men and women becoming parents differentiate themselves as "mothers" and "fathers" by how much they think (or think they should think) about their babies.

I am suggesting here a different spin on new parents' apparent identification with gender-differentiated parental functions. Ehrensaft (1987), for example, suggests that men perceive fathering as something they "do," while women experience mothering as something they "are." Cowan and Cowan (1992) report that new mothers experience a subsuming of themselves into mothering while new fathers become more preoccupied with their abilities as breadwinners. Rather than simply identifying with gender-differentiated images of mothers and fathers, I suggest that new parents feel accountable to these images and reinforce their partner's accountability to these images in order to accomplish parenting and gender at the same time (see Fenstermaker, West, and Zimmerman 1991; West and Fenstermaker 1993).

Whether still employed or not, being in charge of baby care places mothers in a different relationship to paid work than their male partners, whose accountability to the breadwinner image may induce more distance between themselves and their babies. A father can be perceived as a "good" father without thinking about his baby; in fact, his baby may pose a distraction to his doing what he is expected to do. Mothers, on the other hand, are expected to think about their babies. They perform a disproportionate amount of mental baby care not because they are "good" mothers, but in order to be.

Conclusion

This discussion has been an attempt to suggest some of the interactional and institutional processes underlying differences in how men and women who become parents together think about babies as well as to highlight the importance of this issue for marital relationships. To the extent that the discussion has emphasized common experiences by gender, this has been intentional, though not necessarily an expected finding. In embarking on the larger study of gender differentiation in transitions into parenthood from which this paper is derived, I expected to find variations in the couples in my sample. Although there were indeed variations in how couples approached the care of their babies, the tendency for mothers to be responsible for a variety of forms of mental baby care emerged strikingly in my data as a source of gender differentiation, even in situations of relatively shared physical care.

While this pattern appeared in my sample across employment statuses and family experiences, this study does not claim to be a test of the mediating power of work, family, and other variables, which might be areas for future research. These data are part of a theory-generating study about gender-differentiation in the transition to parenthood and should not be seen as a test of hypotheses. Rather I have tried here to make a theoretical case for the importance of recognizing the mental labor that accompanies physical infant care; I suggest that the way mental labor is divided in male-female couples in transition to parenthood is a way in which women and men recreate motherhood and fatherhood as differentiated social experiences.

Finally, I have suggested that gendered divisions of mental labor may be an under-recognized factor in decreases in marital satisfaction following the birth of a first baby. Women who experience marital dissatisfaction upon becoming new mothers will not necessarily be relieved simply by trading off diaper changes. Only when the work of thinking about the baby is shared can new fathers claim to be truly equal participants and new mothers able to make their economic and other contributions to their babies with less stress and guilt.

References

Belsky, Jay. 1985. "Exploring individual differences in marital change across the transition to parenthood: The role of violated expectations." Journal of Marriage and the Family, November: 1037–1044.

Belsky, Jay, and John Kelly. 1994. The Transition to Parenthood. New York: Delacorte Press.

Belsky, Jay, Mary Lang, and Ted L. Huston. 1986. "Sex typing and division of labor as determinants of marital change across the transition to parenthood. Journal of Personality and Social Psychology 50:517–522.

Belsky, Jay, and Brenda L. Volling. 1987. "Mothering, fathering, and martial interaction in the family triad during infancy: Exploring family systems processes." In Men's Transitions to Parenthood, eds. Phyllis W. Berman and Frank A. Pedersen, 37–63. Hillsdale, N.J.: Lawrence Erlbaum Associates, Inc.

Benson, Leonard. 1968. Fatherhood: A Sociological Perspective. New York: Random House.

Berk, Sarah Fenstermaker. 1985. The Gender Factory. New York: Plenum Press.

Berman, Phyllis W., and Frank W. Pedersen. 1987. "Research on Men's transitions to parenthood: An integrative discussion." In Men's Transitions to Parenthood, eds. Phyllis W. Berman and Frank A. Pedersen, 217–242. Hillsdale, N.J.: Lawrence Erlbaum Associates, Inc.

Blumberg, Rae Lesser, and Marion Tolbert Coleman. 1989. "A theoretical look at the gender balance of power in the American couple." Journal of Family Issues 10:225–250.

Coltrane, Scott. 1989. "Household labor and the routine production of gender." Social Problems 36: 473–490.

Coontz, Stephanie. 1992. The Way We Never Were: American Families and the Nostalgia Trap. New York: BasicBooks.

Cowan, Carolyn Pape, and Philip A. Cowan. 1988. "Who does what when partners become parents: Implications for men, women, and marriage." Marriage and Family Review 12:105–131.

———.1992. When Partners Become Parents. New York: BasicBooks.

Daniels, Arlene Kaplan. 1987. "Invisible work." Social Problems 34:403–414.

DeVault, Marjorie L. 1991. Feeding the Family. Chicago: University of Chicago Press.

Dickie, Jane R. 1987. "Interrelationships within the mother-father-infant triad." In Men's Transitions to Parenthood, eds. Phyllis W. Berman and Frank A. Pedersen, 113–143. Hillsdale, N.J.: Lawrence Erlbaum Associates, Inc.

Ehrensaft, Diane. 1987. Parenting Together. New York: The Free Press.

Eisenberg, Arlene, Heidi E. Murkoff, and Sandee E. Hathaway. 1989. What To Expect The First Year. New York: Workman Publishing.

Fenstermaker, Sarah, Candace West, and Don H. Zimmerman. 1991. "Gender inequality: New conceptual terrain." In Gender, Family and Economy: The Triple Overlap, ed. Rae Lesser Blumberg, 289–307. Newbury Park, Calif.: Sage Publication, Inc.

Ferree, Myra Marx. 1991. "Feminism and family research." In Contemporary Families, ed. Alan Booth. Minneapolis, Minn.: National Council on Family Relations.

Glaser, Barney G., and Anselm L. Strauss. 1967. The Discovery of Grounded Theory. New York: Aldine De Gruyter.

Glenn, Evelyn Nakano. 1994. "Social constructions of mothering: A thematic overview." In Mothering: Ideology, Experience, and Agency, eds. Evelyn Nakano Glenn, Grace Chang, and Linda Rennie Forcey, 1–29. New York: Routledge.

Harriman, Lynda Cooper. 1985. "Marital adjustment as related to personal and marital changes accompanying parenthood." Family Relations 34:233–239.

Hartmann, Heidi I. 1981. "The family as the locus of gender, class, and political struggle: The example of housework." Signs: Journal of Women in Culture and Society 6:366–394.

Hays, Sharon. 1993. "The cultural contradictions of contemporary motherhood: The social construction and paradoxical persistence of intensive child-rearing." Ph.D. dissertation, University of California, San Diego.

Hochschild, Arlie Russell. 1983. The Managed Heart: Commercialization of Human Feeling. Berkeley: University of California Press.

Hochschild, Arlie, with Anne Machung. 1989. The Second Shift. New York: Viking Press.

Kranichfeld, Marion L. 1987. "Rethinking family power." Journal of Family Issues 8:42–56.

Lamb, Michael E. 1978. "Influence of the child on marital quality and family interaction during the prenatal, perinatal, and infancy periods." In Child Influences on Marital and Family Interaction, eds. Richard M. Lerner and Graham B. Spanier, 137–164. New York: Academic Press.

LaRossa, Ralph. 1986. Becoming a Parent. Beverly Hills, Calif.: Sage Publications.

LaRossa, Ralph, and Maureen Mulligan LaRossa. 1989. "Baby care: Fathers vs. mothers." In Gender in Intimate Relationships: A Microstructural Approach, eds. Barbara J. Risman and Pepper Schwartz, 138–154. Belmont, Calif.: Wadsworth Publishing Company.

Luxton, Meg. 1980. More Than a Labour of Love: Three Generations of Women's Work in the Home. Toronto: Women's Press.

Marshall, Harriette. 1991. "The social construction of motherhood: An analysis of childcare and parenting manuals." In Motherhood: Meanings, Practices, and Ideologies, eds. Ann Phoenix, Anne Woollett, and Eva Lloyd, 66–85. Newbury Park, Calif.: Sage Publications.

Marshall, Nancy L., and Rosalind C. Barnett. 1995. "Child care, division of labor, and parental emotional well-being among two-earner couples." Paper presented at the 90th Annual Meeting of the American Sociological Association, Washington, D.C.

McMahon, Martha. 1995. Engendering Motherhood: Identity and Self-Transformation in Women's Lives. New York: The Guilford Press.

Mederer, Helen J. 1993. "Division of labor in two-earner homes: Task accomplishment versus household management as critical variables in perceptions about family work." Journal of Marriage and the Family 55:133–145.

Osmond, Marie Withers, and Barrie Thorne. 1993. "Feminist theories: The social construction of gender in families and society." In Sourcebook of Family Theories and Methods: A Contextual Approach, eds. P. G. Boss, W. J. Doherty, R. LaRossa, W. R. Schumm, and S. K. Steinmetz, 591–623. New York: Plenum Press.

Parke, Ross D., and Douglass B. Swain. 1976. "The father's role in infancy: A re-evaluation." The Family Coordinator 25:365–371.

Reskin, Barbara, and Irene Padavic. 1994. Women and Men at Work. Thousand Oaks, Calif.: Pine Forge Press.

Risman, Barbara J., and Pepper Schwartz. 1989. "Being gendered: A microstructural view of intimate relationships." In Gender in Intimate Relationships: A Microstructural Approach, 1–9. Belmont, Calif.: Wadsworth Publishing Company.

Ross, Catherine E., John Mirowsky, and Joan Huber. 1983. "Dividing work, sharing work, and in-between: Marriage patterns and depression." American Sociological Review 48:809–823.

Rossi, Alice S. 1985. "Gender and parenthood." In Gender and the Life Course, ed. Alice S. Rossi, 161–191. New York: Aldine Publishing Co.

Ruble, Diane N., Alison S. Fleming, Lisa S. Hackel, and Charles Stangor. 1988. "Changes in the marital relationship during the transition to first time motherhood: Effects of violated expectations concerning division of household labor." Journal of Personality and Social Psychology 55:78–87.

Ruddick, Sara. 1983. "Maternal thinking." In Mothering: Essays in Feminist Theory, 213–230. Savage, MD: Rowman & Littlefield Publishers, Inc.

Schuchts, Robert A., and Stanley L. Witkin. 1989. "Assessing marital change during the transition to parenthood." Social Casework: The Journal of Contemporary Social Work, February:67–75.

South, Scott J. and Glenna Spitze. 1994. "Housework in marital and nonmarital households." American Sociological Review 59:327–347.

Thompson, Linda. 1991. "Family work: Women's sense of fairness." Journal of Family Issues 12:181–196.

Thompson, Linda, and Alexis J. Walker. 1989. "Gender in families: Women and men in marriage, work, and parenthood." Journal of Marriage and the Family 51:845–871.

Waldron, Holly, and Donald K. Routh. 1981. "The effect of the first child on the marital relationship." Journal of Marriage and the Family, November: 785–788.

West, Candace, and Sarah Fenstermaker. 1993. "Power, inequality, and the accomplishment of gender: An ethnomethodological view." In Theory On Gender/Feminism On Theory, ed. Paula England, 151–174. New York: Aldine de Gruyter.

West, Candace, and Don H. Zimmerman. 1987. "Doing gender." Gender and Society 1:125–151.

Discussion Questions

1. (If you have children): Compare your experiences with those found by Walzer. Are they similar or dissimilar? Share your considerations with someone in your class who doesn't have children, and compare his or her expectations with your experiences.

   (If you don't have children): Compare your expectations as to who will do the mental work with the experiences reported by Walzer. Are they similar or dissimilar? Share your considerations with someone in your class who has children, and compare his or her experiences with your expectations.

2. How would the stress level of a single parent with an infant compare to that of a couple in which most of the mental work was done by one spouse? What might be the outcome of a single parent's increase in physical infant care but a decrease in at least part of the mental aspects of care? In which situation would you prefer to be? Why?

$$C\ h\ a\ p\ t\ e\ r\quad 13$$

Education and Religion

The Rist research on tracking in schools is discussed in your textbook. Walter Schafer and his colleagues carried out a similar study at about the same time Rist was conducting his. The Schafer research began with an acknowledged fact: Most high school programs in the United States separate students into two or more levels, one of them aimed at preparation for college. While it is true that there are achievement differences among the tracks, the question of why this difference exists is open to research. Does the tracking simply divide students along the lines of their natural aptitudes and intelligence, or is it the tracking itself that causes the differences?

The findings of both the Rist and Schafer studies pointed to one of the most interesting processes discovered by sociologists, the self-fulfilling prophecy. Examples of the phenomenon can be found in a wide variety of social settings. In the case of tracking, it looks something like this: (1) Students are stereotyped by teachers and counselors according to certain characteristics, such as race/ethnicity or social class; (2) Students are placed in an educational track that seems appropriate to the stereotype; (3) Expectations for achievement conform to the track level—college preparatory students encounter high expectations, while students in other tracks face moderate to low expectations; (4) Teachers and counselors act on what they expect to find through encouragement and help, or criticism and withdrawal; (5) No one is surprised when the students perform according to expectations. Thus, there is a self-fulfilling prophecy.

In reading the Schafer article, note how this process was uncovered and how it worked in the two schools under study.

Programmed for Social Class: Tracking in High School

WALTER E. SCHAFER   CAROL OLEXA   KENNETH POLK

Since the turn of the century, a number of trends have converged to increase enormously the pressure on American adolescents to graduate from high school: declining opportunity in jobs, the upgrading of educational requirements for job entry, and the diminishing need for teenagers to contribute to family income. While some school systems, especially in the large cities, have adapted to this vast increase in enrollment by creating separate high schools for students with different interests, abilities or occupational goals, most communities have developed comprehensive high schools serving all the youngsters within a neighborhood or community.

In about half the high schools in the United States today, the method for handling these large and varied student populations is through some form of tracking system. Under this arrangement, the entire student body is divided into two or more relatively distinct career lines, or tracks, with such titles as college preparatory, vocational, technical, industrial, business, general, basic, and remedial. While students on different tracks may take some courses together in the same classroom, they are usually separated into entirely different courses or different sections of the same course.

School personnel offer several different justifications for tracking systems. Common to most, however, is the notion that college-bound students are academically more able, learn more rapidly, should not be deterred in their progress by slower, non-college-bound students, and need courses for college preparation which non-college-bound students do not need. By the same token, it is thought that non-college-bound students are less bright, learn more slowly, should not be expected to progress as fast or learn as much as college-bound students, and need only a general education or work-oriented training to prepare themselves for immediate entry into the world of work or a business or vocational school.

Schafer, Walter, Carol Olexa, and Kenneth Polk. Programmed for Social Class: Tracking in High School. *Transaction, 7,* 12, 1970. By permission of Transaction Publishers.

In reply, the numerous critics of tracking usually contend that while the college-bound are often encouraged by the tracking system to improve their performance, non-college-bound students, largely as a result of being placed in a lower-rated track, are discouraged from living up to their potential or from showing an interest in academic values. What makes the system especially pernicious, these critics say, is that non-college-bound students more often come from low-income and minority group families. As a result, high schools, through the tracking system, inadvertently close off opportunities for large numbers of students from lower social strata, and thereby contribute to the low achievement, lack of interest, delinquency and rebellion which schools' personnel frequently deplore in their non-college track students.

Tracks and Who Gets Put on Them

We collected data from official school transcripts of the recently graduated senior classes of two midwestern three-year high schools. The larger school, located in a predominantly middle-class, academic community of about 70,000, had a graduating class that year of 753 students. The smaller school, with a graduating class of 404, was located nearby in a predominantly working-class, industrial community of about 20,000. Both schools placed their students into either a college prep or general track.

Just how students in the two schools were assigned to—or chose—tracks is somewhat of a mystery. When we interviewed people both in the high schools and in their feeder junior highs, we were told that whether a student went into one track or another depended on various factors, such as his own desires and aspirations, teacher advice, achievement test scores, pressure from parents, and counselor assessment of academic promise. One is hard put to say which of these weighs most heavily, but we must note that one team of researchers, Cicourei and Kitsuse, showed in their study of *The Educational Decision-Makers* the assumptions made by counselors about the character, adjustment, and potential of in-coming students are vitally important in track assignment.

Whatever the precise dynamics of this decision, the outcome was clear in the schools we studied: socioeconomic and racial background had an effect on which track a student took, quite apart from either his achievement in junior high or his ability as measured by IQ scores. In the smaller, working-class school, 58 percent of the incoming students were assigned to the college prep track; in the larger, middle-class school, 71 percent were placed in the college prep. And, taking the two schools together, whereas 83 percent of students from white-collar homes were assigned to the college prep track, this was the case with only 48 percent of students from blue-collar homes. The relationship of race to track assignment was even stronger: 71 percent of the whites and only 38 percent of the blacks were assigned to the college prep track. In the two schools studied, the evidence is plain: Children from low income and minority group families more often found themselves in low ability groups and non-college-bound tracks than in high ability groups or college-bound tracks.

Furthermore, this decision point early in the students' high school careers was of great significance for their futures, since it was virtually irreversible. Only 7 percent of those who began on the college prep track moved down to the non-college prep track, while only 7 percent of those assigned to the lower, non-college track, moved up. Clearly, these small figures indicate a high degree of rigid segregation within each of the two schools.

Differences Between Tracks

Track position is noticeably related to academic performance. Thirty-seven percent of the college prep students graduated in the top quarter of their class (measured by grade point average throughout high school), while a mere 2 percent of the non-college group achieved the top quarter. By contrast, half the non-college prep students fell in the lowest quarter, as opposed to only 12 percent of the college prep.

Track position is also strikingly related to whether a student's academic performance improves or deteriorates during high school. The grade point average of all sample students in their ninth year—that is, prior to their being assigned to tracks—was compared with their grade point averages over the next three years. While there was a slight difference in the ninth year between those who would subsequently enter the college and non-college tracks, this difference had increased by the senior year. This widening gap in academic performance resulted from the fact that a higher percentage of students subsequently placed in the college prep track improved their grade point average by the time they reached the senior year.

When compared with college prep students, non-college prep students also show lower achievement, greater deterioration of achievement, less participation in extracurricular activities, a greater tendency to drop out, more misbehavior in school, and more delinquency outside of school. Since students are assigned to different tracks largely on the basis of presumed differences in intellectual ability and inclination for further study, the crucial question is whether assignment to different tracks helped to meet the needs of groups of students who were already different, as many educators would claim, or actually contributed to and reinforced such differences, as critics contend.

The simplest way to explain the differences we have just seen is to attribute them to characteristics already inherent in the individual students, or—at a more sophisticated level—to students' cultural and educational backgrounds.

It can be argued, for example, that the difference in academic achievement between the college and non-college groups can be explained by the fact that college prep students are simply brighter; after all, this is one of the reasons they were taken into college prep courses. Others would argue that non-college-bound students do less well in school work because of family background: they more often come from blue-collar homes where less value is placed on grades and college, where books and help in schoolwork are less readily available, and verbal expression limited. Still others would contend that lower track students get lower grades because they performed less well in elementary and junior high, have fallen behind, and probably try less hard.

Fortunately, it was possible with our data to separate out the influence of track position from the other suggested factors of social class background (measured by father's occupation), intelligence (measured by IQ), and previous academic performance (measured by grade point average for the last semester of the ninth year). Through use of a weighted percentage technique known as test factor standardization, we found that even when the effects of IQ, social class, and previous performance are ruled out, there is still a sizable difference in grade point average between the two tracks. With the influence of the first three factors eliminated we nevertheless find that 30 percent of the college prep, as opposed to a mere 4 percent of the non-college group, attained the top quarter of their class; and that only 12 percent of the college prep, as opposed to 35 percent of the non-college group, fell into the bottom quarter. These figures, which are similar for boys and girls, further show that track position has an independent effect on academic achievement which is greater than the effect of each of the other three factors—social class, IQ, and past performance. In particular, assignment to the non-college track has a strong negative influence on a student's grades.

Looking at dropout rates, and again controlling for social class background, IQ, and past performance, we find that track position in itself has an independent influence which is higher than the effect of any of the other three factors. In other words, even when we rule out the effect of these three factors, non-college-bound students still dropped out in considerably greater proportion than college-bound students (19 percent vs. 4 percent).

When the Forecasters Make the Weather

So our evidence points to the conclusion that the superior academic performance of the college-bound students, and the inferior performance of the non-college students is partly caused by the tracking system. Our data do not explain how this happens, but several studies of similar educational arrangements, as well as basic principles of social psychology do provide a number of probable explanations. The first point has to do with the pupil's self-image.

Stigma

Assignment to the lower track in the schools we studied carried with it a strong stigma. As David Mallory was told by an American boy, "Around here you are *nothing* if you're not college prep." A non-college prep girl in one of the schools we studied told me that she always carried her "general" track books upside down because of the humiliation she felt at being seen with them as she walked through the halls.

One ex-delinquent in Washington, D.C., told one of us how the stigma from this low track affected him.

> *It really don't have to be the tests, but after the tests, there shouldn't be no separation in the classes. Because, as I say again, I felt good when I was with my class, but when they went and separated us—that changed us. That changed our ideas, our thinking, the way we thought about each other and turned us to enemies toward each other—because they said I was dumb and they were smart.*
>
> *When you first go to junior high school you do feel something inside—it's like ego. You have been from elementary to junior high, you feel great inside. You say, well daggone, I'm going to deal with the people here now, I am in junior high school. You get this shirt that says Brown Junior High or whatever the name is and you are proud of that shirt. But then you go up there and the teacher says—"Well, so and so, you're in the basic section, you can't go with the other kids." The*

devil with the whole thing—you lose—something in you—just like it just goes out of you.

Did you think the other guys were smarter than you?
Not at first—I used to think I was just as smart as anybody in the school—I knew I was smart. I knew some people were smarter, and I wanted *to go to school, I wanted to get a diploma and go to college and help people and everything. I stepped into there in junior high—I felt like a fool going to school—I really felt like a fool.*

Why?
Because I felt like I wasn't a part of the school. I couldn't get on special patrols, because I wasn't qualified.

What happened between the seventh and ninth grades?
I started losing faith in myself—after the teachers kept downing me. You hear "a guy's in basic section, he's dumb" and all this. Each year—"you're ignorant— you're stupid."

Considerable research shows that such erosion of self-esteem greatly increases the chances of academic failure, as well as dropping out and causing "trouble" both inside and outside of school.

Moreover, this lowered self-image is reinforced by the expectations that others have toward a person in the non-college group.

The Self-fulfilling Prophecy

A related explanation rich in implications comes from David Hargreaves' *Social Relations in a Secondary School,* a study of the psychological, behavioral, and educational consequences of the student's position in the streaming system of an English secondary modern school. In "Lumley School," the students (all boys) were assigned to one of five streams on the basis of ability and achievement, with the score on the "11-plus" examination playing the major role.

Like the schools we studied, students in the different streams were publicly recognized as high or low in status and were fairly rigidly segregated, both formally in different classes and informally in friendship groups. It is quite probable, then, that Hargreaves' explanations for the greater antischool attitudes, animosity toward teachers, academic failure, disruptive behavior, and delinquency among the low stream boys apply to the non-college prep students we studied as well. In fact, the negative effects of the tracking system on non-college-bound students may be even stronger in our two high schools, since the Lumley streaming system was much more open and flexible, with students moving from one stream to another several times during their four-year careers.

Hargreaves provides a convincing case for the position that whatever the differences in skills, ambition, self-esteem, or educational commitment that the students brought to school, they were magnified by what happened to them in school, largely because low stream boys were the victims of a self-fulfilling prophecy in their relations with teachers, with respect to both academic performance and classroom behavior. Teachers of higher stream boys expected higher performance and got it. Similarly, boys who wore the label of streams "C" or "D" were more likely to be seen by teachers as limited in ability and troublemakers, and were treated accordingly.

In a streamed school the teacher categorizes the pupils not only in terms of the inferences he makes of the child's classroom behavior but also from the child's stream level. It is for this reason that the teacher can rebuke an "A" stream boy for being like a "D" stream boy. The teacher has learned to *expect* certain kinds of behavior from members of different streams. . . . It would be hardly surprising if "good" pupils thus become "better" and the "bad" pupils become "worse." It is, in short, an example of a self-fulfilling prophecy.

A recent study by Rosenthal and Jacobson in an American elementary school lends further evidence to the position that teacher expectations influence student's performance. In this study, the influence is a positive one. Teachers of children randomly assigned to experimental groups were told at the beginning of the year to expect "unusual intellectual" gains, while teachers of the control group children were told nothing. After eight months, and again after two years, the experimental group children, the "intellectual spurters," showed significantly greater gains in IQ and grades. Further, they were rated by the teachers as being significantly more curious, interesting, happy, and more likely to succeed in the future. Such findings are consistent with theories of interpersonal influence and with the interactional or labelling view of deviant behavior.

If, as often claimed, American teachers underestimate the learning potential of low track students and expect more negative attitudes and greater trouble from them, it may well be that they partially cause the very failure, alienation, lack of involvement, dropping out, and rebellion they are seeking to prevent.

Two further consequences of the expectation that students in the non-college group will learn less well are differences in grading policies and in teacher effectiveness.

Grading Policies

In the two schools we studied, our interview at the existence of grade ceilings for non-college prep students. That is, by virtue of being located in a college section or course, college prep students could seldom receive any grade lower than "B" or "C," while students in non-college-bound sections or courses found it difficult to gain any grade higher than "C," even though their objective performance may have been equivalent to a college prep "B." Several teachers explicitly called our attention to this practice, the rationale being that non-college prep students do not deserve the same objective grade rewards as college prep students, since they "clearly" are less bright and perform less well. To the extent that grade ceilings do operate for non-college-bound students, the lower grades that result from this policy, almost by definition, can hardly have a beneficial effect on motivation and commitment.

Teaching Effectiveness

Teachers of higher ability groups are likely to teach in a more interesting and effective manner than teachers of lower ability groups. Such a difference is predictable from what we know about the effects of reciprocal interaction between teacher and class. Even when the same individual teaches both types of classes in the course of the day, as was the case for most teachers in the two schools in this study, he is likely to be "up" for college prep classes and "down" for non-college prep classes and to bring out the same reaction from his students.

Future Payoff

Non-college-bound students often develop progressively more negative attitudes toward school, especially formal academic work, because they see grades—and indeed school itself—as having little future relevance or payoff. This is not the case for college prep students. For them, grades are a means toward the identifiable and meaningful end of qualifying for college, while among the non-college-bound, grades are seen as far less important for entry into an occupation or a vocational school. This difference in the practical importance of grades is magnified by the perception among non-college-bound students that it is pointless to put much effort into school work, since it will be unrelated to the later world of work anyway.

Being on the lower track has other negative consequences for the student which go beyond the depressing influence on his academic performance and motivation. We can use the principles just discussed to explain our finding with regard to different rates of participation in school activities and acts of misbehavior.

Tracks: Conformity & Deviance

For example, the explanations having to do with self-image and the expectations of others suggest that assignment to the non-college-bound track has a dampening effect on commitment to school in general, since it is the school which originally categorized these students as inferior. Thus, assignment to the lower track may be seen as independently contributing to resentment, frustration and hostility in school, leading to lack of involvement in all school activities, and finally ending in active withdrawal. The self-exclusion of the non-college group from the mainstream of student life is probably enhanced by intentional or unintentional exclusion by other students and teachers.

Using the same type of reasons, while we cannot prove a definite causal linkage between track position and misbehavior, it seems highly likely that assignment to the non-college prep track often leads to resentment, declining commitment to school, and rebellion against it, expressed in lack of respect for the school's authority or acts of disobedience against it. As Albert Cohen argued over a decade ago in *Delinquent Boys,* delinquency may well be largely a rebellion against the school and its standards by teenagers who feel they cannot get anywhere by attempting to adhere to such standards. Our analysis suggests that a key factor in such rebellion is non-college prep status in the school's tracking system, with the vicious cycle of low achievement and inferior self-image that go along with it.

This conclusion is further supported by Hargreaves' findings on the effect of streaming at Lumley. Assignment to a lower stream at Lumley meant a boy was immediately immersed in a student subculture that stressed and rewarded antagonistic attitudes and behavior toward teachers and all they stood for. If a boy was assigned to the "A" stream, he was drawn toward the values of teachers, not only by the higher expectations and more positive rewards from the teachers themselves, but from other students as well. The converse was true of lower stream boys, who accorded each other high status for doing the opposite of what teachers wanted. Because of class scheduling, little opportunity developed for interaction and friendship across streams. The result was a progressive polarization and hardening of the high and low stream subcultures between first and fourth years and a progressively greater negative attitude across stream lines, with quite predictable consequences.

The informal pressures within the low streams tend to work directly against the assumption of the teachers that boys will regard promotion into a higher stream as a desirable goal. The boys from the low streams were very reluctant to ascend to higher streams because their stereotypes of "A" and "B" stream boys were defined in terms of values alien to their own and because promotion would involve rejection by their low stream friends. The teachers were not fully aware that this unwillingness to be promoted to a higher stream led the high informal status boys to depress their performance in examinations. This fear of promotion adds to our list of factors leading to the formation of anti-academic attitudes among low stream boys.

Observations and interviews in the two American schools we studied confirmed a similar polarization and reluctance by non-college prep students to pursue the academic goals rewarded by teachers and college prep students. Teachers, however, seldom saw the anti-school attitudes of non-college prep students as arising out of the tracking system—or anything else about the school—but out of adverse home influences, limited intelligence or psychological problems.

Implications

These, then, are some of the ways the schools we studied contributed to the greater rates of failure, academic decline, uninvolvement in school activities, misbehavior and delinquency among non-college-bound students. To the extent the findings are valid and general, they strongly suggest that, through their tracking system, the schools are partly causing many of the very problems they are trying to solve and are posing an important barrier to equal educational opportunity to lower income and black students, who are disproportionately assigned to the non-college prep track.

Discussion Questions

1. To what extent do you think the findings of Schafer and his colleagues reflect the high school you attended? Were there tracks? Did the students believe that college prep students were the most intelligent and the highest achievers? If there were tracks in your high school, to what extent do you think they represented natural aptitudes and abilities?

2. As the Schafer article points out, it can be argued that tracking benefits the students in a variety of ways, or that it blocks opportunities for minority and lower-class students. Choose a partner and debate the issue. Of course, both sides of the argument have some merit, so when you finish debating, try to come to an agreement on the degree to which each position is accurate.

$$Chapter \quad 14$$

Population and Urbanization

U.S. cities, at the end of the twentieth century, have come to be symbols of failure and decay. The image includes crime, noise and air pollution, poverty, gang violence, and even urban bankruptcy. The list of ills contained in this vision of the city touches almost every facet of urban life. To select one aspect of this grim picture of our cities, consider the state of urban schools. There is a growing consensus that schools in the United States, especially in large cities, are failures. In this essay by Ravitch and Vitteritti, the weakness of urban education is taken seriously, but there is a difference between the authors' views and those of most commentators on the future of United States cities. Surprisingly, Ravitch and Vitteritti argue that urban education can be saved! In fact, they believe a reversal has already begun. See if you agree that the six proposals in their agenda for change would be enough to revitalize at least this one crucial sector of our cities.

A New Vision for City Schools

DIANE RAVITCH   *JOSEPH VITERITTI*

Yes, there is hope for urban education. A wave of reform is spreading from city to city and state to state. Rather than aiming to alter isolated practices or to fix one piece of a jerry-built system, these changes are meant to transform the basic character of public schooling. When taken together, the ambitious range of initiatives currently under way can be structured into an integrated program for reforming urban education—one that shifts from a bureaucratic system that prizes compliance to a deregulated system that focuses on student performance.

A century ago, progressive reformers reshaped big-city schools according to the era's widely shared vision of efficient administration. To get schools "out of politics," they created tightly controlled bureaucracies. At the apex of authority were "professional experts," who managed a top-down system designed to impose uniform rules on teachers and students alike. The model for this system was the factory, which, at that time in history, was considered the acme of scientific management. The raw materials for these educational factories were the children of immigrants, who were pouring into American cities in unprecedented numbers, in need of instruction in literacy, hygiene, and basic Americanization. The workers in these factories were teachers, whose views about what or how to teach were not solicited. Nor did the experts see any need to consult parents about anything regarding their children, since many of them were barely literate.

These turn-of-the-century efforts to create what historian David Tyack called "the one best system" were remarkably effective for at least the first half of the century. Big-city schools offered unparalleled educational opportunity to millions of children and helped to generate a vast middle class. At mid-century, the nation's urban schools were considered to be a great success. But no more. The system that transformed an earlier generation of impoverished children into prosperous adults has become sclerotic, the bureaucratic organization created to impose efficiency and order has grown tired and inefficient, tangled helplessly in rules and regulations devised by the courts, state governments, federal government, union contracts, and its own minions.

Ravitch, Diane and Joseph Vitteretti. A New Vision for the Cities. *The Public Interest, 122,* Summer 1996, 3–16. By permission of the publisher.

In city after city, the reports of corruption, disorder, neglect, and low educational achievement are legion. Urban education is in deep trouble, in part because of inept big-city bureaucracies inherited from the past, but also because the public's expectations for the schools are higher now than they were earlier in the century. Fifty years ago, the public was neither surprised nor alarmed by the large numbers of young people who did not graduate from high school, they believed that the numbers would continually improve over time. Today, the public expects a large majority of students to complete high school, especially since the jobs available for high-school dropouts are diminishing.

Convinced that the structure of public education contributes to its ineffectiveness in educating a larger proportion of students, imaginative leaders in cities and states across the country are implementing systemic changes. The new reforms proceed on the conviction that the century-old bureaucratic structures of urban education cannot succeed in today's society. The century-old system of schools cannot work today because it was designed to function in a very different society, with different social mores and different problems, where supervisors instructed teachers, teachers instructed students, and parents expected their children to mind what they were told.

The factory is no longer a useful model for urban education; teachers and children are not interchangeable parts to be moved around to fit the requirements of administrators. The reforms that are now being enacted in many cities incorporate such principles as diversity, quality, choice, and accountability. Instead of a system that regulates identical schools, reformers seek a system in which academic standards are the same for all but where schools vary widely. In the new reform vision, the schools are as diverse as teachers' imagination and will, students and their families choose the school that best meets their needs and interests, and central authorities perform a monitoring and auditing function to assure educational quality and fiscal integrity. In such a reconfigured system, the role of the local superintendent shifts from regulating behavior to auditing results. The bottom line is not whether everyone has complied with the same rules and procedures but whether children are learning.

Charter Schools

Not since the beginning of the twentieth century has there been such a burst of bold experimentation in the organization and governance of schools as there has been in just the last half decade. Among the most notable initiatives on the current scene are charter schools, the contracting of instructional services, and a variety of school-choice programs. These innovations are driven by demands from parents and elected officials for higher levels of educational success. However, few of these innovations are based on hard evidence that they will succeed. But that is the nature of innovation: one purpose of these experiments is to identify what will work and what will not. Most of these initiatives, however, are based on well-documented evidence that the current institutional arrangement does not work very well for large numbers of children.

One of the most promising ideas to appear on the national horizon is charter schools. Charter schools are semi-autonomous, public entities, that are freed from most bureaucratic rules and regulations by state and local authorities in return for a commitment to meet explicit performance goals. They are established under a contract between a group that manages a school and a sponsoring authority that oversees it. The contractor might consist of parents, teachers, a labor union, a college, a museum, or other nonprofit or for-profit entities. The sponsor might be a school board, a state education department, a state university campus, or a government agency. In Arizona, the legislature has created a special governing body authorized to grant or deny a request for a charter, thus such power is not limited to the state or local school boards, which may have a stake in restricting the number of these institutions.

Charter schools may be either new schools or existing ones. Their development will contribute to both the number and variety of quality institutions. In Detroit, the Drug Enforcement Administration is creating a residential school for 200 at-risk students, a school called Metro Deaf serves the hearing impaired in St. Paul. In Wilmington, Delaware, five corporations and a medical center have cooperated in a joint venture to run a new high school for math and science. Boston University runs a school for homeless children in Massachusetts; and the Denver Youth Academy was created for at-risk, middle-school children and their families in Colorado. The possibilities seem endless.

A charter serves as a negotiated, legal agreement that sets standards and expectations for the school. School professionals are authorized to manage their own budget and to choose their own staff, but the degree of autonomy varies from state to state. The Education Commission of the States, in conjunction with the Humphrey Institute at the University of Minnesota, recently completed a survey of 110 charter schools in seven states. It found that educators at these schools are quite willing to be held more accountable for improved student performance, so long as they are permitted to enjoy more autonomy. A majority of these schools focus their attention on at-risk populations.

Presently 19 stated have charter-school laws. Minnesota passed the first one as recently as 1991, with eight schools participating, there are now 40 participating. California approved the establishment of 100 charter schools in 1992. Michigan has 30. Among the states that grant the most autonomy to charter schools are Arizona, California, Colorado, Delaware, Massachusetts, Michigan, Minnesota, New Hampshire, and Texas. (The other states with charter laws are Alaska, Arkansas, Georgia, Hawaii, Kansas, Louisiana, New Mexico, Rhode Island, Wisconsin, and Wyoming.)

Charter schools are public schools. They are accountable to a public authority. In fact, the charter, which defines academic expectations and other legal responsibilities, often serves as a more powerful instrument for accountability than anything that exists for most ordinary public schools. If a charter school fails educationally or misuses its funds, the charter can be revoked, as was the case with one Los Angeles school last year. Most charter schools must accept any student who applies, or they select students by lottery if there are more applicants than places. All are bound by the usual state laws and regulations requiring schools to be nondiscriminatory and protective of civil rights.

Contracts for Performance

Unlike charter-school laws, which begin as state initiatives, contracting-out arrangements usually originate with a local school board. It is not unusual for school boards to contract with private vendors for the performance of non-instructional functions—e.g., transportation, food, supplies, facilities, and custodial and administrative services. What is novel about recent developments is for school boards to arrange to have instructional programs provided by outsiders. This approach has given rise to new entepreneurial organizations on the education scene. Educational Alternatives, Inc. (EAI), for example, is under contract to run nine public schools in Baltimore, as well as a single school in Duluth. It will also overhaul six schools in Hartford (eventually all 32) and assume general responsibility for the management of the district. The Edison Project has contracted to operate individual schools in Wichita, Kansas, Mt. Clemens, Michigan, Sherman, Texas, and Boston. Washington, D.C., has recently contracted with Sylvan Learning Systems to offer remedial reading for a limited number of students; and Sabis, an international group, runs a school in Springfield, Massachusetts.

These arrangements are similar to charter schools in that they are brought into being by a performance agreement between a school organization and a public authority. Some contracts allow more autonomy than others. EAI, for instance, ran into great difficulty implementing changes in Baltimore after it agreed to hire all the existing teachers in what were supposed to be reconstituted schools; moreover, the teachers, union was antagonistic to the project from the beginning. And some argue that EAI committed a major strategic error when it took on general responsibility for running the entire Hartford school district. The approach adopted by the Edison Project, involving the development of new schools, one at a time, with a staff that it has hired and trained, seems to hold more promise.

As with most innovations in public education, the more profound changes exacted through contracting tend to generate the strongest opposition. Wilkinsburg, Pennsylvania, a working-class suburb of Pittsburgh, where 78 percent of the children qualify economically for a free-lunch program, is a case in point. It became the scene of an intense political and legal battle when a newly elected, reform-minded school board announced its intention to contract with Alternative Public School Strategies to operate one of its three elementary schools. The local teachers' union and the National Education Association fiercely opposed its reform proposals: an extended school year, new after-school programs, merit pay for teachers.

Some observers have confused the contracting approach with privatization. Contract schools are public institutions, supported with public funds, accountable to a public authority—usually a local school board. As is the case with charter schools, they are expected to meet specific standards of academic performance defined in a legal agreement. If they do not perform adequately, they can be put out of business. When Baltimore Mayor Kurt Schmoke became dissatisfied with student performance at EAI-operated schools in Baltimore, he said he would rethink the contract. It is a rare occurrence for a city public school to be shut down for poor performance, regardless of its record over time. Contracting arrangements, whether they result from state charter laws or local initiatives, mark a new threshold of aspiration and accountability for public education.

Dimensions of Choice

Choice programs aɪ ɘ designed to enhance the options made available to parents in selecting a school for their children. The most common form of choice program allows parents to choose a public school that lies outside the ordinary range of geographical options. The objective is to improve the chances for students to be placed in settings that suit their needs. It is also assumed that giving parents choice will induce competition among schools. Minnesota adopted the first statewide inter-district choice program in 1985. By 1991, 10 states had approved some form of open-enrollment program; and now, more than two-thirds of the states have enacted public school-choice programs. The first city-wide choice program was developed in 1981 in Cambridge, Massachusetts, perhaps the most celebrated success story at the local level is found in District 4 of East Harlem.

The basic shortcoming of public school-choice programs is that those jurisdictions that have the greatest need for expanding opportunities usually offer the fewest number of satisfactory options. For example, in Massachusetts, where voluntary inter-district choice has existed since 1991, only 25 percent of the districts participate, and none of the 29 on the suburban rim of Boston is included in this group. Supposedly, New York City has had a city-wide choice program since 1992 but, in reality, choice is permitted in only six of 32 districts, and the availability of space is extremely limited. Without measures designed to increase the total number of quality institutions, public school choice promotes competition among parents and children, not educators. It raises expectations but often leads to disappointment.

In 1990, Wisconsin passed innovative legislation that would expand parental choice among low-income parents in Milwaukee. Families who met income criteria ($18,000 or less) were given a state voucher for $2,987, which they might use in either a public school or a participating private school. By the end of the 1994–1995 school year, there were 1,500 children participating in the program that involved 12 nonpublic schools. Last spring, the legislation was amended to increase the value of the voucher to $3,600 and to permit schools with religious affiliations to participate. By next year, 15,000 low-income students are expected to take advantage of this unusual opportunity.

Similarly, last spring, the Ohio legislature enacted a law that will permit up to 2,000 low-income students in Cleveland to use a $2,500 state voucher in a school of choice—public, private, or sectarian. As in Wisconsin, the law was passed at the urging of minority parents dissatisfied with the quality of education in inner-city public schools. Like parents in Milwaukee, they had been frustrated with court-imposed integration plans that led to longer bus rides, rather than better schools. For the first time, many poor children whose life chances would have been determined by assignment to a failing public school were given the opportunity for real choices that gave them access to quality institutions (choices that were formerly available only to the middle class). In the meantime, the Milwaukee program is being challenged in state court, and a legal contest is expected in Cleveland.

Opponents of these programs claim that they violate requirements for the Constitutional separation of church and state. But there is nothing in the First Amendment of the Constitution that prohibits parents who want to send their children to religious schools from receiving public support. Since 1983, rulings by the Supreme Court have held that such support is legally permissible provided that aid goes directly to the parents (not the school), that the choice of school is freely made by parents, and that the system of funding is neutral. Cognizant of these rulings, opponents of choice have resorted to legal arguments based on provisions found in state law, many of which may be incompatible with federal Constitutional standards.

Some critics of choice fear that providing families with private-school options will spell the doom of public education. They predict a mass exodus of children and dollars from public schools. This is highly unlikely, indeed impossible, since the number of children permitted to participate has been limited. Let us keep in mind that every choice program that has gotten serious consideration by policy makers thus far—including those in Wisconsin and Ohio—has targeted a limited portion of the school populations, those on the lowest rung of the economic ladder. Most public-school children were not even eligible according to these criteria.

Traditionally, school reformers have asked how we can improve the existing system. Today many ask, instead, what we can do that is in the best interest of students who are at risk of failing. Since the ground-breaking work by the late sociologist James S. Coleman and his colleagues at the University of Chicago in 1982 (1) there is evidence that private and parochial schools are more educationally effective than public schools. Some scholars have attributed the difference to the selectivity of private schools. However, more recent research on Catholic schools by Bryk, Lee, and Holland (2) indicates that the differences are more the result of characteristics identified within the schools themselves, e.g., high standards, a strong academic curriculum, autonomy, an orderly environment, and a sense of community. Other studies by Coleman, Greeley, and Hoffer (3) rather persuasively that Catholic schools have been particularly effective in educating at-risk, inner-city students who have performed poorly in public schools.

An Agenda for Change

In light of the wide range of reforms currently under way in cities across the country, we propose a six-point agenda to improve educational opportunities for all children. Some of these proposals will require strong legislative action at the state level. Implementation will require an "hourglass strategy," allowing schools to escape one by one from the bureaucratic system. The best schools would function as charter schools and the worst schools would be replaced by institutions with performance contracts. Over time, more and more schools will seek the autonomy and performance agreements that charter schools have, and educational authorities will incrementally replace ineffective schools with new schools that have committed themselves to meet performance goals. The net effect of this approach would be to increase the number of desirable schools that children can attend.

1. Setting Standards

What matters most is whether children are learning, and this can only be assured by having real accountability at the school level. Each school district should establish clear performance standards and administer regular assessments to determine whether students are learning what they should at each grade level. By standards, we mean objective outcome measures that prescribe what should be expected from every school at regular intervals. For example, we would focus on such items as test scores in reading and math, attendance rates, and dropout rates. We would be especially interested in measuring "value added" or "gain scores"—the progress made over a given academic year—rather than unfairly comparing schools with children from vastly different social circumstances. We would not involve district-level administrators in defining basic inputs like instructional approaches or building specifications beyond code requirements designed to protect safety.

2. *School Closings*

The public school that once served as a gateway of opportunity for immigrant populations now serves as a custodial institution for disadvantaged children. Even as national achievement-test scores creep slowly upward, the gap between black and white students' scores remains shamefully wide, and those of Hispanic children are actually declining. As a matter of public policy, no child should be forced to go to a failing school. We cannot ask parents of children who are trapped in floundering institutions to be patient while we work things out. Educators and political leaders should not expect poor parents to accept educational standards for their children that the middle class would not tolerate for their own.

Any school that shows a consistent record of failure over several years should be a candidate for closure. The first step must be to define objective standards for placing a school on probation. Most school systems already have the basic data needed to develop appropriate criteria. A combination of attendance rates, test scores, dropout rates, improvement ratings, and similar markers will identify those schools that must be placed on probation or eventually closed.

3. *School Autonomy*

Schools that are working well should receive a performance contract and control over their budget and personnel. Subject to due process, principals should be able to select and remove staff. They should be allowed to purchase supplies and support services of their choosing, though central authorities will audit these purchases.

All schools, whether autonomous or not, should be liberated from unnecessary and cumbersome mandates. In New York, the state Education Department recently identified more than 120 regulations that are not related to health, safety, or civil rights. California, Michigan, and Florida have taken the lead on regulatory reform; their governors have called for sunsetting the entire education code and starting over, enacting only those regulations that are essential. Illinois is one of 10 states that have set up a procedure where local school districts can request waivers from outdated requirements. School superintendents should conduct a top-to-bottom review of local regulations to eliminate those that are not necessary. The goal should be to minimize the burden on teachers and principals and to grant schools greater independence in providing education.

Many school systems in the United States are experimenting with site-based management that moves decision making out of the administrative structure of the bureaucracy down to the school level. When implemented seriously, site-based management can improve both flexibility and accountability. However, a key question is whether central school authorities will actually concede the power to which they have become accustomed. A recent evaluation of the Los Angeles autonomy program, by McKinsey & Company, identified significant delays at the district level in implementing the reforms. Several years ago, New York City launched a modest experiment in school-based management without reducing the power of the central bureaucracy. It resulted in neither real autonomy for participating schools nor increased accountability for student performance.

Worth consideration is the city of London's opt-out program, in which a majority of parents in a school can vote to remove the school from the supervision of the local school district. Independence means that the school gets control over its own budget and a portion of the administrative overhead, so long as it continues to meet well-defined performance standards based on the national curriculum and national tests. All big-city school districts should have a similar plan, enabling schools to "opt out" of the present bureaucratic structure. We would propose, however, that approval require a majority vote of both parents and teachers. Teachers are important members of the school community, and their support is essential for success.

Not all schools are ready for such autonomy. But, if the parents and professionals at a school apply for approval as a charter school, then such a request should be evaluated by the local superintendent, the state education commissioner, or by an independent chartering agency on the basis of established criteria. In exchange for autonomy, the school administration would be required to sign a compact defining educational and financial standards to which the school would be held accountable. Greater autonomy would permit the school to hire staff, choose its teaching materials, set its fiscal priorities, and decide where it wants to purchase supplies and support services. Decisions about what to buy and where to buy it would be made by educators at the school level, not bureaucrats at central headquarters.

4. New Schools

If we intend to close failing schools, we need to provide alternatives to students who attend them. School superintendents should be given the power to solicit proposals for new institutions, either to replace failing schools or to grant contracts for increasing the total number of quality institutions. Proposals would be received from groups of teachers or parents, universities, libraries or museums, nonprofit organizations, or private entrepreneurs who demonstrate a professional capacity to administer a school. They may be progressive schools, family-style schools, Outward Bound schools, single-sex schools, back-to-basics schools, classical academies: The range is as vast as the imagination of creative educators.

These should, of course, be schools of choice. If they attract enough students, they will succeed; if they don't, they won't. These new schools would be established under the same terms as the charter schools described above. They would be granted autonomy in exchange for signing a compact outlining the educational and financial standards to which they would be held accountable. But, if the marketplace prevails, parents will become the ultimate judges of success or failure at the school level.

5. Central Administration

In a recent article in the *Wall Street Journal,* Peter Drucker predicts that in 10 to 15 years, most organizations will be "outsourcing" all of their support activities to specialist groups, thus allowing executives to avoid distractions and focus on functions that are directly related to their central mission. We share a similar vision for public education, where the role of central authorities will be transformed. Over time, the central administrative institution will significantly reduce its role as a provider of support services to schools. It would not be in charge of supplies, leasing, meals, building repairs, transportation, personnel, and other functions that can be performed better by others. Depending on the outcome of the competitive market, support services will either be provided by a private vendor or administered by an appropriate municipal agency. Marriot, for example, already provides food services to schools in Baltimore and Salt Lake City; and most municipal governments are well equipped to assume responsibility for such functions as personnel administration, procurement, transportation, or building maintenance.

According to our plan, the central school administration will become a monitoring agency with clearly focused and limited responsibilities. It will be responsible for educational standards, city-wide assessments, fiscal accountability, capital improvements, the authorization of new schools, and negotiation of union contracts that are specific enough to protect members' rights but flexible enough to permit school-by-school variations. The school system's chief executive should concentrate on setting standards, monitoring performance, and identifying those schools that either should be put on probation or closed. The chief executive would also be responsible for financial monitoring to protect against corruption and malfeasance. In a system where every school has its own budget, this is a formidable task, and it will probably require some form of administrative decentralization.

6. Real Choice for the Poor

Parents whose children attend the worst schools—those targeted for closure—should be given scholarships on a means-tested basis to use in any accredited school, be it public, private, or religious. Middle-class parents exercise such options for their children all the time; poor children should have the same. Priority for financial aid should go first to children in failing institutions whose families are on public assistance. The amount of a scholarship should not exceed the per capita cost of sending a child to public school. Schools receiving scholarship students should accept the award as a full fee for tuition. Students who get public scholarships should be regularly tested to assess their progress, in order to assure accountability and to exclude inadequate schools from participation.

Schools for the Twenty-First Century

We believe that these proposals, taken together, will strengthen and energize public education—freeing professionals and students from counterproductive regulations, shifting resources from the district level to the schools, providing alternative means for the delivery of vital support services, assuring choice for the students who now receive the least educational opportunity, rewarding success, encouraging creativity, requiring accountability for results, phasing out schools that are not conducive environments for teaching or learning, and placing institutions on the line by putting students first.

The public education system as currently structured is archaic. It cannot reform itself, nor can it be reformed by even the most talented chief executive. Trying to do so would be like trying to convert an old-fashioned linotype machine into a word-processor: It can't be done. They perform the same function, but their methods and technologies are so different that one cannot be turned into the other. Instead of a school system that attempts to impose uniform rules and regulations, one needs a system of schools that is dynamic, diverse, performance based, and accountable. The school system that we now have may have been right for the age in which it was created; it is not right for the twenty-first century.

Discussion Questions

1. Assume that Ravitch and Vitteritti are right, that urban education can be saved. Would this be enough to start a revitalization of U.S. cities? If so, why? If not, what more would it take to start a renewal of our cities?

2. Do you think the extremely negative image of U.S. cities, including its schools, is completely warranted? Or is it a distorted view held by those who live somewhere else? To whatever degree the image is accurate, what would you consider the most pressing urban problem? If you selected something other than the failure of city schools, where do you think it ranks in importance among all the problems facing our cities? Why did you rank it where you did?

(1) James S. Coleman, Thomas Hoffer, and Sally Kilgore, *High School Achievement: Public, Catholic, and Private Schools* (New York: Basic Books, 1982). (2) Anthony Bryk, Valerie E. Lee, and Peter B. Holland, *Catholic Schools and the Common Good* (Cambridge: Harvard University Press, 1993). (3) Andrew M. Greeley, *Catholic High Schools and Minority Students* (Rutgers: Transaction, 1982); Thomas Hoffer, Andrew M. Greeley, and James S. Coleman, "Achievement Growth in Public and Catholic Schools," *Sociology of Education* 58 (1985): 74–97.

$$Chapter \quad 15$$

Social Change: Technology, Social Movements, and the Environment

Auguste Comte, who gave sociology its name, stated that the study of society should entail two objects of study, social statics and social dynamics. Although we call them social structure and social change, modern sociologists do study these two aspects of society. Perhaps the most fascinating, and the least understood, is the latter—social change, the subject of this essay by Lester Brown. While Comte, writing a century and a half ago, was optimistic that social engineering would bring about a Utopia, Brown concerns himself with the very real problems present at the end of the twentieth century, which social engineering has not solved. The specific global issue discussed by Brown is a decline in food supply and economic growth in the face of an ever growing population.

As you read the essay, try to evaluate the analysis and see if you agree with the conclusion that population growth must be curtailed.

A Decade of Discontinuity

LESTER R. BROWN

The 1980s may have been the last decade in which humankind could anticipate a future of ever-increasing productivity on all fronts. By one measure after another, the boom we have experienced since mid-century is coming to an end.

When the history of the late 20th century is written, the 1990s will be seen as a decade of discontinuity—a time when familiar trends that had seemed likely to go on forever, like smooth straight roads climbing toward an ever-receding horizon, came to abrupt bends or junctures and began descending abruptly. The world's production of steel, for example, had risen almost as reliably each year as the sun rises in the morning. The amount of coal extracted had risen almost uninterruptedly ever since the Industrial Revolution began. Since the middle of this century, the harvest of grain had grown even faster than population, steadily increasing the amount available both for direct consumption and for conversion into livestock products. The oceanic fish catch, likewise, had more than quadrupled during this period, doubling the consumption of seafood per person.

These rising curves were seen as basic measures of human progress; we expected them to rise. But now, within just a few years, these trends have reversed—and with consequences we have yet to grasp. Meanwhile, other trends that were going nowhere, or at most rising slowly, are suddenly soaring.

That such basic agricultural and industrial outputs should begin to decline, while population continues to grow, has engendered disquieting doubts about the future. These reversals, and others likely to follow, are dwarfing the discontinuities that occurred during the 1970s in the wake of the 1973 rise in oil prices. At that time, an overnight tripling of oil prices boosted energy prices across the board, slowed the growth in automobile production, and spurred investment in energy-efficient technologies, creating a whole new industry.

The discontinuities of the 1990s are far more profound, originating not with a handful of national political leaders as with the OPEC ministers of the 1970s, but in the collision

Brown, Lester R. A Decade of Discontinuity. *World Watch,* July/Aug. 1993. By permission of The World Watch Institute.

between expanding human numbers and needs on the one hand and the constraints of the earth's natural systems on the other. Among these constraints are the capacity of the oceans to yield seafood, of grasslands to produce beef and mutton, of the hydrological cycle to produce fresh water, of crops to use fertilizer, of the atmosphere to absorb CFCs, carbon dioxide, and other greenhouse gases, of people to breathe polluted air, and of forests to withstand acid rain.

Though we may not have noticed them, these constraints drew dramatically closer between 1950 and 1990, as the global economy expanded nearly fivefold. Expansion on this scale inevitably put excessive pressure on the earth's natural systems, upsetting the natural balances that had lent some stability to historical economic trends. The trends were driven, in part by unprecedented population growth. Those of us born before 1950 have seen world population double. In 1950, 37 million people were added to the world's population. Last year, it was 91 million.

Against the Grain

The production of grain, perhaps the most basic economic measure of human well-being, increased 2.6 fold from 1950 to 1984. Expanding at nearly 3 percent per year, it outstripped population growth, raising per capita grain consumption by 40 percent over the 34-year period, improving nutrition and boosting consumption of livestock products—meat, milk, eggs, and cheese—throughout the world.

That period came to an end, ironically, around the time the United States withdrew its funding from the United Nations Population Fund. During the eight years since 1984, world grain output has expanded perhaps one percent per year. In per capita terms, this means grain production has shifted from its steady rise over the previous 34 years to a decline of one percent per year since then—a particularly troubling change both because grain is a basic source of human sustenance and because of the likely difficulty in reversing it.

This faltering of basic foodstuffs was triggered by other, earlier discontinuities of growth—in the supply of cropland, irrigation water, and agricultural technologies. Cropland, measured in terms of grain harvested area, expanded more or less continuously from the beginning of agriculture until 1981. The spread of agriculture, initially from valley to valley and eventually from continent to continent, had come to a halt. Since 1981, it has not increased. Gains of cropland in some countries have been offset by losses in others, as land is converted to nonfarm uses and abandoned because of erosion.

Irrigation, which set the stage for the emergence of early civilization, expanded gradually over a span of at least 5,000 years. After the middle of this century, the growth in irrigated area accelerated, averaging nearly 3 percent per year until 1978. Around that time, however, as the number of prime dam construction sites diminished and underground aquifers were depleted by overpumping, the growth of irrigated area fell behind that of population. Faced with a steady shrinkage of cropland area per person from mid-century onward, the world's farmers since 1978 have faced a shrinking irrigated area per person as well.

Although there was little new land to plow from mid-century onward, the world's farmers were able to achieve the largest expansion of food output in history by dramatically raising land productivity. The engine of growth was fertilizer use, which increased ninefold in three decades—from 14 million tons in 1950 to 126 million tons in 1984—before starting to slow.

In 1990, the rise in fertilizer use—what had been one of the most predictable trends in the world economy—was abruptly reversed. It has fallen some 10 percent during the three years since the 1989 peak of 146 million tons. Economic reforms in the former Soviet Union, which removed heavy fertilizer subsidies, account for most of the decline. Letting fertilizer prices move up to world market levels, combined with weakened demand for farm products, dropped fertilizer use in the former Soviet Union by exactly half between 1988 and 1992. This was an anomalous decline, from which there should eventually be at least a partial recovery.

More broadly, however, growth in world fertilizer use has slowed simply because existing grain varieties in the United States, Western Europe, and Japan cannot economically use much more fertilizer. U.S. farmers, matching applications more precisely to crop needs, actually used nearly one-tenth less fertilizer from 1990 to 1992 than they did a decade earlier. Using more fertilizer in agriculturally advanced countries does not have much effect on production with available varieties.

The backlog of unused agricultural technology that began to expand rapidly in the mid-19th century now appears to be diminishing. In 1847, German agricultural chemist Justus von Leibig discovered that all the nutrients removed by plants could be returned to the soil in their pure form. A decade later, Gregor Mendel discovered the basic principles of genetics, setting the stage for the eventual development of high-yielding, fertilizer-responsive crop varieties. As the geographic frontiers of agricultural expansion disappeared in the mid-20th century, the adoption of high-yielding varieties and rapid growth in fertilizer use boosted land productivity dramatically. In the 1960s, an array of advanced technologies for both wheat and rice producers was introduced into the Third World—giving rise to a growth in grain output that was more rapid than anything that had occurred earlier, even in the industrial countries.

Although it cannot be precisely charted, the backlog of unused agricultural technology must have peaked at least a decade ago. Most of the known means of raising food output are in wide use. The highest-yielding rice variety available to farmers in Asia in 1993 was released in 1966—more than a quarter-century ago. Today, the more progressive farmers are peering over the shoulders of agricultural scientists looking for new help in boosting production, only to find that not much is forth-coming. Agricultural scientists are worried that the rapid advance in technology characterizing the middle decades of this century may not be sustainable.

Less Meat and Less Fish

The growth in meat production, like that of grain, is slowing. Between 1950 and 1987, world meat production increased from 46 million tons to 161 million tons—boosting the amount per person from 18 kilograms in 1980 to 32 kilograms (about 70 pounds) in 1987. Since then, however, it has not increased at all. The one percent decline in per capita production in 1992 may be the beginning of a gradual world decline in per capita meat production, another major discontinuity.

Underlying this slowdown in overall meat production is a rather dramatic slowdown in the production of beef and mutton, resulting from the inability of grasslands to support more cattle and sheep. From 1950 to 1990, world beef output increased 2.5-fold. Now, with grasslands almost fully used—or overused—on every continent, this growth may be nearing an end. From 1990 to 1992, per capita beef production world fell 6 percent.

The supply of fish, like that of meat, no longer keeps pace with increases in human numbers. Here, too, there has been a reversal of the historic trend. Between 1950 and 1989, the global catch expanded from 22 million tons to 100 million tons. The per capita seafood supply increased from 9 to 19 kilograms during this period. Since 1989, the catch has actually declined slightly, totalling an estimated 97 million tons in 1992. United Nations marine biologists believe that the oceans have reached their limit and may not be a able to sustain a yield of more than 100 million tons per year

Throughout this century, it has been possible to increase the fish take by sending out more ships, using more sophisticated fishing technologies, and going, literally, to the farthest reaches of the ocean. That expansion has now come to an end. The world's ocean catch per capita declined 7 percent from 1989 until 1992, and is likely to continue declining as long as population continues to grow. As a result, seafood prices are rising steadily.

Getting more animal protein, whether it be in the form of beef or farm-raised fish, now depends on feeding grain and soybean meal. Those desiring to maintain animal protein intake now compete with those trying to consume more grain directly.

Fossil Fuels: The Beginning of the End

While biological constraints are forcing discontinuities in agriculture and oceanic fisheries, it is atmospheric constraints—the mounting risks associated with pollution and global warming—that are altering energy trends. Throughout the world energy economy, there are signs that a major restructuring is imminent. On the broadest level, this will entail a shifting of investment from fossil fuels and nuclear power toward renewables—and toward greater energy efficiency in every human activity.

We cannot yet see the end of the fossil fuel age, but we can see the beginning of its decline. World oil production peaked in 1979 (see Table 15.1). Output in 1992 was four percent below that historical high. World coal production dropped in 1990, in 1991, and again in 1992 (partly because of the recession), interrupting a growth trend that had spanned two centuries. If strong global warming policies are implemented, this could be the beginning of a long-term decline in coal dependence.

Of the three fossil fuels, only natural gas is expanding output rapidly and is assured of substantial future growth. Gas burns cleanly and produces less carbon dioxide than the others, and is therefore less likely to be constrained by stricter environmental policies. While oil production has fallen since 1979, gas production has risen by one-third.

With oil, it was the higher price that initially arrested growth. More recently, it has been the pall of automotive air pollution in cities like Los Angeles, Mexico City and Rome that has slowed the once-unrestrained growth in motor vehicle use and, therefore, in oil use. With coal, it was neither supply nor price (the world has at least a few centuries of coal reserves left), but the effects of air pollution on human health, of acid rain on forests and

TABLE 15.1   Growth and Decline in Production of Fossil Fuels, 1950–92

Fossil Fuel	Growth Period		Decline Period	
	Years	Annual Rate (percent)	Years	Annual Rate (percent)
Oil	1950–79	+6.4	1979–92	–0.5
Coal	1950–89	+2.2	1989–92	–0.6
Natural Gas	1950–92	+6.2		

crops, and of rising CO_2 concentrations on the earth's climate that have sent the industry into decline. Several industrial countries have committed themselves to reducing carbon emissions. Germany, for example, plans to cut carbon emissions 25 percent by 2005. Switzerland is shooting for a 10 percent cut by 2000, and Australia for 20 percent by 2005. Others, including the United States, may soon join them.

With the beginning of the end of the fossil fuel age in sight, what then will be used to power the world economy? Fifteen years ago, many would have said, with little hesitation, that nuclear power will. Once widely thought to be the energy source of the future, it has failed to live up to its promise (the problems of waste disposal and safety have proved expensive and intractable) and is being challenged on economic grounds in most of the countries where it is produced.

Nuclear generating capacity reached its historical peak in 1990. Though it has declined only slightly since then, it now seems unlikely that there will be much, if any, additional growth in nuclear generating capacity during this decade—and perhaps ever.

The Winds of Change

Even as the nuclear and fossil fuel industries have faltered, three new technologies that harness energy directly or indirectly from the sun to produce electricity—solar thermal power plants, photovoltaic cells, and wind generators—are surging. In wind power, particularly, breakthroughs in turbine technology are setting the stage for rapid expansion in the years ahead. Wind electricity generated in California already produces enough electricity to satisfy the residential needs of San Francisco and Washington, D.C. Indeed, it now seems likely that during the 1990s, the growth in wind generating capacity will exceed that in nuclear generating capacity. Three countries—Denmark, the Netherlands, and Germany—have plans to develop a minimum of a thousand megawatts of wind generating capacity by 2005. China claims to reach the same goal by 2000. Given the rapid advances in the efficiency of wind generating machines and the falling costs of wind generated electricity, the growth in wind power over the remainder of this decade could dwarf even current expectations.

The potential for wind power far exceeds that of hydropower, which currently supplies the world with one-fifth of its electricity. England and Scotland alone have enough wind generating potential to satisfy half of Europe's electricity needs. Two U.S. states—

Montana and Texas—each have enough wind to satisfy the whole country's electricity needs. The upper Midwest (the Dakotas east through Ohio) could supply the country's electricity without siting any wind turbines in either densely populated or environmentally sensitive areas, And wind resource assessments by the government of China have documented 472,000 megawatts of wind generating potential, enough to raise China's electricity supply threefold.

For Third World villages not yet connected to a grid, a more practical source is photovoltaic arrays, which may already have a competitive advantage. With the World Bank beginning to support this technology, costs will fall fast, making photovoltaic cells even more competitive. Wind, photovoltaic cells, and solar thermal power plants all promise inexpensive electricity as the technologies continue to advance and as the economies of scale expand. Over the longer term, cheap solar electricity in various forms will permit the conversion of electricity into hydrogen, which will offer an efficient means of energy transportation and storage.

Technological advances that increase the efficiency of energy use are in some ways even more dramatic than the advances in harnessing solar and wind resources. Striking gains have been made in the energy efficiency of electric lighting, electric motors, the thermal efficiency of windows, and cogenerating technologies that produce both electricity and heat. One of the most dramatic, as recently noted in World Watch (May/June 1993), is the new compact fluorescent light bulb—which can supply the same amount of light as an incandescent bulb while using only one-fourth as much electricity. The 134 million compact fluorescent bulbs sold worldwide in 1992 saved enough electricity to close 10 large coal-fired power plants.

The discontinuities that have wreaked havoc with once-reliable trends are not random, but reflect an escalating awareness of the need to transform the global economy into one that is sustainable. They reflect the unavoidable reality that we have entered an era in which satisfying the needs of the 91 million people being added each year depends on reducing consumption among those already here. At this rate, by the year 2010, this growth will amount to a net addition equal to nearly 200 cities the size of New York, or 100 countries the size of Iraq—dramatically reducing the per capita availability of cropland and irrigation water. At some point, as people begin to grasp the implications of this new reality, population policy will become a central concern national governments.

Economic Entropy

Whether in basic foodstuffs and fresh water, or in overall economic output, the decade of discontinuity has begun. Growth in the world economy reached its historical high at 5.2 percent per year during the 1960s (see Table 15.2). It then slowed to 3.4 percent per year in the 1970s, and 2.9 percent in the 1980s. Despite this slowdown, the per capita output of goods and services rose as overall economic growth stayed ahead of population growth. Now that, too, may be reversing.

From 1990 to 1992, the world economy expanded at 0.6 percent per year. If the International Monetary Fund's recent projection of 2.2 percent in world economic growth for 1993 materializes, we will find ourselves three years into this decade with an income per

TABLE 15.2   World Economic Growth by Decade, 1950–93

Decade	Annual Growth of World Economy	Annual Growth Per Person
1950–60	4.9	3.1
1960–70	5.2	3.2
1970–80	3.4	1.6
1980–90	2.9	1.1
1990–93 (prel.)	0.9	–0.8

person nearly 2 percent lower than it was when the decade began. Even using an economic accounting system that overstates progress because it omits environmental degradation and the depletion of natural capital, living standards are falling.

Evidence is accumulating that the world economy is not growing as easily in the 1990s as it once did. The conventional economic wisdom concerning the recession of the early 1990s attributes it to economic mismanagement in the advanced industrial countries (particularly the United States, Germany, and Japan) and to the disruption associated with economic reform in the centrally planned economies. These are obviously the dominant forces slowing world economic growth, but they are not the only ones. As noted above, growth in the fishing industry, which supplies much of the world's animal protein, may have stopped. Growth in the production of beef, mutton, and other livestock products from the world's rangelands may also be close to an end. The world grain harvest shows little prospect of being able to keep pace with population, much less to eliminate hunger. And scarcities of fresh water are limiting economic expansion in many countries. With constraints emerging in these primary economic sectors—sectors on which much of the Third World depends—we may be moving into an era of slower economic growth overall.

The popular question of "growth or no growth" now seems largely irrelevant. A more fundamental question is how to satisfy the basic needs of the world's people without further disrupting or destroying the economy's support systems. The real challenge for the 1990s is that of deciding how the basic needs of all people can be satisfied without jeopardizing the prospects of future generations.

Of all the discontinuities that have become apparent in the past few years, however, it is an upward shift in the population growth trend itself that may be most disturbing. The progress in slowing human population growth so evident in the 1970s has stalled—with alarming implications for the long-term population trajectory. Throughout the 1960s and 1970s, declining fertility held out hope for getting the brakes on population growth before it began to undermine living standards. The 1980s, however, turned out to be a lost decade, one in which the United States not only abdicated its leadership role, but also withdrew all financial support from the U.N. Population Fund and the International Planned Parenthood Federation. This deprived millions of couples in the Third World of access to the family planning services needed to control the number or timing of their children.

The concern that population growth could undermine living standards has become a reality in this decade of discontinuity. There is now a distinct possibility that the grain supply per person will be lower at the end of this decade than at the beginning, that the amount of seafood per person will be substantially less, and that the amount of meat per person will also be far less than it is today.

The absence of any technology to reestablish the rapid growth in food production that existed from 1950 to 1984 is a matter of deepening concern. In early 1992, the U.S. National Academy of Sciences and the Royal Society of London together issued a report that warned: "If current predictions of population growth prove accurate and patterns of human activity on the planet remain unchanged, science and technology may not be able to prevent either irreversible degradation of the environment or continued poverty for much of the world."

Later in the year, the Union of Concerned Scientists issued a statement signed by nearly 1,600 of the world's leading scientists, including 96 Nobel Prize recipients, noting that the continuation of destructive human activities "may so alter the living world that it mill be unable to sustain life in the manner that we know." The statement warned: "A great change in our stewardship of the earth and the life on it is required, if vast human misery is to be avoided and our global home on this planet is not to be irretrievably mutilated."

The discontinuities reshaping the global economy define the challenge facing humanity in the next few years. It is a challenge not to the survival of our species, but to civilization as we know it. The question we can no longer avoid asking is whether our social institutions are capable of quickly slowing and stabilizing population growth without infringing on human rights. Even as that effort gets underway, the same institutions face the complex issue of how to distribute those resources that are no longer expanding, among a population that is continuing to grow by record numbers each year.

Discussion Questions

1. In light of what you have learned by being introduced to sociology, what do you think will be the greatest global problem in the next 50 years? How important do you think the joint problems of population growth and decline in the food supply are? Do you think it's possible to solve them? If so, how? If not, why not?

2. Gather a group of people and work with them to build an ideal society. What place does population growth, economic growth, food supply, and the environment have in your Utopia? Now, can you get to your ideal? Exchange your vision of the future with that of another group and critique the plans as to the adequacy of their society to solve crucial problems and the likelihood that the vision could be attained.